# Motherhood and War

# Motherhood and War

## International Perspectives

Edited by Dana Cooper and Claire Phelan

palgrave
macmillan

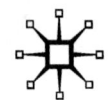

MOTHERHOOD AND WAR
Copyright © Dana Cooper and Claire Phelan, 2014.

All rights reserved.

First published in 2014 by PALGRAVE MACMILLAN® in the United States—a division of St. Martin's Press LLC, 175 Fifth Avenue, New York, NY 10010.

Where this book is distributed in the UK, Europe and the rest of the world, this is by Palgrave Macmillan, a division of Macmillan Publishers Limited, registered in England, company number 785998, of Houndmills, Basingstoke, Hampshire RG21 6XS.

Palgrave Macmillan is the global academic imprint of the above companies and has companies and representatives throughout the world.

Palgrave® and Macmillan® are registered trademarks in the United States, the United Kingdom, Europe and other countries.

ISBN: 978-1-137-43795-2

Library of Congress Cataloging-in-Publication Data

Motherhood and war : international perspectives / edited by Dana Cooper and Claire Phelan.
    pages cm
  Includes bibliographical references and index.
    ISBN 978-1-137-43795-2 (hardback : alk. paper) 1. Women and war. 2. Mothers of soldiers. 3. Mothers of war casualties. 4. Women soldiers—Family relationships. 5. Mother and child. 6. Women in war. I. Cooper, Dana, 1977–, editor of compilation. II. Phelan, Claire, editor of compilation. III. Title.

JZ6405.W66M65 2017
306.874'3088355—dc23                                            2014002899

A catalogue record of the book is available from the British Library.

Design by Scribe Inc.

First edition: July 2014

10 9 8 7 6 5 4 3 2 1

For my precious son,
Christian

For my mother and father,
Pauline and Raymond Horton

# Contents

Acknowledgments ix
Prologue: Mother xi
*Amitabh Vikram Dwivedi*

1 Introduction: The Shenandoah Doctrine:
  Sons, Soldiers, and Service to the Nation 1
  *Dana Cooper*

2 Mothers, Warfare, and Captivity in the Eastern
  Woodlands of North America, 1607–1763 15
  *John J. Navin*

3 Sailing Sons: The Personal Consequences of
  Impressment 45
  *Claire Phelan*

4 *Las Madres Guerreras*: Testimonial Writing on
  Militant Motherhood in Latin America 61
  *Tracy Crowe Morey and Cristina Santos*

5 The Women's Resistance Movement in Argentina:
  *Las Madres de Plaza de Mayo* 85
  *Elena Shabliy*

6 Japanese Mothers and Rural Settlement in
  Wartime Manchukuo: Gendered Reflections of
  Labor and Productivity in *Manshû Gurafu*
  (Manchuria Graph), 1936–43 95
  *Annika A. Culver*

7 Dear Okāsan . . . : An Analysis of Farewell Letters
  from Kamikaze Pilots to Their Mothers 115
  *Salvador Jimenez Murguia and Benjamin A. Peters*

| | | |
|---|---|---|
| 8 | Social Trauma and Motherhood in Postwar Spain<br>*Lorraine Ryan* | 127 |
| 9 | Barbara Hepworth and War: Themes of Motherhood and Sacrifice in Hepworth's *Madonna and Child*, St. Ives Parish Church<br>*Lyrica Taylor* | 145 |
| 10 | War Opponents and Proponents: Israeli Military Mothers from Rivka Guber to "Four Mothers"<br>*Udi Lebel* | 159 |
| 11 | Reproducing a Culture of Martyrdom: The Role of the Palestinian Mother in Discourse Construction, Transmission, and Legitimization<br>*Michael Loadenthal* | 181 |
| 12 | Motherhood as a Space of Political Activism: Iraqi Mothers and the Religious Narrative of Karbala<br>*Fatin Shabbar* | 207 |
| 13 | Mothers and Memory: Suffering, Survival, and Sustainability in Somali Clan Wars<br>*Mohamed Haji Ingiriis* | 225 |
| 14 | Grieving US Mothers and the Political Representations of Protest during the Iraq War and Beyond<br>*Francis Shor* | 241 |
| Notes on Contributors | | 253 |
| Index | | 259 |

# Acknowledgments

## Dana Cooper

My interest in women's history has been a back-door journey of sheer luck and constant discovery. For all women, irrespective of nation or era, known and yet to be discovered, thank you for your contributions to and shaping of history.

I would also like to acknowledge the exceptional collegiality and great friendships I have been so lucky to enjoy at Stephen F. Austin State University. The Department of History, College of Liberal and Applied Arts, and Gender Studies Advisory Board have provided generous support and encouraged me on innumerable occasions. Rare are such personal and professional relationships, for which I am incredibly thankful.

## Claire Phelan

I first became interested in the subject of impressment as a graduate student of Gene A. Smith at Texas Christian University. His enthusiastic mentorship of my career continues to this day, and I am honored to count him as both a close friend and trusted advisor.

I would also like to acknowledge the generous support given to me by the University of Mary Hardin-Baylor. Provost Steve Oldham and Dean Danny Mynatt have encouraged me at every turn, and I am indeed indebted to them. I also consider myself extremely fortunate to be a member of the Department of History and Political Science led by Department Chair David Chrisman. A happier group of people would be hard to find.

\*\*\*

We would both also like to recognize our friends at Palgrave Macmillan: Editorial Assistant Mike Aperauch and Senior Editor Chris Chappell. Both have worked tirelessly on our behalf and we are most grateful.

Finally, we would like to acknowledge the invaluable assistance given to us by Jay Knarr, a colleague and friend. His counsel on all matters practical and technical allowed us to devote our time to exploring the history of some extraordinary women, whose stories are found within this work.

# Prologue

## Mother

*Amitabh Vikram Dwivedi*

O Mother! Wipe your eyes as your son is alive
Don't think of death as poor mortals do
Remember, you are not only a mother but a daughter too
And we all are paying a debt to and we will do
To our beautiful country who seeks life
In the veins of your son and in our blood
We live and die in Her arms, and are reborn in Her breast
O Mother! Don't think of life as wretched mortals do
There is a life when we die for our land
God embraces us and keeps us in his hands
As we live only for our country
Wipe your eyes as I will never die as poor mortals do

# Chapter 1

## Introduction:
## The Shenandoah Doctrine
### Sons, Soldiers, and Service to the Nation

*Dana Cooper*

When the movie *Shenandoah* was released in the summer of 1965, few Americans watched the film with much thought toward the slow but escalating tensions in Vietnam. Though one of Jimmy Stewart's lesser-acclaimed movies, the film presents Stewart in the lead role as Charlie Anderson, a widower with seven children, including six sons, who desperately tries to maintain his neutral status during the Civil War. His primary goal throughout is to remain uninvolved in the conflict, and he repeatedly explains that his family will not take part in the war until it concerns them. Even as he tries valiantly to keep all his sons on the family farm in war-torn Virginia, and thereby out of the fighting, the conflict continues to rage around them.

Though *Shenandoah* was not intended to take a stand on the situation in Southeast Asia or promote a national dialogue about military service, compulsory or otherwise, a brief but notable statement by Stewart foreshadowed the controversial decision to draft young men into the Vietnam War. When a Virginia State lieutenant comes to collect Stewart's sons, the lieutenant smugly and presumptively explains that "Virginia needs all her sons." Vengefully justifying his decision to keep his sons on the family farm regardless of the war, Stewart passionately retorts, "They don't belong to the state. They belong to ME! When they were babies, I never saw the state comin' around here with a spare tit!"[1] Thus the Shenandoah doctrine was born, which raises two crucial questions: To whom does a young man belong in a time of war? And does he suddenly bear an obligation to his state or nation because of a domestic or diplomatic conflict? The idea of military service as an obligation of citizenry can be traced back to the Greco-Roman period.[2] As military service and citizenship has long maintained a reciprocal relationship, the authority of the state to conscript residents in order to fulfill an army defined and validated this implicit connection. Similar military forces existed around the world over time, as seen with the rise of the Qin Empire and the Anglo-Saxon fyrd in England.[3] But as "the professional military caste of the Middle Ages . . . collapsed before the mass armies of the new nation-states," explains George Flynn, the expectation and justification of military conscription reached new heights.[4] In 1789, the French National Assembly issued a report, candidly demanding that "every citizen must be a soldier and every soldier a citizen or we shall never have a constitution."[5] With Napoleon's utilization of conscripted forces and the resulting decimation of European powers, France crushed their longtime rivals, which decidedly quashed any remaining questions as to the use of citizens in the interest of the nation. Notably, no army since that time has successfully fought a significant war without the mass drafting of civilians. In 1935, Emperor Haile Selassie made his expectations clear for all men and women of Ethiopia when he issued the following edict: "Everyone will now be mobilized, and all boys old enough to carry a spear will be sent to [the capital] Addis Ababa. Married men will take their wives to carry food and cook. Those without wives will take any woman without a husband. Anyone found at home after the receipt of this order will be hanged."[6] The notion of military service in the name of the nation is an established concept through history.[7]

And yet the idea of armed obligation among men as citizen soldiers took its own unique form in the American colonial period. A version of conscription existed among the colonists, though it could not be enforced or supervised. The colonies (and eventual states), with the exception of Quaker Pennsylvania, handled this soldierly responsibility at the state level with militias.[8] Not until the American Civil War did the United States impose a federal level conscription policy, which met with intense resistance, as the New York City draft riots proved.[9] But the raising of troops by both the North and South during the Civil War, as James Geary contends, "contributed significantly to later periods of military mobilization."[10] A national draft did not occur again in the United States until World War I, and again a short time later in World War II. The onset of the Cold War in the late 1940s revived the

INTRODUCTION: THE SHENANDOAH DOCTRINE 3

legislation once more. The final wave of military conscription, notably without a declaration of war, ended with the termination of efforts in South Vietnam in 1973, which witnessed some of the most visible and volatile backlash against such policies in American history.[11] Controversy concerning the draft continued when the nation returned to a compulsory draft registration under President Jimmy Carter, and Ronald Reagan's presidential administration chose to prosecute those who resisted registration; thus the draft continued as a contentious issue even in the absence of war.[12]

Much of the national perception and discussion of compulsory service is often shaped by the commander in chief of US military forces, or the president of the United States. Not surprisingly, the vast majority of American presidents, particularly those who dealt with combat issues during their tenure in the White House, presented an honorable and duty-focused perspective of military service. As one with firsthand experience of war, George Washington described such service as "a primary position, and the basis of our system, that every Citizen who enjoys the protection of a free Government, owes not only a proportion of his property, but even of his personal services to the defence [sic] of it."[13] More than a hundred years later, President Woodrow Wilson reiterated Washington's focus on the obligations of the citizenry when he said, "We must depend in every time of national peril, in the future as in the past, not upon a standing army, not yet a reserve army, but upon a citizenry trained and accustomed to arms."[14] Finding himself in a world war like Wilson, President Franklin Delano Roosevelt announced in 1940 that by adopting a conscription law in peacetime, America "has broadened and enriched our basic concepts of citizenship. Besides the clear and equal opportunities, we have set forth the underlying other duties, obligations and responsibilities of equal service."[15] Focusing less on the idea of citizenry and more on the benefit of military service to the individual solider, President Harry S. Truman claimed that universal military training "would provide a democratic and efficient military force . . . [and that it] would be a constant bulwark in support of our ideals of government."[16] Finally, President Lyndon Johnson echoed Truman's belief of the benefit of such service to each soldier, explaining that "local citizens can perform a valuable service to the Government . . . we cannot lightly discard an institution with so valuable a record of effectiveness and integrity."[17]

While American presidents maintain an enthusiastic stance on military service in various forms, the fulfillment of such a noble service, at present, varies a great deal from a global perspective. While the United States, United Kingdom, and much of Western Europe require no military service to the nation, other rising and arguably ambitious nations, including Brazil, Israel, North Korea, South Korea, Mexico, Greece, Russia, Austria, Egypt, and Iran all have some level of mandatory military service. Notably, Israel, Norway, and China require that men *and* women serve in the military. Given the events of September 11, 2001, the subsequent and ongoing wars on terror, seismic changes to military power, and the reach and abilities of resulting intelligence, the mere discussion of military obligation can incite passionate debates on the expectations of society and obligations of citizens around the world. Just as mandatory military service claims to rely equally on an entire populace to support the nation, the very same and seemingly democratic process has its drawbacks. As a Greek army captain recently remarked, "Greece could never have gone into Iraq. Because every mother in the country would need to know why."[18]

For all citizens of any nation, military service often connotes strong gendered expectations, especially for women. Whether it was the "white, middle-aged American 'Mom' [that functioned as] the predominant image of womanhood in the war culture of the First World War," as Susan Zeiger maintains, or the "eroticized and youthful 'pinup girl'" who served as the face of "wartime femininity in the 1940s," military service, as a cultural byproduct of the nation at hand, has often demanded a particular response from its female citizenry, but particularly from mothers of military men.[19] As an example of the reliance on mothers to support the national war effort, and specifically to bolster military recruitment efforts, a 1916 Canadian advertisement boldly asked, "Have you Mothered a Man?" and went on to describe a man as one who wore "the King's Khaki somewhere in France." The advertisement pressured mothers "not to use their influence against the enlistment of sons" but rather to provide a man for the front who would fight "for Freedom and Liberty and civilization . . . [and] for the sacredness of Home and Womanhood."[20]

Given the heavily gendered attachments to ideas such as masculinity, militarism, and maternalism, much is at stake for individuals—men and women, mothers and sons—as they seek to find a balance between private provocations and national needs.[21] Whether such participation is labeled as compulsory or is compelled by societal pressures, whether an individual is coerced or otherwise shamed into "volunteering," as was often the case with the White Feather Brigade in Great Britain during World War I, much is on the line for individual respectability and family honor, not only for sons, but for mothers as well.[22] Such "gender ridicule," as Kathleen Kennedy describes it, "was a common tactic in American politics . . . [which emphasizes] the close relationship between the family, citizenship, and the states."[23] Consequently, the nature of military service as a result of war is highly dependent on the political and societal forces, and especially culturally constructed ideas of gender, in place at the time of military conflict. Consequently, the use of universal military training, conscription, or the Selective Service System is arguably more controversial than once thought. As George Flynn argues, "[T]urning civilians into soldiers involves political and social issues more than military strategy."[24]

Men have wrestled with these issues for centuries, but women, and specifically mothers, occupy a unique position within such debates, as war and peace affect women differently.[25] As the sex that gestates and bears children, many women feel a vehement reaction to protect their offspring from military service, and particularly their sons from combat. The sense of ownership, loyalty, duty, and responsibility take on new meaning during wartime regardless of national borders or historic period. Thus the questions posed by the Shenandoah doctrine apply globally. How could national politicians, military leaders, or any society at large possibly expect mothers to dedicate their lives to home and hearth, dutifully create a family, dedicate themselves to the molding of daughters, and faithfully raise sons for decades, and then, without question or hesitation, turn their children over to the military and/or government and send them off to potentially face their own deaths? "Only my mother," as they say in Turkish, "can cry for me sincerely."[26] Hence this shared urge to protect one's own becomes a double-edged sword, as mothers have tried to defend their children even as the state has called on them to defend their respective nations.

When compared to the long history of military service and conscription, the mobilization of mothers by mothers to protest war is a relatively recent phenomenon. One such group, though not limited to mothers, was Women Strike for Peace (WSP). Founded in 1961 by Bella Abzug and Dagmar Wilson, WSP promoted the slogan "Not My Son, Not Your Son, Not Their Sons" throughout the Vietnam War.[27] Focusing on their roles as mothers as the primary protectors of their sons, WSP concentrated their efforts in 1967 on the White House and published an open letter to President Lyndon Johnson in the *New York Times*. The letter passionately implored the president, asking, "What must we mothers do to reach the ear, to reach the heart of our president? We women gave you our sons, lovingly raised to live, to learn, and to create a better world." WSP publically shamed the president and blamed him for using their sons "to kill and . . . return[ing] 12,269 caskets and 74,818 casualties to heart-broken mothers." Calling on the protective and maternal instincts of mothers, and comparing themselves to lionesses protecting their cubs, WSP warned President Johnson that they would "walk where you can see us. We will walk where you can hear us . . . a mother in defense of her family is not easily turned aside."[28]

Even as the WSP put the president on notice, another group of concerned mothers mobilized. In 1967, a group of 15 mothers organized to create Another Mother for Peace. In a short five years, this small but powerful group maintained a mailing list of more than 250,000 people and had Hollywood celebrities such as Debbie Reynolds, Joanna Woodward, and Paul Newman promoting the cause. Academy Award–winner Barbara Avedon, the founder of the organization, saw the war in a different light after having a son. She was suddenly concerned that "before I know it, he will be old enough to go to war. I wonder which one will be his and where it will be and what it will be about." As her maternal perspective collided with the current events of the day, she reflected that "we are the ones who create life, and we should be the ones to preserve it; yet, here we are, accepting the idea that war is inevitable."[29]

Holding their first annual meeting on Mother's Day in 1969, Another Mother for Peace advocates gathered in Los Angeles, and the leadership of the organization revealed their vision for a Pax Materna as "a permanent irrevocable condition of amnesty and understanding among mothers of the world."[30] The Pax Materna pledged,

> I join with my sisters in every land
> In the Pax Materna—
> A permanent declaration of peace
> That transcends our ideological differences.
> In the nuclear shadow, war is obsolete.
> I will no longer suffer it in silence.
> Nor sustain it by complicity.
> They shall not send my son
> To fight another mother's son.
> For now, forever, there is no mother
> Who is an enemy to another mother.[31]

Most recently, the Committee of Soldiers' Mothers (CSM) in Russia took a bold stand against the war in Chechnya and marched into the war-torn country and literally dragged their sons from military bases and thus waging war in the name of the nation. Such striking images garnered terrific publicity for the organization and provided traction for the group to take an active role in military policy making, which in turn abolished the national draft and created an alternative national service plan. Notably, these developments occurred during a period of great political and economic unrest; thus most of the institutional and ideological basis of the country was in flux, which provided CSM a rare opportunity for influence. It was not long, however, before the rhetoric of CSM was used against the organization, as opponents argued that mothers did not belong in politics and that their actions were unpatriotic.[32]

As these maternally motivated groups demonstrate, and Harriet Hyman Alonso argues, "The motherhood theme has been an essential element in the women's rights (or feminist) peace movement for several reasons. It has provided women a societally acceptable cover for their highly political work. It has also allowed women to be angry and to express that anger within this acceptable context, giving them a certain amount of credibility. In addition, it has given women a unique position that men cannot share and therefore cannot really argue against."[33]

But even as motherhood provides a base by which many a woman has argued against armed warfare, the irony is that conscription seems to contradict much of the foundational ideas of the United States and claims of American individualism alongside the pursuit of life, liberty, and happiness. In the words of John Chambers, how did a "national draft come to a country that traditionally emphasized the liberty of individuals, and is suspicious of centralized governmental power, of standing armies, and of national conscription?"[34] The very idea of conscription violates the essence of an American tradition of individual freedom.[35] For the United States to impose any form of national service is arguably incompatible with American ideologies. The potential "theory of national service is that everyone owes a year's unpaid or poorly paid labor to the state," as Eliot Cohen argues, "in other words, *corvée*. Whether such a proposal would be constitutional or not . . . it would likely meet with indignation from parents and children."[36] These sentiments seem to echo the words of a prominent nineteenth-century American politician. "Where is it written in the Constitution, in what article or section is it contained, that you may take children from their parents," Daniel Webster boldly asked in the midst of the War of 1812, "and parents from their children, and compel them to fight the battles of any war, in which the folly or the wickedness of Government may engage it?"[37] These questions, in various forms, continued to be posed by citizens of all backgrounds and experiences in the twentieth and twenty-first centuries. As Mildred

Scott Olmsted, a mother, pacifist, and Women's International League for Peace and Freedom member, once reflected, "I have often wondered why it is that a family which would make a great protest if the government took away their automobile or even the dog, says nothing when the government takes away their sons."[38]

And yet many see military service, according to Michael Foley, "as one of the few duties of citizenship in America that fosters a sense of civic responsibility in those who participate."[39] Similarly, Soviets of the interwar period viewed military service, according to Amy Caiazza, as a means by which all its citizenry "would develop a sense of national identity, patriotism and civic duty . . . [which would] lead to a new sense of Soviet citizenship and public-mindedness."[40] Just as military service is revered as an honorable and formative experience for soldiers, Israeli fathers have closely identify with the military experiences of their sons, which often results in a unique bond.[41]

Correspondingly, the bond between mothers of soldiers currently serving and deceased is exceptionally strong; thus not all mothers wanted to protect their sons from war or various forms of conflict. Instead, some mothers strongly advocate for their sons' such service and see themselves as nurturers of "sons to be sacrificed on the altar of civil need."[42] As evidence of such maternal enthusiasm, mothers from Israel, Palestine, Northern Ireland, Argentina, and El Salvador serve as prime examples of women who have championed their sons' deaths as an honorable sacrifice on behalf of the nation.[43] Similarly, Canadian mothers who lost sons during World War I were presented with the Silver Cross medal, which symbolized their sons' ultimate sacrifice for the nation, which in turn noted their sacrifice as well.[44] This tangible and visible honoring of mothers also helped mothers maintain connections with the nation, as the state wished to continue to call on their support in the future. One World War I poster in Canada pointedly asked mothers, "Do you expect other mothers' sons to defend you and your son?"[45] Another poster praised the national devotion of a mother who "sacrificed the life of my boy" and accordingly proclaimed her "The Greatest Mother in the World."[46] This sense of unity among mothers was praised throughout the United Kingdom as those "who mother the men" and thus have the "most important job in the world" as the ones who defend "the honour and traditions not only of our Empire but of the whole civilized world."[47] Thus, as Amy Caiazza maintains, "traditional gender ideologies provided a resource creating solidarity among women."[48]

In a similar maternal unification, the Gold Star Mothers Club and Blue Star Mothers Club were formed in the United States after

World War I and during World War II, respectively. The clubs provide support for mothers of children in the military and followed a tradition of hanging a banner, or service flag, in a window at their home. Each blue star represents a family member in the military, while each gold star signifies a child who died while in service. Such a public effort to honor military service at the family level clearly indicates the shared sacrifice of families, but especially mothers. As the individual and shared sacrifice of such mothers and organizations prove and the Marine Family Network Parents attest, "It can't always be someone else's son."[49]

Just as such sacrifice cannot always fall on another's shoulders, such sacrifice is not limited to narrow definitions of traditional warfare. As the Vietnam War and current wars on terror demonstrate, an official declaration of war is not necessary for men to lose their lives and mothers to lose their sons. Neither is formal participation in a recognized military branch necessary for a man to face his own mortality, nor is a uniform needed for him to be pressured, shamed, or otherwise compelled into armed conflict; a man does not need to be recognized as a solider to serve as a combatant in warfare. Thus the chapters presented in this book demonstrate the limits of the word *war* and broaden the concept of international combat into a much more encompassing definition of conflict. The chapters that follow present a comprehensive understanding of armed encounters around the world and the roles that mothers acquired, assumed, or adopted within such situations.

Beginning in North America, John Navin's examination of mothers and warfare in the early colonial period presents the varied roles that mothers and children—white and Native American—endured due to interracial and intertribal violence in the eastern woodlands. As pawns, prisoners, and peacemakers, Navin reveals the diverse range of experiences that mothers and their offspring faced due to hostile forces. Claire Phelan presents the heartbreak faced by American families of impressed sailors during the late eighteenth and early nineteenth centuries. By analyzing letters between impressed sons and their mothers, she discloses the harsh reality of life at sea and the strength of maternal love that time, hardship, or circumstance could never undermine.

Moving to Latin America, Tracy Crowe Morey and Cristina Santos examine the testimonial writings of militant mothers in Latin America. As women, and specifically mothers, played key roles as political activists and militants during numerous Latin American uprisings in the 1970s and 1980s, such written statements illustrate shared maternal experiences and strategies across a diverse set of revolutionary movements. Evidence of such activism can be seen in Elena Shabliy's discussion of the Mothers of Plaza de Mayo. In response to national turbulence and the "Dirty War" between 1976 and 1983, the public response by Argentinean mothers radically changed the image of the private woman in Latin America and arguably served as a catalyst for the transition to democracy across the country.

Unlike the revolutions in Latin America, traditional definitions and experiences of warfare devastated the whole of Asia during the twentieth century. Annika Culver investigates the colonization and settlement activities of rural Japanese women as a significant contribution to the war effort in Manchukuo. Her analysis of propaganda pictorials displays the expressed desirable behaviors for women in settlement areas as mothers raising future soldiers and as evidence of imperial Japan's success during the war. Such themes of strength and sacrifice continue in the consideration of farewell letters from kamikaze pilots to their mothers, which suggest a predominant loyalty to mothers and families rather than to the nation. Utilizing a content analysis strategy, Salvador Jimenez Murguia and Benjamin A. Peters document the relationship between Japanese mothers and sons during World War II and challenge the long-standing belief in blind nationalism as the sole motivation for such wartime suicide missions.

From a European perspective, Lorraine Ryan analyzes the effects of social trauma on motherhood in postwar Spain. By dissecting the responses of Republican mothers during and after the war, she proves that maternal resourcefulness served as a determining factor in the survival of the Republican family. Producing a very different response, British artist Barbara Hepworth used her art as a means of survival due to wartime experiences. Lyrica Taylor's deconstruction of Hepworth's sculpture addresses how such art served to validate the individual and collective loss of Britons during and after World War II.

A Middle Eastern and African examination offers a very different perspective of motherhood during national and international conflict. Udi Lebel presents the victimological militarism of Israeli mothers; as Lebel contends, their distress preserves a cultural militarism, which in turn grants them prominence in public discourse. Likewise, Palestinian mothers earn and maintain such a revered role through their perpetuation of a culture of martyrdom. Michael Loadenthal argues that Palestinian mothers play a passionate role as the reproducers of future fighters as they carry the cultural narrative that serves to perpetuate the intifada. Fatin Shabbar discusses the effect of ongoing political conflicts in Iraq and subsequence influence on the definition and practice of motherhood in that country. She maintains that religious practice of mourning ceremonies and the cultural tradition of storytelling help Iraqi mothers resist the impact of wars and militarization on their children and communities. Mohamed Haji Ingiriis provides an African perspective concerning the historical status and social position of Somali women during the civil war and shows how mothers assumed a significant degree of authority on social and economic movements during the conflict.

Finally, Francis Shor presents the established power of the image of grieving mothers through the long history of warfare. His examination focuses on the recent grieving process of Americans Lila Lipscomb and Cindy Sheehan, mothers of sons who were killed in action as part of the war on terror. Their public articulation and criticism of the Iraq War transformed them into iconic media and maternally motivated figures. Their political representation of antiwar protests illustrates the different approaches to a shared opposition to international conflict.

Thus the question of ownership and obligation of young men, and specifically sons, is one that is not specific to American history or traditional notions of war, or any one group of mothers within a specific era or national boundary. The permanent and devastating effects of war, and the many variations of deadly conflict, are known to all people of any age in any country. Yet the versatile perspectives and malleable queries presented in the movie *Shenandoah* prove useful in analyzing questions of duty and sacrifice on behalf of a nation. In a sentimental monologue to his deceased wife, Jimmy Stewart forlornly describes the situation in the Civil War, though the nature of his words could be applied to most any conflict: "I don't even know what to say to you, Martha. There's nothing much I can tell you about this war. It's like all wars, I suppose. The undertakers are winning it. Politicians talk a lot about the glory of it. The soldiers, they just want to go home."[50] The mothers of such warriors, in many cases, would concur.

## NOTES

1. *Shenandoah*, directed by Andrew V. McLaglen (1965; Universal City, CA: MCA Universal Home Video, 2003), DVD.
2. Eliot A. Cohen, *Citizens and Soldiers: The Dilemmas of Military Service* (Ithaca: Cornell University Press, 1985), 122.
3. Rita J. Simon and Mohamed Alaa Abdel-Moneim, *A Handbook of Military Conscription and Composition the World Over* (Lanham: Lexington, 2011), 182; R. J. Q. Adams and Philip P. Poirier, *The Conscription Controversy in Great Britain, 1900–18* (Columbus: Ohio State University Press, 1987), ix.

4. George Q. Flynn, *The Draft, 1940–1973* (Lawrence: University Press of Kansas, 1993), 1.
5. Ibid., 2.
6. *Time*, "On Being Citizens and Soldiers," June 9, 1980.
7. Flynn, *The Draft*, 1–2.
8. John O'Sullivan and Alan M. Meckler, eds., *The Draft and Its Enemies: A Documentary History* (Urbana: University of Illinois Press, 1974), xv.
9. Allan R. Millett and Peter Maslowski, *For the Common Defense: A Military History of the United States of America* (New York: Free Press, 1984), 201; *New York Times*, "Making War on the Draft," October 13, 2013.
10. James W. Geary, *We Need Men* (DeKalb: Northern Illinois University Press, 1991), 174.
11. O'Sullivan and Meckler, eds., *The Draft and Its Enemies*, xi–xii.
12. John Whiteclay Chambers II, *To Raise an Army: The Draft Comes to Modern America* (New York: Free Press, 1987), vii.
13. O'Sullivan and Meckler, eds., *The Draft and Its Enemies*, xv.
14. Cohen, *Citizens and Soldiers*, 123.
15. Flynn, *The Draft*, 2.
16. O'Sullivan and Meckler, eds., *The Draft and Its Enemies*, xv.
17. Flynn, *The Draft*, 4.
18. *Guardian*, "Bring Back Mandatory Military Service in the US and UK," August 30, 2013.
19. Susan Zeiger, "She Didn't Raise Her Boy to Be a Slacker: Motherhood, Conscription, and the Culture of the First World War," *Feminist Studies* 22, no. 1 (Spring 1996): 7.
20. Suzanne Evans, *Mothers of Heroes, Mothers of Martyrs: World War I and the Politics of Grief* (Montreal: McGill-Queens University Press, 2007), 83.
21. *Christian Science Monitor*, "Feelings Mixed for Israeli Mothers as Sons go to War," August 10, 2006.
22. Nicoletta F. Gullace, "White Feathers and Wounded Men: Female Patriotism and the Memory of the Great War," *Journal of British Studies* 36, no. 2 (April 1997): 178–206.
23. Kathleen Kennedy, *Disloyal Mothers and Scurrilous Citizens: Women and Subversion during World War I* (Bloomington: Indiana University Press, 1999), 9–10.
24. Flynn, *The Draft*, 1.
25. Cheryl Benard, "Assessing the Truths and Myths of Women in War and Peace," delivered at the United States Institute of Peace Conference, *Perspectives on Grassroots Peacebuilding: The Roles of Women in War and Peace*, Washington, DC, September 14, 1999, 6.
26. Berk Çektir, "Compulsory Military Service," *Today's Zaman*, May 6, 2009.

INTRODUCTION: THE SHENANDOAH DOCTRINE    13

27. Amy Swerdlow, *Women Strike for Peace: Traditional Motherhood and Radical Politics in the 1960s* (Chicago: University of Chicago Press, 1993), 178.
28. Ibid.
29. Harriet Hyman Alonso, *Peace as a Woman's Issue: A History of the U.S. Movement for World Peace and Women's Rights* (Syracuse: Syracuse University Press, 1993), 216.
30. Ibid., 218.
31. Another Mother for Peace website, http://www.anothermother.org, accessed December 19, 2013.
32. Amy Caiazza, *Mothers and Soldiers: Gender, Citizenship, and Civil Society in Contemporary Russia* (New York: Routledge, 2002), 123, 143.
33. Alonso, *Peace as a Woman's Issue*, 11.
34. Chambers, *To Raise an Army*, ix.
35. O'Sullivan and Meckler, eds., *The Draft and Its Enemies*, xviii.
36. Cohen, *Citizens and Soldiers*, 185.
37. Kenneth Lasson, *Your Rights and the Draft* (New York: Pocket Books, 1980), 12.
38. Alonso, *Peace as a Woman's Issue*, vii.
39. Michael S. Foley, *Confronting the War Machine: Draft Resistance during the Vietnam War* (Chapel Hill: University of North Carolina Press, 2003), 344.
40. Caiazza, *Mothers and Soldiers*, 102.
41. Amia Lieblich, *Transition to Adulthood during Military Service: The Israeli Case* (Albany: State University of New York Press, 1989), 191.
42. Jean Belthke Elshtain, *Women and War* (Chicago: University of Chicago Press), 62.
43. Caiazza, *Mothers and Soldiers*, 113, 143.
44. Evans, *Mothers of Heroes, Mothers of Martyrs*, x.
45. Ibid., 79.
46. Ibid., 86.
47. Ibid., 88.
48. Caiazza, *Mothers and Soldiers*, 143.
49. Marine Family Network, "It Can't Always Be Someone Else's Son," http://marinefamilynetwork.com, accessed July 15, 2013.
50. *Shenandoah*, dir. McLaglen.

## Selected Bibliography

Adams, R. J. Q., and Philip P. Poirier. *The Conscription Controversy in Great Britain, 1900–18*. Columbus: Ohio State University Press, 1987.

Alonso, Harriet Hyman. *Peace as a Woman's Issue: A History of the U.S. Movement for World Peace and Women's Rights*. Syracuse: Syracuse University Press, 1993.

Caiazza, Amy. *Mothers and Soldiers: Gender, Citizenship, and Civil Society in Contemporary Russia*. New York: Routledge, 2002.

Chambers, John Whiteclay, II. *To Raise an Army: The Draft Comes to Modern America*. New York: Free Press, 1987.

Cohen, Eliot A. *Citizens and Soldiers: The Dilemmas of Military Service*. Ithaca: Cornell University Press, 1985.

Elshtain, Jean Belthke. *Women and War*. Chicago: University of Chicago Press, 1995.

Evans, Suzanne. *Mothers of Heroes, Mothers of Martyrs: World War I and the Politics of Grief*. Montreal: McGill-Queens University Press, 2007.

Flynn, George Q. *The Draft, 1940–1973*. Lawrence: University Press of Kansas, 1993.

Foley, Michael S. *Confronting the War Machine: Draft Resistance during the Vietnam War*. Chapel Hill: University of North Carolina Press, 2003.

Geary, James W. *We Need Men*. DeKalb: Northern Illinois University Press, 1991.

Gullace, Nicoletta F. "White Feathers and Wounded Men: Female Patriotism and the Memory of the Great War." *Journal of British Studies* 36, no. 2 (April 1997): 178–206.

Kennedy, Kathleen. *Disloyal Mothers and Scurrilous Citizens: Women and Subversion during World War I*. Bloomington: Indiana University Press, 1999.

Lasson, Kenneth. *Your Rights and the Draft*. New York: Pocket, 1980.

Lieblich, Amia. *Transition to Adulthood during Military Service: The Israeli Case*. Albany: State University of New York Press, 1989.

Millett, Allan R., and Peter Maslowski. *For the Common Defense: A Military History of the United States of America*. New York: Free Press, 1984.

O'Sullivan, John, and Alan M. Meckler, eds. *The Draft and Its Enemies: A Documentary History*. Urbana: University of Illinois Press, 1974.

Simon, Rita J., and Mohamed Alaa Abdel-Moneim. *A Handbook of Military Conscription and Composition the World Over*. Lanham: Lexington Books, 2011.

Swerdlow, Amy. *Women Strike for Peace: Traditional Motherhood and Radical Politics in the 1960s*. Chicago: University of Chicago Press, 1993.

Zeiger, Susan. "She Didn't Raise Her Boy to Be a Slacker: Motherhood, Conscription, and the Culture of the First World War." *Feminist Studies* 22, no. 1 (Spring 1996): 6–39.

Chapter 2

———⸙———

Mothers, Warfare, and Captivity in the Eastern Woodlands of North America, 1607–1763

*John J. Navin*

On August 9, 1610, colonists from Jamestown launched a surprise attack on the main settlement of the Paspahegh tribe, intent on avenging the deaths of 17 Englishmen the previous year. The attackers killed "fifteen or sixteen" Paspahegh, burned their houses, and cut down their corn. Most inhabitants fled, but those captured included the wife and children of Wowinchapuncke, the Paspahegh sachem. On the return trip "it was agreed upon to put the Children to death . . . by throwing them overboard and shooting out their brains in the water" while their mother watched in horror. At Jamestown, Sir Thomas Gates, the colony's governor, "seemed to be discontent because the queen was spared." He "thought [it] best to burn her," but George Percy opted to give the woman "a quicker dispatch." Three of his soldiers took the grieving mother into the woods and "put her to the sword."[1]

As colonists penetrated the interior of North America, women and children often found themselves at the center of bloody encounters—not just white women and children, but Native American women and children as well. In times of war, mothers became victims, warriors, prisoners, pawns, peacemakers, caregivers, tormentors, martyrs, mourners, and more. This essay focuses on the experience of mothers who were drawn into the maelstrom of interracial and intertribal violence in the eastern woodlands from the early seventeenth century to 1763, the end of the Colonial period. It is especially concerned with mothers who were taken captive or whose children fell into the hands of hostile forces, though the two events often coincided. Their husbands and older sons often figure prominently in these terrifying ordeals, but the captivity experiences of adult males tended to be brief and indescribably harsh.

Historian Gary Ebersole's contention that "captivity represents an ultimate boundary situation where human existence, identity, and ultimate meaning are called into question" was written with the captivity of whites by Native Americans in mind, but the loss of freedom and autonomy, social status, and cultural accouterments and markers was potentially devastating for all captives regardless of race or gender. They were often "reduced to abject poverty, subjected to great physical deprivation, extreme hunger, and psychological stress, and divested of all status and power."[2] How much greater, then, must the stress have been for *mothers* who were taken captive? For those women, there existed an array of possible scenarios, none of them good. A great number, the majority in some settlements, witnessed the deaths of their husbands and neighbors during the initial assault. Some mothers were carried off by the enemy, left to wonder how their children fared in their absence. Worse yet and far more frequent, mothers were captured *with* their children, pressed to care for them under the most adverse circumstances. Many were separated from their sons and/or daughters while in captivity, left to agonize over their fate. Others saw their children perish due to illness, exposure, injury, or other hazards. The least fortunate mothers witnessed the outright murder of one or more of their offspring; infants were especially at risk. Captivity also involved mothers who escaped capture but whose children fell into the hands of their enemies; uncertainty and dread must have been their constant companions. For white mothers, the fact that Native Americans often adopted young captives fostered both hope and dismay; the prospect that a son or daughter remained alive and well was offset by the likelihood that he or she might never be recovered. This apprehension was exacerbated by the fact that white adoptees frequently became "Indianized," preferring to remain with their captors.

Native American mothers were in the unenviable position of having to fear not only their tribe's enemies but also their supposed allies. Spanish, French, and English colonists and clergy—and later, American religious and civil authorities and philanthropists—were sometimes inclined to "help" Indians by placing their children in missions, schools, convents, apprenticeships, servitude, or other situations that separated parents from their offspring. Like the mothers of white captives, Native American women had to fear aggressive forms of acculturation and the permanent loss of their children. It is telling that Indians relied on adoption and affective bonds to integrate children into their culture, whereas whites institutionalized the process, relying on indoctrination (with significantly less success). Those affective bonds were a double-edged sword: Native American women who accepted white captives as substitutes for lost family members sometimes had to surrender them as a result of negotiation or force. As surrogate mothers, their grief at the loss of a child, even an adoptive one, was genuine.

Pocahontas, daughter of Powhatan, was the most famous Indian captive in Colonial America. Taken hostage by Captain Samuel Argall at Jamestown in 1612, her captivity led to her religious conversion, marriage to colonist John Rolfe, delivery of a son, and death by disease in England. The earliest account of white female captivity in the eastern woodlands stemmed from the Jamestown massacre of 1622, a bloodletting that provoked more than two decades of interracial warfare in the Chesapeake. Hundreds of colonists were killed and at least 19 women were captured and held "in great slavery" among the Powhatan Indians; some were redeemed years later but others presumably died in captivity.[3] When Pequot Indians attacked Wethersfield, Connecticut, in 1637 they killed nine colonists and captured "two maids" whom they exchanged for seven members of their own tribe.[4] A month later, more than four hundred Pequot women and children were surrounded and deliberately "broiled to death" or shot while trying to escape their burning encampment near the Mystic River. The slaughter occurred despite the fact that Miantonomi, sachem of the Narragansett tribe allied to the English, had requested "that women and children be spared."[5] Captain John Underhill later attempted to justify the carnage, noting that "sometimes the Scripture declareth women and children must perish with their parents."[6] Subsequent battles resulted in hundreds of additional Native American casualties and the capture of three hundred or so Pequot women and children. Puritan leaders made servants of some, allocated others to their Native American allies, and sold an unfortunate few into slavery off the Nicaraguan coast.[7] The wife of the Pequot sachem Mononotto begged that "the English would not abuse her body and that her children might not be taken from her."[8] Many Pequot women who were thrust into servitude later attempted escape, a crime for which they were branded if recaptured. Roger Williams, founder of Rhode Island, counseled a Pequot runaway who had been raped, branded, and "beaten with firesticks."[9] A tract published in London in 1643 alleged that many Pequot children were "much in love" with their English families; six years into their captivity, they were "long since civilized," grounded in Christianity, fluent in the English language, and unable to "endure to returne any more to the Indians."[10]

Native American mothers sometimes seemed to be surrounded by enemies on all sides. In 1643, Wickquasgeck and Tappan Indians fled to New Netherland seeking protection from fierce Mohawk warriors. However, the murder of a colonist prompted Dutch authorities to unleash their troops in a nighttime attack on the refugees' encampment at Pavonia: "[I]nfants were torn from their mother's breasts, and hacked to pieces in the presence of their parents . . . and other sucklings, being bound to small boards, were cut, stuck, and pierced, and miserably massacred . . . Some were thrown into the river, and when the fathers and mothers endeavored to save them, the soldiers . . . made both parents and children drown."[11] After 20 members of their tribe were sold into slavery in 1663, Esopus Indians attacked two Dutch settlements; 20 colonists were slain and 44 women and children were taken prisoner.[12] Dutch reprisals were severe: a report described nine large pits into which fleeing Esopus had cast their dead. One unfortunate mother and child "lay unburied . . . almost wholly devoured by the ravens and the wolves."[13]

Native American social customs emphasized clan responsibility: when someone was killed or captured, a victim's male kin were compelled to seek revenge.[14] One cause of King Philip's War—New England's second interracial war—was a false report that colonists had slaughtered a group of Indian women who were gathering corn. Not surprisingly, members of the victims' tribe "took up arms to revenge that supposed injury."[15] Another provocation occurred in 1672 when Englishmen allegedly overturned the canoe in which an Indian mother and child were travelling to test the rumor that "children of the Indians . . . could swim as naturally as any other creatures." The child drowned and his enraged father, the sachem of Saco, then "was never . . . willing to be reconciled."[16] The war proved a long and bloody affair (1675–78) in which atrocities occurred on both sides. In October 1675, Captain Mosely informed Governor Leverett that an "old Indian squaw" his men had captured "was ordered to be tourne in peeces by dogs."[17] The following year English militia killed at least one hundred Native American women and children at the battle of Turner's Falls. In his *Brief History of the Warr*, Reverend Increase Mather described yet another massacre—the Great Swamp Fight: "There were hundreds of *Wigwams* (or Indian houses) within the

Fort, which our Souldiers set on fire, in the which men, women and Children (no man knoweth how many hundreds of them) were burnt to death . . . it is supposed that not less then a thousand Indian Souls perished at that time."[18] The identities of Native American women and children who died in these clashes remains unknown, whereas the names and fates of their English counterparts were often captured in correspondence, official documents, or in print. Mary Rowlandson's famous narrative, *The Sovereignty and Goodness of God*, described the assault on her Lancaster, Massachusetts, home in early 1675: "Some in our house were fighting for their lives, others wallowing in their blood, the house on fire over our heads, and the bloody heathen ready to knock us on the head if we stirred out. Now might we hear mothers and children crying out for themselves and one another, 'Lord, what shall we do?'"[19]

For mothers in the eastern woodlands, white and Indian alike, interracial wars were local affairs—even in their homes they and their families were not safe.[20] To the dismay of Rowlandson and other frontier matriarchs, Indian raiding parties, sometimes abetted by French allies, pillaged and often burned outlying settlements. They killed colonists who resisted and took the rest as prisoners, especially after 1689 when most adult English captives could be redeemed for a set price.[21] Historians estimate that nearly four hundred white women in the northeast were captured by Indians between 1675 and 1763, when the Treaty of Paris ended Anglo-French conflict in North America.[22] That total was likely surpassed by the number of women seized in Western Pennsylvania and Virginia during the French and Indian War (1754–60). In just a few years, some two thousand settlers— nearly 1 percent of the entire population of those colonies—were killed or taken captive. Virginia's Governor Morris wrote in 1756, "[I]t is difficult to conceive . . . what a multitude of inhabitants, of all ages and both sexes, they have carried into captivity." After Shawnee warriors took 150 prisoners at Fort Vause in Augusta County, William Preston was dismayed by the "Confusion and Disorder [of] the Poor People . . . Mothers with [a] train of helpless Children at their heels straggling through woods & mountains to escape the fury of those merciless savages."[23] Women and children in the Carolinas also suffered grievously during this period. In February 1760, the *South Carolina Gazette* reported that settlers fleeing from Long Cane had been attacked by Cherokees on horseback. The dead included about "50 persons, chiefly Women and Children"; the following week's paper reported, "Many children have been found wandering in the woods . . . some of them terribly cut with tomahawks and left for dead, and other scalp'd, yet alive."[24]

Captivity often proved a terrifying ordeal, but many mothers and children did not even survive the initial assault. Of the 37 people in the garrison house with Mary Rowlandson, only one escaped death or capture. Rowlandson herself was shot through the side, the same bullet piercing "the bowels and hand of my dear child in my arms."[25] Accounts of similar episodes punctuate the records of towns on the northeast frontier. When the garrison at Falmouth, Maine, surrendered to French and Indian attackers in 1690, all but a handful of the approximately 70 men and 130 women and children were massacred. A survivor related that "the French suffered our women and children and especially the wounded men to be cruelly murdered or destroyed after the surrender."[26] That same year a similar raiding party "murther'd Sixty men women and Children most Barbarously" at Schenectady, taking 27 others captive.[27] Extant documents reveal countless personal tragedies. In 1704, Eunice Williams of Deerfield watched her captors slay two of her children and her servant.[28] In Easthampton, the wife of Benjamin Janes witnessed the slaughter of her four young children as well as her in-laws and their three children just before she was tomahawked, scalped, and left for dead.[29] When Indians attacked Dover Township in 1724, two "barbarous savages" came into Elizabeth Hanson's house in a "great fury" and killed one of her children immediately, "thinking thereby to strike in us the greater terror." Because her four-year-old child "continued screeching," the attackers "knocked its brains out . . . Now having killed two of my children, they scalped them."[30]

Once they breached the defenses and killed or neutralized any defenders, Native American raiding parties were usually quick to seize plunder and prisoners and then take flight. According to one estimate, at least one-fifth of the women captured in New England were either pregnant or had just given birth.[31] When militiamen were in hot pursuit, slower captives and noisy infants were a liability, so pregnant women and newborns were sometimes sacrificed in the interests of speed and stealth. Increase Mather described an incident in 1676 when "those barbarous wretches hasted to run away, but before that they knocked the two Children on the head, as they were sucking their mothers breasts, and then knocked their Mothers on the head."[32] Following a raid on Schenectady, Peter Schuyler reported "women bigg with Childe rip'd up, and the Children alive thrown into the flames, and their heads dashed to pieces against the Doors and windows."[33] During a 1703 raid in Maine, the attackers "ript up one Goody Webber that was big with child and laid her child to her breast and so left her."[34] Benjamin Church elaborated on the incident, saying the infant, "seized fast with strings to her chest . . . had no apparent wound, which doubtless was left alive to suck its dead mother's breast, and so miserably to perish and die."[35]

Surviving the initial assault and entering captivity was no guarantee of survival for mothers or their offspring. What followed was often a forced march that tested the endurance of everyone involved; in the northeast, the destination was often Canada. Captives faced a long, arduous journey across steep snow-covered hills and icy streams; many would last no more than a few days in the wilderness. Catherine Adams, just eight days past childbirth, was "up to her neck in Water six times" during the first day's twenty-mile trek; her two children had been killed because they were deemed "too young to travel."[36] John Searle's wife had travelled just a short distance when her captors "finding that she was pregnant and thinking that she would not be able to travel to Canada, tomahawked her."[37] Eunice Williams, taken prisoner two weeks after giving birth, was executed after she plunged "over head and ears" in a freezing river. Two days later the Indians murdered a pregnant woman who had "wearied with her journey." The next day's march proved "long and tedious," and four exhausted women were slain. Mary Brooks, a "pious young woman" from Deerfield, informed Reverend John Williams that "by my falls on the Ice yesterday I wrong'd my self, causing an Abortion this Night, so that now I am not able to Travel far." Brooks told Williams that "I know they will kill me today," a prediction that proved true.[38] Mary Furguson, "overburdened with plunder," was scalped and decapitated when she insisted she could travel no further.[39] Many of her companions met a similar fate: concerns about the "English Pursueing of them" caused the raiding party "to nock all the captives on the head, Save 5 or 6."[40] Mary Rowlandson described the "sad end" of a female companion "very big with child, having but one week to reckon, and another child in her arm two years old": "[The Indians] stripped her naked, and set her in the midst of them. And when they had sung and danced about her (in their hellish manner) as long as they pleased they knocked her on head, and the child in her arms with her . . . they made a fire and put them both into it."[41] In some cases the mother was preserved but her child was not. Mary Plaisted's "Diabolical master" seized her baby, "dash'd out its Brains and then flang it into the river"; Margaret Teuxbury's infant was "burnt on the fire."[42] Mehetable Goodwin's baby was tomahawked because it cried too much.[43]

Ann Jenkins testified that "in one miles goeing" three children were killed by their captors.[44]

Some women faced the daunting prospect of giving birth while in a state of captivity in the wilderness and on the run. Tamsen Drew's child, "born in the open air and in a violent snowstorm," was killed by her captors.[45] The wife of John Smead "was delivered a child on ye road" just one day after her capture; both she and her newborn died in captivity.[46] When Susannah Johnson delivered a child on the second day of her forced march, her Indian master clapped his hands with joy, crying "two monies for me, two monies for me." Johnson later observed, "None but mothers can figure to themselves my unhappy fortune."[47] The hardships posed by the rapid pace and challenging terrain were compounded by the lack of food, proper clothing, and shelter. During her forced march, Susannah Fitch nursed not only her 16-month-old child but also her four- and six-year-old sons.[48] Elizabeth Hanson's milk dried up; her infant "grew very poor and weak, just skin and bones." Caring for children under such dire circumstances was extraordinarily difficult, but separation from sons and daughters proved even more excruciating for many mothers. Captured in 1724, Hanson later recalled, "I suffered, in being under various fears and doubts concerning my children that were separated from me, which helped to add to and greatly increase my troubles."[49] Jemima Howe, taken captive with her children in 1755, was forced to "pluck" her nursing infant from her breast and deliver it "shrieking and screaming" to its "new owners." At night she could "hear its incessant cries and heart-rending lamentations." Howe preserved her milk "in hopes of seeing my child again"; she did, but it was "greatly emaciated and almost starved." Howe later recalled, "I often imagined . . . that I plainly saw the naked carcasses of my deceased children hanging upon the limbs of the trees, as the Indians are wont to hang the raw hides of those beasts which they take in hunting."[50] Such horrific images were sometimes all too real. After the 1704 raid on Deerfield, Benjamin Church was distressed to see "poor children, hanging upon fences, dead, of either sex, in their own poor rags."[51] When residents of Shenandoah country, Virginia, were attacked by Frenchmen and Native Americans in 1758, the latter "forced from the arms of their mothers four infant children, hung them up in trees, shot them in savage sport, and left them hanging."[52] Indians on the Pennsylvania frontier reportedly pinned colonists' scalps to trees and mutilated women and children, leaving their bodies on display at crossroads.[53]

Colonial tracts and captivity narratives focused on "outrages" committed by marauding Indians, but they inadvertently exposed some of the hardships that Native American mothers and their children faced as they fled pursuing militia. Mary Rowlandson noted, "They marched on furiously with their old and with their young; some carried their old decrepit mothers; some carried one and some another."[54] Deerfield captive John Williams observed, "They were many hundreds, old and young, some sick and some lame; many had papooses at their backs; the greatest number at this time with us were squaws; and yet they travelled with all they had, bag and baggage, and they got over this river aforesaid; and on Monday they set their wigwams on fire, and away they went."[55] The English viewed noncombatants as their enemy's Achilles heel; Increase Mather lamented, "Had the *English* pursued the Enemy they might easily have overtaken the Women and Children that were with *Philip*, yea and himself also, and so have put an end to these tumults."[56] Mary Rowlandson thought the English militia should have been able to track the Indians by detecting where they had been "rooting the ground for ground-nuts whilst they were flying for their lives."[57] With so many Indian women in flight for weeks and even months at a time, births, miscarriages, and premature deaths were inevitable. James Corse recalled "an old squaw, pregnant, that traveled with us, stoped alone & was delivered of a child and by Monday overtook us with a living child upon her back."[58] Shortly after Mary Rowlandson's Indian "mistress" attended the burial of a friend's papoose, her own baby died. The women who came to "mourn and howl" with Weetamoo evoked little sympathy from Rowlandson, whose own child had died in captivity. She also described a Native American papoose whose parents had been killed: the infant, almost dead, had been "turned out" of the wigwam, "quivering in the cold . . . stretched out with his eyes, nose, and mouth full of dirt and yet alive and groaning." One rainy evening Rowlandson's captors "quickly got up a bark wigwam where I lay dry"; in the morning she realized "many of them had laid in the rain all night." On that and many other occasions, "I fared better than many of them."[59] The English tactic of destroying villages and crops and waging war on entire tribes meant that Native American mothers and children were constantly on the run, suffering from exposure, exhaustion, and near starvation. The Dutch also employed this strategy in their wars with the Esopus Indians, noting in 1663 that their enemy was "deprived of all means of subsistence through the destruction of their corn."[60] Rowlandson said her captors would eat items "that a hog or dog would hardly touch."[61] When English militiamen destroyed their enemy's stock of fish in 1704, the Indians "set up a hideous cry" and fled into the woods.[62] In these and other ways, Native American mothers and their offspring endured untold hardships and perished in great numbers, but unlike many of their white counterparts, they left no written accounts of their sufferings.

Because they formed close bonds with their adopted children, Native American mothers were often reluctant to part with them despite generous ransom offers. Captives replaced lost family members not just physically but also in spirit, status, and role. Rituals such as running the gauntlet, symbolic washing, and donning Native American attire enabled white captives to shed their former identities and become fully adopted into Indian families.[63] During the Esopus War, a woman refused to allow two Dutch captives to be ransomed because "she is very sick and hath no children."[64] Eunice Williams was adopted by a Mohawk whose daughter had died of smallpox; despite being offered "an hundred pieces of eight" and even "an Indian girl in her stead," Williams' captors informed negotiators that they would "as soon part with their hearts as the child."[65] In 1714 when Ebenezer Nims boarded a ship to return from ten years of captivity in Canada, his Native American mother hurried to Quebec to demand his return.[66] John Handson redeemed two of his captive sons, but he was unable to ransom his daughter, "for the Indians would not consent to part with her on any terms."[67] Mary Woodwell's adoptive mother refused all ransom offers until Mary suddenly fell gravely ill (a physician having administered a potion to deceive the woman).[68] During ransom negotiations for Eleanor Noble, her Native American mother pointed out that she had paid for a wet nurse, stayed home from hunting to care for the infant, and bought French food "when she would not eat Indian." The woman was coerced into accepting one-third the amount she sought, but the next morning she and the little girl had vanished and the ransom money lay on the table.[69] Elizabeth Hanson's husband was unable to redeem one of her daughters, because she had been "given to an old squaw who intended to marry her in time to her son."[70] In a striking example of maternal affection, the "squaw-mothers" of Mary Adams and Mary Sheldon, two redeemed captives, travelled from Canada to Massachusetts to visit their adoptive daughters.[71] Some Indian converts had their white children baptized and attended church weddings when they had grown.[72]

The affection that Native American mothers felt for their adopted children often worked in both directions. One tribulation for English settlers in the Colonial period was the frequency with which captives became "Indianized" (and in some cases converted to Catholicism).

Peter Schuyler's efforts to redeem colonists seized in King William's War were frustrated when all but "two or three" of the English captives then residing in Canada "unanimously refused to return." When Schuyler demanded the children under 14, they were "reluctantly given to them," but even some of these "still remained who hid themselves." In 1698 the Iroquois surrendered their French captives "except the little children, who are become almost Iroquois."[73] The parents of captives often went to great effort and expense to recover their offspring, only to find they had become fully assimilated into Native American culture. Many could no longer speak their native tongue, and when taken back to English settlements against their will, they often proved unhappy and attempted to return to their Indian families. Benjamin Franklin noted in 1753 that unless carefully watched, former captives "seized the first good opportunity of escaping again into the Woods, from whence there is no reclaiming them."[74]

Maternal instincts sometimes transcended racial animosities. When 24 shipwrecked Quakers became the prisoners of Ais Indians in Florida, a native woman insisted on nursing the Dickinson's six-month-old son. Fearful at first, the parents came to appreciate her intervention because "its mother's milk was almost gone . . . And our child, which had been at death's door, from the time of its birth, until we were cast away, began now to be cheerful and have an appetite for food."[75] When Elizabeth Hanson was unable to breastfeed her child, one of her female captors showed her how to prepare a mixture of walnuts and water that caused her infant "to thrive and look well."[76] But despite such acts of kindness, it must be remembered that Native American mothers were involved in interracial violence not just as victims but as participants as well. Given the emotional stress placed on Indian women, many of whom suffered extreme hardships and physical deprivation as they fled with their children, captives never knew whether they would meet compassion or abuse at their hands. In matrilineal tribes, women often determined which captives would live or die.[77] Bereaved mothers and widows could choose to adopt a prisoner, or they could seek satisfaction in rituals of torture and execution.[78] One former captive's description of the infamous gauntlet that male prisoners had to run included "a heap of squaws and childring who stand ready for to receive them with their sticks, clubbs, pols and fir-brands, who lay on with all the force and might."[79] Numerous accounts of ritual torture portray Native American women and children burning captives with firebrands or piercing their bodies with "blazing fagots of pine."[80] Ottawa women were said to be "more ingenious and subtle in inventing tortures" than their male counterparts; they also encouraged their children to participate in ritual torture, shooting arrows into their victims.[81] Native American mothers could even be involved in offensive operations. In 1689 "two squaws" reconnoitered garrison houses in Dover, New Hampshire; while the English slept, the women "opened the gates and gave the signal" to waiting warriors.[82] During a bloody encounter at Pemaquid, a daring Indian woman "caught up a bundle of guns, and run for the woods."[83] But these women were exceptions; the majority of Native American mothers and children were not directly involved in any raids, though they were frequently the victims of their enemies' forays against the Indians. In 1724 English troops invaded the home of the sachem Bomazeen; they "killed his daughter, and then captivated his wife." When a "famous Indian warrior" shot one of their Mohawk allies, the English "in a rage killed his squaw and two helpless children."[84]

English mothers also took up arms (or whatever else was at hand) to defend themselves and their families. Elizabeth Tozier was boiling soap when two Indians attempted to seize her; she threw the scalding liquid on them and made her escape. Tozier sometimes "dressed in man's clothes with gun in hand" and acted as sentry.[85] Hannah Bradley used hot soap to even greater effect; aided by a male companion, she poured "a good quantity of scalding Soap" on an Indian attacker "whereby he was kill'd immediately." When another warrior "stabb'd the English man to the Heart," Bradley "dispensed also a quantity of her Sope which, not killing him, she with the other Women and Children ran into the Chamber." She was taken captive (for the second time) and "with the Snow under her and the Heaven over her," gave birth to her fourth child.[86] Cotton Mather wrote that during the assault on Wells, Maine, in 1692, women "not only brought ammunition to the Men, but also with a Manly resolution fired several Times upon the Enemy."[87] In 1706 women in New Hampshire "put on the Habit [clothing] of men, and acted their part so manfully," that their attackers withdrew; another report stated that they "fired so briskly that they struck a terror in the enemy."[88] A woman in a Dover garrison shouted "orders and alarms" to imaginary companions, persuading Native American raiders to retreat. In Gorham, women stood guard when an epidemic struck down most male inhabitants.[89]

Once a female colonist was taken captive, further resistance often proved fatal. Even so, some women attempted escape. Few succeeded, but one notable exception was Mary Draper Ingles, captured by Shawnee warriors in 1755. After her children were taken away from her, Ingles sneaked off and reached her Blacksburg, Virginia, home following a six-week, 800-mile trek.[90] Another captive mother—Hannah Duston (or Dustin)—gained enduring fame in 1697. Six days after giving birth to her twelfth child, Duston was one of 39 settlers seized in a raid on Haverhill, Massachusetts. According to Cotton Mather, the Indians "dash'd out the Brains of the Infant, against a Tree" and killed several other captives "as they began to Tire." Duston was claimed by a Native American family consisting of "Two stout men, Three Women, and Seven Children." That night, as their captors slept, Duston and two fellow prisoners killed ten of their "Sleeping Oppressors" with the Indians' own hatchets; one woman and boy escaped the slaughter. The three whites then scalped their victims and carried their grisly trophies back to Haverhill. As "Recompence of their Action" the General Assembly of Massachusetts awarded Duston 25 pounds and half that amount to her companions; they also received "many presents of Congratulation" from their friends and even from the Governor of Maryland.[91] Duston was not the only female colonist to indulge in retaliatory violence. In 1677, Indians in Maine seized a number of English fishing vessels, prompting rumors that the crews had been murdered. When a ketch sailed into Marblehead harbor with two Native American prisoners on board, women rushed out of the meetinghouse and "demanded why we kept them alive and why we had not killed them." The crew intended to take their captives to the authorities, but the women "with stones, billets of wood, and what else they might, they made an end of these Indians." A witness later deposed that "we found them with their heads off and gone, and their flesh in a manner pulled from their bones." The women declared that "if there had been forty of the best Indians in the country here, they would have killed them all, though they should be hanged for it."[92]

No one knows how many Native American mothers and children in the eastern woodlands were captured by whites during the Colonial period, though that total would undoubtedly pale in comparison to the number whose lives were disrupted and endangered. On occasion they were seized in great numbers, as was the case with hundreds of Pequot women and children taken prisoner in 1637, or in 1676 when Major Richard Waldron used treachery to capture "80 fighting men & 20 old men, 250 women and children" in New Hampshire.[93] In 1687 the French Governor of Canada used treachery to seize 51 Mohawk warriors and 150 women and children, many of whom died in captivity.[94] Three years later, 16 Native American women and children and 5 male captives were "sent by water to Boston" from Saco, prompting their tribe to seize English colonists who could be used in a prisoner exchange.[95] Sometimes Native American women were seized as interpreters or for interrogation about the number, whereabouts, or intent of their tribal companions. The commander of Fort Loudoun in South Carolina informed Governor Henry Lyttleton that "intelligence from women among the Indians are always best."[96] Native American women and children were occasionally taken as hostages, especially if they were members of an important Sachem's family. In 1690, Benjamin Church's troops captured the wives and children of two sachems; the mothers pleaded that Church spare their lives and those of their children, promising that if he did, 80 or so white captives would be returned. Church saved "two old squaws" to use as messengers but ordered that the rest of his prisoners be "knocked on the head . . . for an example."[97] During Queen Anne's War, the wife of a Norridgewock chief and her children were exchanged for four English captives.[98] In 1723, Jane Edgar and Margaret Watt petitioned Massachusetts authorities that "an Indian woman named Elizabeth with her children now in the hands of this Government" be exchanged for their husbands and seven children held captive in Canada.[99] Several years later, two Native American women were released on the condition that they return with captive whites; a "young son" of one of them was kept as hostage.[100] In his history of King Philip's War, Increase Mather wrote, "*Philip* hardly escaped with his life . . . his *Squaw and his Son were taken Captives* . . . It must needs be bitter as death to him, to loose [sic] his Wife and only Son (for the Indians are marvellous fond and affectionate towards their Children)."[101] In the wake of the Pequot War and King Philip's War, many Native American women and children from defeated tribes were assimilated when they fled to neighboring tribes or were awarded to Indian allies of the English. Mothers who were forced into servitude or sold abroad as slaves often became separated from their sons and daughters.

Though many were killed or driven from their homes, the number of Native American mothers and children taken captive in the northeast woodlands actually paled in comparison to the number seized in the southeast. Faced with a shortage of indentured servants, some Virginia colonists used enslaved Indians on their plantations; women were preferred due to their traditional agricultural roles. In 1682, Virginia's Burgesses defined all non-Christians—Indians and Africans alike—as eligible for perpetual slavery.[102] South Carolinians negotiated a treaty whereby the Westos tribe would supply deerskins and Indian slaves.[103] Within a decade the alliance crumbled and colonists were selling Westos women and children to Caribbean sugar planters. Carolina authorities were quick to establish other alliances, and the trade in enslaved Indians boomed; in 1700 a Muklasa Indian noted that "the greatest traffic between the English and the savages is the trade of slaves . . . the [Indian] men take the women and children away and sell them to the English."[104] Chickasaw raiders received "a Gun, ammunition, horse, hatchet, and a suit of Cloathes" for just one captive.[105] Carolina's proprietors in England criticized the colonists for persuading Native Americans "to make war upon their neighbors, to ravish the wife from the Husband, kill the father to get to the Child, and to burn and Destroy the habitations of these poor people." They denounced the fact that "poor Innocent women and children [were] Barbarously murdered, taken and sent to be sold as slaves."[106] In 1711 a Creek warned his fellow warriors that a defeat at the hands of the approaching Apalachee would result in "inexpressible groans and screeches" of captive Creek women and children who would be "abused before your eyes." But should they defeat the Apalachee raiders, "our wives and children shall dance, whoop and sing to see them dying and howling." The Creek leader noted that as a young man he "began with the slaughter of women and children" before collecting the 15 male scalps on his girdle.[107]

The majority of Indians that were sold into slavery in the southeast were noncombatants. Benard de La Harpe reported that the English and their Chickasaw allies took 300 women and children captive in just one of three major raids on Choctaw settlements between 1706 and 1711.[108] When North Carolinians needed assistance in their war with the Tuscarora, Governor Hyde encouraged South Carolinians to send extra men, because there were "hundreds of women and children . . . perhaps 3 or 4 thousand" that could be enslaved.[109] Though they continued to value the ritual torture of male prisoners, Native American slave raiders in the southeast often preferred mothers and children because they proved less troublesome while being conveyed over long distances (slave raids reached all the way south from Carolina to Florida and west to the Mississippi).[110] Not all captives were exported; a 1708 census showed that South Carolina's 9,580 inhabitants included 1,400 enslaved Indians.[111] Carolina's Indian slave trade diminished significantly after the Yamassee War (1715–16), but intermittent hostilities continued. In 1759 the rape of Cherokee women by white officers provoked reprisals; following a bayonet attack at Little Keeowee the British commander remarked that some women and children "could Not Be Saved." That action and a subsequent battle at Sugar Town left scores of Cherokee dead and forty men, women, and children in captivity.[112] Three years later the Catawba complained to the British that the Cherokee had been stealing their women.[113]

Like their northern counterparts, Native American women in the southeast were not just victims but actors as well. They traditionally determined which prisoners would be adopted, though the rise of the Indian slave trade meant many indigenous captives were secured for sale, not adoption.[114] During the "scalp dance" Creek women received scalps, war clubs, and captives from male kin; afterward mothers and children joined in the torment of those prisoners who were not to be adopted, sold, or kept as slaves. A contemporary noted, "Not a soul, of whatever age or sex, manifests the least pity during the prisoner's tortures: the women sing with religious joy, all the while they are torturing the devoted victim."[115] Some women joined in actual combat: a Cherokee named Cuhtahlutah led her tribe to victory after her husband was killed.[116] A stream in Georgia called "War Woman's Creek" was so named after a victory credited to another Cherokee woman.[117] Some women served their tribes as leaders, diplomats, interpreters, or peacemakers.[118] In Virginia the English had to negotiate with Cockacoeske, the Queen of Pamunkey; in the northeast, several Algonquian "Sunksqaws" assumed leadership roles in the mid- to late seventeenth century.[119] Prior to King Philip's War, both Metacomet (King Philip) and his English enemies courted the allegiance of Awashunkes and Weetamoo, two "Squaw Sachems."[120] In 1725 the Creek sent a captive Cherokee to persuade her tribe to join in an alliance against the English.[121] In some Cherokee villages there was one woman who "by the wave of a swan's wing could deliver a wretch already condemned by the Council, and already tied to the stake."[122] This was a "War Woman" or "Beloved Women," the most famous of whom was Nanye'hi, known to whites as Nancy Ward. The mother of two young children, she had replaced her fallen husband in a battle against Creek warriors.[123] During negotiations in 1781, Nanye'hi spoke on behalf of her Cherokee sisters: "You know that women are always looked upon as nothing: but we are your mothers; and you are our sons. Our cry is all for peace; let it continue. This peace must last forever. Let your women's sons be ours; our sons be yours. Let your women hear our words." Colonel William Christian replied on behalf of the American negotiators: "Mothers: we have listened well to your talk; it is humane ... We all are descendents of the same women. We will not quarrel with you, because you are our mothers. We will not meddle with your people if they will be still and quiet at home and let us live in peace."[124] Remaining "still and quiet at home" was not an option for many mothers on the Colonial frontier. When wars occurred, women and children were inevitably drawn into the fray as victims, not willing participants. Most historians regard "Total War"—unrestricted warfare against enemy populations—as a phenomenon that emerged in the nineteenth or twentieth century, but the military tactics and strategies employed by both Native Americans and Europeans in the seventeenth and eighteenth centuries shed the distinctions between combatants and noncombatants.[125] When Pequot women and children were incinerated by English militia, when pregnant women and newborn infants were slain by their Indian captors in New England, when homes and crops on both sides in King Philip's War were razed, when enslaved Westos of all ages were deported, and when hundreds of Creek mothers and children fell victim to Apalachee raiders, there was no pretense of limited war.[126] Villages, towns, tribes, and even entire populations became targets up and down the eastern woodlands.

The circumstances in which mothers and their offspring suffered and died were sometimes dictated by race. Although whites and Indians alike perished during assaults on their homes, Native American women were far more likely to be the victims of large-scale operations conducted against villages or encampments. Some historians maintain that the mothers and children killed at Mystic Fort in 1637 and in the Great Swamp Fight in 1675 perished in genocidal campaigns.[127] Such incidents were far different from smaller-scale attacks on frontier settlements, where the desire for booty and ransom sometimes superseded racial animosities, revenge, or blood lust. But in both cases, mothers who had been nursing their infants or tending cooking fires only moments earlier suddenly found themselves and their loved ones in grave danger. From New England to Florida, warfare knew no bounds, and it took only minutes for mothers to become victims, widows, and/or captives.

It has been shown that the experience of captivity also differed by race, gender, age, and location. In the northeast, white women were valued for purposes of ransom or, less frequently, as slaves or potential replacements for lost tribal members. Their weaned children were coveted as adoptees—a circumstance stemming from the extreme population loss suffered by most eastern woodland tribes during the Colonial period. Tragically, infants were often viewed as a liability and murdered outright during the initial assault or early in a forced march. Native American mothers, on the other hand, were not particularly valued as prisoners by whites in the northeast. They and their children were rarely adopted by whites, ransom was seldom a motive for their capture, and their enslavement by colonists proved problematic. In the southeast the situation was far different. There, mothers were swept up (or killed) in widespread slave raids that sent thousands of men, women, and children to plantations in the West Indies. Cross-cultural alliances played a role in New England warfare, but Native American women in the southeast had far more to fear from other Indians.

Whether fleeing from pursuing militia or as prisoners of Native American raiding parties, mothers and children of both races endured exposure, starvation, exhaustion, and injury during forced marches through an unforgiving wilderness. Their common plight was both tragic and ironic—the product of warfare that assigned guilt on the basis of race, not conduct. But even mothers shared some culpability for the violence and bloodshed of the Colonial period—the role of Native American women in initiating raiding parties and in ritual torture must not be overlooked, nor should the contribution of white women to the spread of European influence and settlement at the expense of Native American lives, landholdings, and cultures. Whether casualties among mothers and children could be regarded as "collateral damage" is debatable, since they so often seemed targets, not bystanders, but there is no denying that mothers of both races found themselves in hellacious circumstances that often seemed undeserved.

The Colonial period ended with the termination of the Seven Years War in 1763, but intertribal and interracial violence in the eastern woodlands was far from over. In fact, the negotiated departure of French troops and officials following the 1763 Treaty of Paris precipitated the pan-Indian uprising known as "Pontiac's Rebellion," an affair so sanguinary that King George III issued a proclamation restricting English settlement to the eastern side of the Appalachian Mountains. In the 1770s the American Revolution devastated families throughout the eastern woodlands, white and Indian alike. Then in the closing decades of the eighteenth century, countless settlers on the trans-Appalachian frontier were killed or taken captive; space does not permit their stories, or those of their Native American adversaries, to be told here. Historians and novelists have duly noted that many "pioneers" perished or were captured as settlement pushed westward.[128] In truth, tragedies such as the massacre of 517 whites (mainly women and children) at Fort Mims in Alabama in 1813 proved far less frequent than the slaughter of Native American men, women, and children at sites such as Gnadenhutten, Ohio (1782); San Antonio, Texas (1840); Sand Creek, Colorado (1864); and Wounded Knee, South Dakota (1890). The forced relocation of Native American tribes—many of them mere remnants—and their containment on reservations provided a bloody and shameful coda to the widespread fighting between the races, but not to the animosity that remains even to this day.

The dawning of the twentieth century marked the end of protracted warfare on the North American continent; subsequent conflicts in which the United States would be involved were "foreign wars" that involved few American mothers as combatants or prisoners. Mothers would, of course, continue to experience the dread of sending loved ones off to war and the heartache that accompanied the death or captivity of a father, brother, husband, or son.[129] But the series of conflicts that raged across the eastern woodlands of North America during the Colonial period represented war in its bleakest form, and mothers of both races truly were among those most affected. That many died at the hands of their enemy is certain, but in the present age where post-traumatic stress syndrome is a widely recognized ailment, one is left to wonder exactly what psychological toll the bloodshed and experience of captivity took on those mothers and children who did manage to survive.

## Notes

1. George Percy, "A Trewe Relacyon—Virginia from 1609 to 1612" (1625), *Tyler's Quarterly Historical and Genealogical Magazine* 3 (1922): 271–73.
2. Gary L. Ebersole, *Captured by Texts: Puritan to Postmodern Images of Indian Captivity* (Charlottesville: University Press of Virginia, 1995), 7.
3. J. Frederick Fausz, "The Missing Women of Martin's Hundred," *American History* 33 (1998): 56–62.
4. John Underhill and Paul Royster, eds., *Newes from America* ... (1638), 20–26, Electronic Texts in American Studies Libraries at University of Nebraska-Lincoln, Paper 37.
5. *The Correspondence of Roger Williams*, vol. 1, ed. Glenn W. LaFantasie (Hanover, NH: University Press of New England, 1988), 73.
6. Underhill and Royster, *Newes from America*, 20–26. In 1645, while serving as a mercenary in the war between the Dutch and their Native American neighbors (Kieft's War), Underhill killed three of his Indian captives and brought two others to New Amsterdam, where they were "barbarously tortured and slain in the street in the presence of many lamenting squaws." Mariana Griswold Van Rensselaer, *History of the City of New York in the Seventeenth Century*, Vol. 1, *New Amsterdam* (New York: Cosimo, 2007), 235.
7. *Winthrop's Journal: History of New England, 1630–1649*, 2 vols., ed. James Kendall Hosmer, in *Original Narratives of Early American History* (New York: Charles Scribner's Sons, 1908), 1: 126, 225. In

1638 Narragansett Sachems complained to Roger Williams that the Mohegans were "secretly adopting" Pequots instead of treating them as war captives. Daniel Mandell, *King Philip's War: Colonial Expansion, Native Resistance, and the End of Indian Sovereignty* (Baltimore: Johns Hopkins University Press, 2010), 17. As many as 1,500 Pequot may have been integrated into other tribes; see Shelburne F. Cook, "Interracial Warfare and Population Decline among the New England Indians," *Ethnohistory* 20 (1973): 1–24.

8. John Winthrop, *Winthrop Papers, 1498–1654*, ed. Allyn B. Forbes, 6 vols. (Boston: Massachusetts Historical Society, 1929–47), 3: 457; Samuel Gardner Drake, *Book of the Indians* (Boston: Benjamin B. Mussey, 1845), 2: 109.

9. *The Correspondence of Roger Williams*, ed. Glenn Lafantasie (Hanover, NH: University Press of New England, 1988), 1: 132.

10. Anonymous, *New England's First Fruits* (London: Henry Overton, 1643), 6–7.

11. "Broad Advice, or a Dialogue about the Trade of the West India Company," in David Peterson De Vries, *Voyages from Holland to America, A.D. 1632 to 1644*, trans. Henry Murphy, in *Collections of the New York Historical Society*, 2d. ser., 3 (1856): 115–16. The killing of colonist Claes Swits was in retaliation for the murder of Wickquasgeck Indians in 1641.

12. Theodore Dietz, *Dutch Esopus / Wiltwyck / Kingston Memories* (Pittsburgh: Dorrance, 2012), 4–5.

13. John Romeyn Broadhead et al., *Documents Relative to the Colonial History of the State of New-York . . .* , new ser., 13 vols. (Albany: Weed Parsons, 1881; reprinted AMS Press, 1969), 2: 252, 339.

14. Yasuhide Kawashima, *Puritan Justice and the Indian: White Man's Law in Massachusetts, 1630–1763* (Middletown, CT: Wesleyan University Press, 1986), 5.

15. Increase Mather, *A Brief History of the Warr with the Indians in New-England* (1676), An Online Electronic Text Edition, ed. Paul Royster (*Faculty Publications, UNL Libraries*, Paper 31, http://digitalcommons.unl.edu/libraryscience/31), 46.

16. William Hubbard, *A Narrative of the Indian Wars in New-England . . .* (Stockbridge, MA: Heman Willard, 1803), 302. Daniel Gookin, Indian Superintendent in the Bay Colony, wrote, "If any murther, or other great wrong upon any of their relations or kindred, be committed, all of that stock and consanguinity look upon themselves to revenge that wrong, or murder, unless the business be taken up by the payment of wompompeague, or other satisfaction, which their custom admits, to satisfy for all wrongs, yea for life itself." Daniel Gookin, *Historical Collections of the Indians in New England* (1674), Massachusetts Historical Society, *Collections* [1st ser.] (1792): 149.

17. Samuel Mosely to Governor Leverett, Hadley, October 16, 1675, in Sylvester Judd and Lucius M. Boltwood, *History of Hadley* . . . (Northampton, MA: Metcalf, 1863), 154–55. Mosely was given 15 Algonquian Indians as servants after the war. Pauline Turner Strong, *Captive Selves, Captivating Others: The Politics and Poetics of Colonial American Captivity Narratives* (Boulder, CO: Westview, 1999), 95. In 1528 a similar outrage took place when Panfilio Narvaez threw Chief Hirrihigua's mother to hungry mastiffs. Christina Snyder, *Slavery in Indian Country: The Changing Face of Captivity in Early America* (Cambridge, MA: Harvard University Press, 2010), 35.
18. Mather, *A Brief History of the Warr*, 35.
19. Mary Rowlandson, *The Sovereignty and Goodness of God . . . A Narrative of the Captivity and Restauration [sic] of Mrs. Mary Rowlandson* (Cambridge, MA: Printed by Samuel Green, 1682), in *Puritans among the Indians: Accounts of Captivity and Redemption, 1676–1724*, ed. Alden T. Vaughan and Edward W. Clark (Cambridge, MA: Belknap Press of Harvard University Press, 1981), 34.
20. King Philip's War (1675–78) was New England's second and final "Indian war"; King William's War (1689–97), Queen Anne's War (1702–13), King George's War (1739–48) and the French and Indian War (1754–63) represented the North American phases of larger European conflicts.
21. Ann M. Little, *Abraham in Arms: War and Gender in Colonial New England* (Philadelphia: University of Pennsylvania Press, 2007), 92.
22. Alden Vaughan and Daniel K. Richter, "Crossing the Cultural Divide: Indians and New Englanders, 1605–1763," *Proceedings of the American Antiquarian Society* 90 (April 16, 1980): 53. Vaughan and Richter estimate the total number of whites captured during this period was 1,641.
23. Matthew C. Ward, *Breaking the Backcountry: The Seven Years' War in Virginia and Pennsylvania* (Pittsburgh: University of Pittsburgh Press, 2004), 40–57. By August 1756, French officials estimated that the Ohio Indians alone had taken more than 3,000 English captives; that estimate was probably high, but it reflected the frequency of captivity experiences.
24. *South Carolina Gazette*, February 2–9, 16–23, 1760.
25. Rowlandson, *The Sovereignty and Goodness of God*, 34–35.
26. William Durkee Williamson, *The History of the State of Maine: From Its First Discovery, A. D. 1602, to the Separation, A. D. 1820, Inclusive*, 2 vols. (Hallowell, ME: Glazier, Masters and Smith, 1839), 1: 621. The corpses of some 200 victims lay unburied for two years after the massacre.
27. Schuyler to the Council of Connecticut, February 15, 1690, in Francis Parkman, *Count Frontenac and New France under Louis XIV* (Boston: Little, Brown, 1911), 214.

28. John Williams, *The Redeemed Captive Returning to Zion* . . . (Boston: 1707; reprinted Bedford, MA: Applewood, 1987), 16–17.
29. James Russell Trumbull, *History of Northampton Massachusetts from its Settlement in 1654*, vol. 1 (Northampton, MA: Gazette, 1898), 496.
30. Elizabeth Hanson, *God's Mercy Surmounting Man's Cruelty, Exemplified in the Captivity and Redemption of Elizabeth Hanson* (Philadelphia: Thomas Keimer, 1728), in *Puritans among the Indians*, ed. Vaughan and Clark, 238.
31. Laurel Thatcher Ulrich, *Good Wives: Image and Reality in the Lives of Women in Northern New England, 1650–1750* (New York: Oxford University Press, 1982), 205.
32. Mather, *A Brief History of the Warr*, 42.
33. Schuyler to the Council of Connecticut, February 15, 1690, in Parkman, *Count Frontenac and New France*, 214.
34. Steven Eames, *Rustic Warriors: Warfare and the Provincial Soldier on the New England Frontier, 1689–1748* (New York: New York University Press, 2011), 189–90.
35. Thomas Church, *The History of Philip's War: Commonly Called the Great Indian War of 1675 and 1676* (Boston: 1716; reprinted Exeter, NH: J&B Williams, 1843), 244.
36. Emma Lewis Coleman, *New England Captives Carried to Canada between 1677 and 1760 during the French and Indian Wars*, 2 vols. (Portland, ME: Southworth, 1925), 1: 399–400.
37. Trumbull, *History of Northampton Massachusetts*, 497.
38. Williams, *The Redeemed Captive*, 16–21.
39. Williamson, *History of the State of Maine*, 623.
40. Coleman, *New England Captives Carried to Canada*, 1: 319.
41. Rowlandson, *The Sovereignty and Goodness of God*, 42.
42. Cotton Mather, *Decennium Luctuosum: An History of Remarkable Occurrences in the Long War, which New-England Hath Had with the Indian Salvages, from the Year 1688, to the Year 1698* (Boston: B. Green and J. Allen, 1699), 212; Coleman, *New England Captives Carried to Canada*, 1: 176.
43. Mather, *Decennium Luctuosum*, 210.
44. "Statement of Ann Jenkins, June 11, 1695," in *The New England Historical and Genealogical Register*, vol. 18 (Albany: J. Munsell for the New England Historic Genealogical Society, 1864), 164.
45. Ibid., 1: 272.
46. William Pote and John Fletcher Hurst, eds., *The Journal of Captain William Pote, Jr: During His Captivity in the French and Indian War from May, 1745, to August, 1747* (New York: Dodd, Mead, 1896), 115.
47. Susannah Willard Johnson, *A Narrative of the Captivity of Mrs. Johnson, Containing an Account of Her Sufferings during Four Years with the Indians and French*, 4th ed. (Lowell, MA: Daniel Bixby, 1834), 28.

48. Coleman, *New England Captives Carried to Canada*, 2: 214.
49. Hanson, *God's Mercy Surmounting Man's Cruelty*, 236–38.
50. "A Particular Account of the Captivity and Redemption of Mrs. Jemima Howe . . ." in Samuel G. Drake, *Indian Captivities, or Life in the Wigwam* . . . (Auburn, ME: Derby and Miller, 1839), 159–61.
51. Church, *The History of Philip's War*, 244.
52. Samuel Kercheval, *History of the Valley of Virginia* (Winchester, VA: Samuel H. Davis, 1833), 105.
53. Ward, *Breaking the Backcountry: The Seven Years' War in Virginia and Pennsylvania*, 7.
54. Rowlandson, *The Sovereignty and Goodness of God*, 43.
55. Williams, *The Redeemed Captive*, 45.
56. Mather, *A Brief History of the Warr*, 15.
57. Rowlandson, *The Sovereignty and Goodness of God*, 68.
58. "Journal of James Corse of Deerfield," in George Sheldon, *A History of Deerfield, Massachusetts* . . . , 2 vols. (Deerfield, MA: E.A. Hall, 1895–96), 1: 518.
59. Rowlandson, *The Sovereignty and Goodness of God*, 50–57.
60. Broadhead et al., *Documents Relative to the Colonial History of the State of New-York*, 2: 323. During the American Revolution, Major General John Sullivan's 3,200 Continentals, acting on George Washington's orders, destroyed at least forty Iroquois villages and 160,000 bushels of corn (planted and harvested primarily by Indian women) in western New York in 1779. Daniel Broadhead to [John] Sullivan, October 10, 1779, in Otis G. Hammond, ed., *The Letters and Papers of Major General John Sullivan, Continental Army*, 3 vols. (Concord: New Hampshire Historical Society, 1939), 3: 148.
61. Rowlandson, *The Sovereignty and Goodness of God*, 69.
62. Church, *The History of Philip's War*, 270.
63. Gail D. MacLeitch, *Imperial Entanglements: Iroquois Change and Persistence on the Frontiers of Empire* (Philadelphia: University of Pennsylvania Press, 2011), 161. Captive women and children were often spared the running of the gauntlet or were allowed to do so unharmed.
64. Broadhead et al., *Documents Relative to the Colonial History of the State of New-York*, 2: 352.
65. Coleman, *New England Captives Carried to Canada*, 2: 54.
66. Ibid., 2: 103.
67. Ibid., 2: 164.
68. Ibid., 2: 188–89.
69. Ibid., 2: 254–55. The captive, Eleanor Noble, was later redeemed and placed in a convent by a French couple.
70. Hanson, *God's Mercy Surmounting Man's Cruelty*, 243. Hanson's daughter married a Frenchman, since "those captives married by the French are by that marriage made free."

71. Coleman, *New England Captives Carried to Canada*, 2: 117–18; Trumbull, *History of Northampton, Massachusetts*, 485.
72. Coleman, *New England Captives Carried to Canada*, 2: 104; 1: 174.
73. Ibid., 2: 79, 122.
74. Benjamin Franklin to Peter Collinson, May 9, 1753, in Dorothy A. Mays, *Women in Early America: Struggle, Survival, and Freedom in a New World* (Santa Barbara, CA: ABC-CLIO, 2004), 201.
75. Linda Colley, *Captives: Britain, Empire, and the World, 1600–1850* (New York: Random House Digital, 2004), 145; Kevin M. McCarthy, *Thirty Florida Shipwrecks* (Sarasota: Pineapple, 1992), 25–26.
76. Hanson, *God's Mercy Surmounting Man's Cruelty*, 237–39.
77. For a description of matrilineal and matrilocal societies, see Snyder, *Slavery in Indian Country*, 196.
78. Daniel Richter, "War and Culture: The Iroquois Experience," *The William and Mary Quarterly*, 3rd ser., 40, no. 4 (October 1983): 532–35. One of the best explanations of the function of ritual torture among eastern woodland Indians appears in José António Brandão, *"Your Fyre Shall Burn No More": Iroquois Policy toward New France and Its Native Allies to 1701* (Lincoln: University of Nebraska Press, 1997), 38–42.
79. John Putnam Demos, *The Unredeemed Captive: A Family Story from Early America* (New York: Random House Digital, 1995), 81.
80. John Wesley Monette, *History of the Discovery and Settlement of the Valley of the Mississippi . . .* , 2 vols. (New York: Harper and Brothers, 1846), 2: 49–50.
81. Henri Raymond Casgrain (J.C.B.), *Travels in New France by J.C.B.*, ed. Sylvester K. Stevens, Donald H. Kent, and Emma Edith Woods (Harrisburg: Pennsylvania Historical Commission, 1941), 72.
82. *Memoirs of Odd Adventures, Strange Deliverances, etc, in the Captivity of John Gyle, Esq. . . .* (Boston: 1736; reprinted Cincinnati: Spiller and Gates, 1869), 15.
83. Williamson, *History of the State of Maine*, 1: 547.
84. Church, *The History of Philip's War*, 329–30.
85. Coleman, *New England Captives Carried to Canada*, 1: 195.
86. Ibid., 1: 346–47.
87. Mather, *Decennium Luctuosum*, 94.
88. Jabez Fitch, *A Brief Narrative of Several Things Respecting the Province of New Hampshire in New-England, 1728–29* (Boston: Massachusetts Historical Society, 1859); Samuel Penhallow, *The History of the Wars of New-England with the Eastern Indians* (Cincinnati: J. Harpel, 1859), 41–42, in Little, *Abraham in Arms*, 89.
89. Eames, *Rustic Warriors*, 45–49.
90. Mays, *Women in Early America*, 200.
91. Mather, *Decennium Luctuosum*, 263–66.

92. James Axtell, "The Vengeful Women of Marblehead: Robert Roule's Deposition of 1677," *The William and Mary Quarterly*, 3rd Series, 31 (October 1974): 647–52.
93. Jenny Hale Pulsipher, *Subjects unto the Same King: Indians, English, and the Contest for Authority in Colonial New England* (Philadelphia: University of Pennsylvania Press, 2005), 226.
94. Parkman, *Count Frontenac and New France*, 142.
95. C. D., *New England's Faction Discovered; or a Brief and True Account of Their Persecution of the Church of England; the Beginning and Progress of the Late War with the Indians; and Other Late Proceedings There* . . . (London: 1690), in *Narratives of the Insurrections, 1675–1690*, ed. Charles M. Andrews, vol. 16 (New York: Charles Scribner's Sons, 1915), 255–56.
96. G. J. Barker-Benfield and Catherine Clinton, *Portraits of American Women: From Settlement to the Present* (New York: Oxford University Press, 1998), 92.
97. Church, *The History of Philip's War*, 188–89.
98. Ibid., 2: 55–56.
99. Coleman, *New England Captives Carried to Canada*, 2: 143–44.
100. Ibid., 2: 12.
101. Mather, *A Brief History of the Warr*, 69.
102. William Waller Hening, comp., *The Statutes as Large; Being a Collection of all the Laws of Virginia* . . . , 13 vols. (New York, Richmond, and Philadelphia: 1809–23), 1: 481–82; also 2: 404, 440, 491–92, in Owen Stanwood, "Captives and Slaves: Indian Labor, Cultural Conversion, and the Plantation Revolution in Virginia," *Virginia Magazine of History and Biography* 114, no. 4 (2006): 442–44.
103. Snyder, *Slavery in Indian Country*, 49.
104. Vernon J. Knight and Sherée L. Adams, "A Voyage to the Mobile and Tomeh in 1700, with Notes on the Interior of Alabama," *Ethnohistory* 28 (1981): 182.
105. *Nairne's Muskhogean Journals: The 1708 Expedition to the Mississippi River*, ed. Alexander Moore (Jackson: University Press of Mississippi, 1988), 48.
106. *The Colonial Records of South Carolina: The Journal of the Commons House of Assembly*, ed. J. Harold Easterby (Columbia: South Carolina Archives Department, 1914), 1: 259, in Alan Gallay, *The Indian Slave Trade: The Rise of the English Empire in the American South, 1670–1717* (New Haven: Yale University Press, 2002), 61.
107. John Stewart to Queen Anne, March 10, 1711, AC, microfilm copies, Manuscript Reading Room, LC, C13C, in Gallay, *The Indian Slave Trade*, 190–91.
108. Gallay, *The Indian Slave Trade*, 312; Jean-Baptiste Benard de La Harpe, *The Historical Journal of the Establishment of the French in Louisiana*, trans. Virginia Koenig and Joan Cain, ed. Glenn R. Conrad

(Lafayette: University of Southwestern Louisiana Press, 1971), 73, in Gallay, *The Indian Slave Trade*, 297.
109. *SCCHJ Journal of the Commons House of Assembly*, 21 vols., ed. Alexander S. Salley Jr. (Columbia: Historical Commission of South Carolina, 1907–46), vol. "August 5, 1712–August 8, 1712," in Gallay, *The Indian Slave Trade*, 274.
110. Gallay, *The Indian Slave Trade*, 200.
111. *Colonial Records of South Carolina*, 2: 203–9, in Gallay, *The Indian Slave Trade*, 200.
112. John Oliphant, *Peace and War on the Anglo-Cherokee Frontier, 1756–63* (Baton Rouge: Louisiana State University Press, 2001), 83–86, 125.
113. Folio 275: General [Jeffrey] Amherst to William Johnson, New York, September 3, 1763, in William L. Lewis and James A. Lewis, *A Guide to Cherokee Documents in Foreign Archives* (Metuchen, NJ: Scarecrow, 1983), 111.
114. Snyder, *Slavery in Indian Country*, 196; "The General Deposition of Greenwood LeFlore, February 24, 1843," Clairborne Papers, box 3, folder 24, Southern Historical Collection, Louis Round Wilson Special Collections Library, University of North Carolina at Chapel Hill.
115. James Adair, *Adair's History of the American Indians*, ed. Samuel C. Williams (Johnson City: Watauga, 1930), 239–42, in Theda Purdue, *Cherokee Women: Gender and Culture Change, 1700–1835* (Lincoln: University of Nebraska Press, 1999), 53.
116. Barker-Benfield and Clinton, *Portraits of American Women*, 88–89.
117. William Bartram, "Observations on the Creek and Cherokee Indians, 1789," in American Ethnological Society, *Transactions* 3, part 1 (1853): 32.
118. English authorities were sometimes compelled to negotiate with clan matrons or even individual Indian women when attempting to recover captives. Joan R. Gunderson, *To Be Useful to the World: Women in Revolutionary America, 1740–1790* (Charlotte: University of North Carolina Press, 2006), 35. Iroquois women held separate "women's councils" to discuss tribal affairs and had a formal role in choosing sachems. Little, *Abraham in Arms*, 99–101.
119. Martha McCartney, "Cockacoeske," in *Dictionary of Virginia Biography*, vol. 3, ed. Sara B. Bearss (Richmond: Library of Virginia, 2006), 321–22. Authorities in England ordered that a jeweled coronet, other jewelry, and a suit of regal attire be presented to Cockacoeske, her son, and her interpreter.
120. Little, *Abraham in Arms*, 30–31.
121. Theda Perdue, *Slavery and the Evolution of Cherokee Society, 1540–1866* (Knoxville: University of Tennessee Press, 1987), 7.
122. Henry Timberlake, *The Memoirs of Lt. Henry Timberlake: The Story of a Soldier, Adventurer, and Emissary to the Cherokees, 1756–1765*, ed.

Duane H. King (Chapel Hill, NC: University of North Carolina Press, 2007), 94.
123. Ibid., 122; Pat Alderman, *Nancy Ward, Cherokee Chieftainess* (Johnson City, TN: Overmountain, 1978), 34. Following her husband's death, Nanye'hi married Bryant Ward, an English trader who had a white wife as well.
124. Samuel Cole Williams, *Tennessee during the Revolutionary War* (Nashville: Tennessee Historical Commission, 1944), 133.
125. David A. Bell, *The First Total War: Napoleon's Europe and the Birth of Modern Warfare* (New York: Houghton Mifflin, 2007); Roger Chickering and Stig Forster, eds., *Great War, Total War: Combat and Mobilization on the Western Front, 1914–1918* (Cambridge: Cambridge University Press, 2000); Charles Winchester, *Total War: Great Battles of the 20th Century* (London: Quercus, 2010); Mark Grimsley, "Modern War/Total War," in *The American Civil War: A Handbook of Literature and Research*, ed. Steven Woodworth (Westport, CT: Greenwood, 1996).
126. Regarding the Apalachee assault, see the testimony of trader John Stewart in Gallay, *The Indian Slave Trade*, 186.
127. Michael Freeman, "Puritans and Pequots: The Question of Genocide," *The New England Quarterly* 68, no. 2 (June 1995): 278–93; Jill Lepore, *The Name of War: King Philip's War and the Origins of American Identity* (New York: Random House, 1998), passim.
128. One notable difference in the treatment of white female captives in the Southwest was the alleged sexual abuse at the hands of the Apache, Comanche, and other Plains Indians. There were no recorded instances of sexual assault on white female captives in seventeenth-century New England. Strong, *Captive Selves, Captivating Others*, 108.
129. The inclusion of women in the modern-day American military has altered this situation, placing women (including mothers) in harm's way as soldiers or in support roles—a recent and somewhat controversial development. Of course, "foreign wars" inevitably involve mothers and children living outside North America.

## Selected Bibliography

Alderman, Pat. *Nancy Ward, Cherokee Chieftainess*. Johnson City, TN: Overmountain, 1978.

Axtell, James. "The Vengeful Women of Marblehead: Robert Roule's Deposition of 1677." *The William and Mary Quarterly*, 3rd ser., 31, no. 4 (October 1974): 647–52.

Barker-Benfield, G. J., and Catherine Clinton. *Portraits of American Women: From Settlement to the Present*. New York: Oxford University Press, 1998.

Bell, David A. *The First Total War: Napoleon's Europe and the Birth of Modern Warfare*. New York: Houghton Mifflin, 2007.

Brandão, José António. *"Your Fyre Shall Burn No More": Iroquois Policy Toward New France and Its Native Allies to 1701*. Lincoln: University of Nebraska Press, 1997.

Chickering, Roger, and Stig Forster, eds. *Great War, Total War: Combat and Mobilization on the Western Front, 1914–1918*. Cambridge: Cambridge University Press, 2000.

Coleman, Emma Lewis. *New England Captives Carried to Canada between 1677 and 1760 during the French and Indian Wars*. 2 vols. Portland, ME: Southworth, 1925.

Colley, Linda. *Captives: Britain, Empire, and the World, 1600–1850*. New York: Random House Digital, 2004.

Cook, Shelburne F. "Interracial Warfare and Population Decline among the New England Indians." *Ethnohistory* 20 (1973): 1–24.

Demos, John Putnam. *The Unredeemed Captive: A Family Story from Early America*. New York: Random House Digital, 1995.

Dietz, Theodore. *Dutch Esopus / Wiltwyck / Kingston Memories*. Pittsburgh: Dorrance, 2012.

Eames, Steven. *Rustic Warriors: Warfare and the Provincial Soldier on the New England Frontier, 1689–1748*. New York: New York University Press, 2011.

Ebersole, Gary L. *Captured by Texts: Puritan to Postmodern Images of Indian Captivity*. Charlottesville: University Press of Virginia, 1995.

Fausz, J. Frederick. "The Missing Women of Martin's Hundred." *American History* 33 (1998): 56–62.

Freeman, Michael. "Puritans and Pequots: The Question of Genocide." *New England Quarterly* 68, no. 2 (June 1995): 278–93.

Gallay, Allan. *The Indian Slave Trade: The Rise of the English Empire in the American South, 1670–1717*. New Haven: Yale University Press, 2002.

Gunderson, Joan R. *To Be Useful to the World: Women in Revolutionary America, 1740–1790*. Charlotte: University of North Carolina Press, 2006.

Kawashima, Yasuhide. *Puritan Justice and the Indian: White Man's Law in Massachusetts, 1630–1763*. Middletown, CT: Wesleyan University Press, 1986.

Knight, Vernon J., and Sherée L. Adams. "A Voyage to the Mobile and Tomeh in 1700, with Notes on the Interior of Alabama." *Ethnohistory* 28, no. 2 (Spring 1981): 179–94.

Lepore, Jill. *The Name of War: King Philip's War and the Origins of American Identity*. New York: Random House, 1998.

Little, Ann M. *Abraham in Arms: War and Gender in Colonial New England*. Philadelphia: University of Pennsylvania Press, 2007.

MacLeitch, Gail D. *Imperial Entanglements: Iroquois Change and Persistence on the Frontiers of Empire*. Philadelphia: University of Pennsylvania Press, 2011.

Mandell, Daniel. *King Philip's War: Colonial Expansion, Native Resistance, and the End of Indian Sovereignty*. Baltimore: Johns Hopkins University Press, 2010.
Mays, Dorothy A. *Women in Early America: Struggle, Survival, and Freedom in a New World*. Santa Barbara, CA: ABC-CLIO, 2004.
McCarthy, Kevin M. *Thirty Florida Shipwrecks*. Sarasota, FL: Pineapple, 1992.
Oliphant, John. *Peace and War on the Anglo-Cherokee Frontier, 1756–63*. Baton Rouge: Louisiana State University Press, 2001.
Pulsipher, Jenny Hale. *Subjects unto the Same King: Indians, English, and the Contest for Authority in Colonial New England*. Philadelphia: University of Pennsylvania Press, 2005.
Purdue, Theda. *Cherokee Women: Gender and Culture Change, 1700–1835*. Lincoln: University of Nebraska Press, 1999.
———. *Slavery and the Evolution of Cherokee Society, 1540–1866*. Knoxville: University of Tennessee Press, 1987.
Richter, Daniel. "War and Culture: The Iroquois Experience." *The William and Mary Quarterly*, 3rd ser., 40, no. 4 (October 1983): 528–59.
Snyder, Christina. *Slavery in Indian Country: The Changing Face of Captivity in Early America*. Cambridge, MA: Harvard University Press, 2010.
Strong, Pauline Turner. *Captive Selves, Captivating Others: The Politics and Poetics of Colonial American Captivity Narratives*. Boulder, CO: Westview Press, 1999.
Ulrich, Laurel Thatcher. *Good Wives: Image and Reality in the Lives of Women in Northern New England, 1650–1750*. New York: Oxford University Press, 1982.
Van Rensselaer, Mariana Griswold. *History of the City of New York in the Seventeenth Century*. Vol. 1, *New Amsterdam*. New York: Cosimo, 2007.
Vaughan, Alden T., and Edward W. Clark, eds. *Puritans among the Indians: Accounts of Captivity and Redemption, 1676–1724*. Cambridge, MA: Belknap Press of Harvard University Press, 1981.
Vaughan, Alden T., and Daniel K. Richter. "Crossing the Cultural Divide: Indians and New Englanders, 1605–1763." *Proceedings of the American Antiquarian Society* 90 (April 16, 1980): 23–99.
Ward, Matthew C. *Breaking the Backcountry: The Seven Years' War in Virginia and Pennsylvania*. Pittsburgh: University of Pittsburgh Press, 2004.
Williams, Samuel Cole. *Tennessee during the Revolutionary War*. Nashville: Tennessee Historical Commission, 1944.
Winchester, Charles. *Total War: Great Battles of the 20th Century*. London: Quercus, 2010.
Woodworth, Steven, ed. *The American Civil War: A Handbook of Literature and Research*. Westport, CT: Greenwood, 1996.

# Chapter 3

## Sailing Sons

### The Personal Consequences of Impressment

### Claire Phelan

In 1810, Charles Vass, the son of a Virginian flour merchant, left the port of Alexandria on a voyage to foreign shores, yet he never arrived at his destination for "he was impressed and dragged on board" a British ship of war. Denied the opportunity of writing to his family to inform them of his "slavery," he "was carried to the East Indies, as is the custom with these man-stealers." Eventually Vass returned to his community. Walking along the streets, unrecognizable to his friends and neighbors, he suddenly caught sight of his father, Ambrose. The ragged sailor called out, but the old man, having given his son up for dead after five years of inquiries, failed to recognize the sailor standing before him. With a "big manly tear rolling down his cheek," Charles identified himself as Ambrose's long lost son. In a flash of recognition, the elated father pressed Charles to his "wounded heart" before taking him inside to reunite a much beloved son with his mother. "Disfigured as he was, the very first glance, like the lightening of heaven, rived her whole frame, and she apparently fell lifeless on the floor." A swift recovery and a joyous embrace ensued, but despite the heartache that his protracted absence had caused, Vass would shortly set sail again, and his mother, like so many others, would count the weeks, months, and sometimes years before knowing if there were to be other such reunions or if the shadowy depths of the sea had claimed yet another son.[1]

The act of impressment involved the forcible removal of a man for service in a vessel, most commonly a man-of-war. In the context of this chapter, impressment relates to the British abduction of American-born seamen and those claiming American citizenship. Impressment was only one of the dangers that a sailor had to face daily. Shipwreck, disease, and death by accident or in a time of war made a seafarer's life one of the most dangerous occupations in the United States in the late 1700s and the early 1800s. The turmoil experienced on the continent during the Napoleonic Wars also made its presence felt in America, via Jefferson's Embargo. The United States suddenly found itself caught between two of the world's great powers, and there was very little it could do to assert its authority over its own mariners, whether on land or at sea.

While it remains impossible to gauge accurately the exact number of Americans impressed by the British, conservative estimates have placed the figure between nine and ten thousand. American anger at British impressment of its sailors from merchant fleets and US naval vessels was listed as a principal cause for declaring war against Great Britain in 1812. In an effort to prevent the impressment of its citizens, the US government issued protection certificates that listed the name, age, height, eye color, and other personal details of a seaman in an effort to prove the holder's legitimate claim to citizenship. Unfortunately, time and the elements often degraded these documents, or they were taken illegally by British officers who determined that they were mere forgeries, as a number of them were.

Articles and editorials in a variety of newspapers ensured that the subject of impressment remained at the forefront of daily life, for such episodes offered tangible examples of Britain's disdain of American sovereignty, and seamen always presented a colorful group on which to write. Sailors of the day held somewhat of a unique place in trans-Atlantic society. The harsh physical demands of a seaman's life ensured that this was essentially a young man's occupation. With the brash nature that accompanies the vigor of youth, the masculine virtue of selfless courage, and a strong sense of *esprit de corps*, these men coalesced to symbolize the raw energy of a new, but nascent, national power. Yet society also derided the common Jack Tar for his hard-drinking and hard-living ways. His bawdy songs and pugnacious nature elicited many a complaint from the more respectable matrons of coastal hamlets and towns; nevertheless, bonds of maternal love and admiration bound the mothers of such men to them. In some cases, mothers were also monetarily dependent on their seafaring sons, should no other family members exist who could sustain them. For many of these mothers, their sons' absence occurred at a critical time of loss in their lives, and an ardent need to have them at their sides coincided with a determination to free them from forced military service in the navy of a perceived belligerent waging informal war against hapless individual American seaman in the decades before declared hostilities in 1812.

Historian Gary Nash described eighteenth-century seamen as "perhaps the most elusive social group in early American history because they moved from port to port with greater frequency than other urban dwellers, shifted occupations, died young, and least often left behind traces of their lives on tax lists and probate records." Our knowledge of seamen's lives in the nineteenth century proves little better, and historian Brian De Toy suggests "few of the letters written by sailors in the nineteenth century survive." Fortunately, the formal record-keeping requirements of the navies of both the United States and Britain and the authority governing US Collectors of Customs required that the captains of both military and merchant vessels make full reports of any impressment incidents. These records contain a voluminous amount of correspondence written by and to sailors and provide an unexpected source of evidence of the close relationship that many seafarers enjoyed with their mothers.[2]

The majority of letters suggests that the authors generally came from working-class families. Unfortunately, a lack of education did hinder the chance for success of those attempting to negotiate their way through a bewildering and lengthy system of appeal. Freeing an impressed man involved visits to officials, written applications, and petitions to those in a position to help support claims of citizenship. Those possessing an education, together with influential connections, obviously stood a better chance of achieving their purpose in a timely manner. When, through necessity, the mothers of impressed men undertook this task, the burden of pursuing the prescribed course, as determined by the Agents for the Relief of Seamen who operated in various foreign ports, must have proved onerous at best.

The correspondence between sailors and their mothers adds a compelling, yet rarely explored, dimension to the impressment story. Men who went to sea must have contributed to broadening the horizons of these women, if only vicariously, but in cases of impressment, it often rested with these poorly educated and generally homebound mothers to agitate for their release. Certainly, few politicians came to the aid of these families by publicly acknowledging or undertaking any significant action to overcome the difficulties they faced as a result of their sons' impressment. In a speech given in Congress on February 6, 1806,

James Elliot chided merchants who called loudly for the redress of economic injuries while neglecting the plight of "another class of injured citizens; [for] while we give [consideration] to the rich, let us not withhold it from the poor." Elliot enjoined the nation to remember "the groans" of its impressed sailors and to make every effort on their behalf. Unfortunately, his appeal did not resonate with much of the population, and, as usual, the families of these men labored valiantly to make what little progress they could.[3]

Struggling simply to exist from day to day could be a time-consuming task for these women, especially after the Embargo Act of 1807, which left many seafarers without work or stranded in foreign countries when ships' captains learned that a return journey would not result in a profit. How these mothers sustained themselves and the remainder of their families in the absence of a steady income from their sons remains a topic for further investigation, but in common with the female relatives of other sailors, they most likely resorted to taking in boarders, doing laundry, or turning their hand to any number of home businesses in which they could best put to use their skills in the domestic arts. In all likelihood, mothers with impressed sons also assumed at least a degree of responsibility for the provision of their daughters-in-law and grandchildren. At the very least, impressed men sometimes relied more on their mothers for help than their wives. In 1814, David Tarr instructed his wife to forward all relevant documents to his mother, Patty, so that she could undertake the responsibility for their distribution to the appropriate officials.[4]

There is some suggestion that wives occasionally used the incarceration of their spouses as a means of achieving freedom from unhappy unions. Isaac Clark wrote some heartfelt missives to his wife regarding his state of mind after spending 17 months on a British vessel. He admonished her not to "rest one day till you got me out of this for you don [sic] know what that I endure." Clark appeared entirely befuddled as to her inaction, for he had first written for help some 17 months earlier. He ended by pledging his undying love and prayed that his wife had not forgotten him but declared that if he could not soon achieve freedom, then he did not care how quickly death came to claim him.[5]

Alexander Boyd also appeared perplexed that his wife had not responded to any of his letters. Of late, he had only received a three-month-old note in which she had complained that a business or social contact had refused to give her the sum of fifty dollars. Nearly a year later, Alexander still worked to get his wife to forward a copy of his protection. Perhaps, then, the maxim that there is no love like a mother's love resonated with David Tarr for very practical reasons. Certainly, no complaints exist regarding the tardy nature of mothers in fulfilling the requests of their impressed sons, unless of course British officers intentionally diverted the letters containing these requests. Such correspondence most frequently included a request for a duplicate protection, but they also sometimes gave evidence of the depths of a man's depression.[6]

In 1812, James Williams wrote a disconsolate letter to his mother, Polly, begging for her help in obtaining a duplicate protection after failing to receive any letters at all from friends or acquaintances. "Long has my absence been from you and even at this period, I have but little or no hopes of ever getting my discharge from this horrid service . . . Pardon me, My Dear Mother for so saying but it is now nearly three years since I was impressed." If his mother could offer no tangible assistance, he determined "to trust in God to soon deliver me out of this torment." Impressed seaman Hugh Irwin estimated that he had written twenty to thirty letters to his mother, yet it appears that only a couple arrived at their destination. Unfortunately, a letter he received from his mother informed him of the deaths of both his uncle and his brother. Irwin felt the loss of his sibling keenly and expressed the wish that he could have traded places with a brother who could have given comfort to a mother in her old age. Instead, he remained her only son—a "miserable" creature after enduring eight years of separation and no release in sight. Of course, when impressed, a man sometimes lacked the opportunity to correspond as often as he may have preferred. In a letter written by impressed sailor Peyton Page, he pauses to consider if any of his relatives are even still alive, for he needs someone to collect a duplicate protection on his behalf, yet he reserves his final thoughts for his mother: "I hope [that] my Dear mother still enjoys her health . . . I hope when I arrive in America to have the satisfaction of seeing her well and happy [but] I do not know who to direct this letter to for I am afraid my mother is Dead."[7]

Some families appeared reconciled that their seagoing relatives seemed less than devoted correspondents who offered little information other than reports on their health and that they still often thought with affection of those at home. Such infrequent communication meant that it sometimes came as a shock to learn of the impressment of a favorite son. The family of Norton Knowles only learned of his incarceration through the kindness of others. A friend wrote to Knowles's mother, Sarah, informing her of Norton's impressment into the *Tribune*, then in Denmark. Although Knowles appeared in good health when last seen, his prospects for release seemed dim, as the impressing officer completely refuted his claim to American citizenship.[8]

Perhaps the most poignant letters in this collection come from the widowed mothers of impressed seamen. Interestingly, these women always noted carefully their status on any legal documents. Some obviously used this information to inject an additional note of pathos into their applications of appeal. Generally, one suspects they merely reflected the social conventions of the day, although more than one widow called attention to her state on numerous occasions.

Many of these mothers found the appeals process particularly trying, both emotionally and, quite possibly, financially. Hannah Brimblecom made a heartfelt application "on behalf of a widowed mother praying" for the release of her son, Philip, but she had almost no chance of succeeding, as British forces had captured him aboard a French vessel. He had originally sailed out of Portland heading to Spain, but two French ships interdicted his schooner before it had reached its destination. Philip consequently took employment aboard a French merchant vessel, which had the misfortune of falling in with a British frigate. He spent some time aboard the Royal Navy ship before the commanding officer sent him to a British prison hulk, a loathsome place where many men lost hope and languished in filthy conditions for months on end. His eventful journey continued when officials subsequently transferred Brimblecom to a man-of-war. His mother dispatched his protection and a number of other relevant documents to the office of the American Consul in London. Unfortunately, she received a reply stating that as her son had served aboard a French privateer, "all applications from this office will avail nothing." It must have been truly heartbreaking for a woman in Brimblecom's circumstances to realize that all the efforts that she had exerted on her son's behalf had proved fruitless. At a time of heightened tension, and only a few short months away from the beginning of the War of 1812, there existed very little impetus for the British to release the young man. Although despised for their squalid nature, Brimblecom's incarceration in a prison hulk may have at least offered Hannah a modicum of comfort, as at least this relieved him from the dangers of crewing a British man-of-war, but one can only imagine the depths of her despair when the Admiralty forced her son to man a British vessel to fight against his own countrymen at the outbreak of hostilities.[9]

Fellow American Warren Hedge similarly found himself in prison after suffering impressment, and like Brimblecom, British officers also forced him into permanent sea service, along with a number of other Americans. He initially refused to labor for the British but eventually consented, for in his opinion he would have otherwise faced starvation in a prison ship. Family obligations may have also forced his hand, for Hedge had a widowed mother and a sister depending on him for their survival. Nevertheless, reviling his situation, he attempted to escape on a number of occasions and allegedly received more than four hundred lashes for his troubles. In a letter written by his brother-in-law to Isaiah Green, his local representative in Congress, he stressed that Hedge "was the sole support of his aged mother, and sister who are looking to him for protection. May you have compassion on the tears of the widow and orphan and may God who is the rewarder of every good deed render them a crown of glory and righteousness."[10]

Unfortunately, no personal appeal to any politician would likely result in a response to a letter written by widow Peggy Bowen, for her son's status as "mulatto" precluded him from having any formal claims to citizenship. African Americans rarely possessed birth certificates, so if they lost their protections, their success in claiming American nationality depended largely on their ability to convince whites to attest on their behalves. In a country where institutional racism still largely prevailed, this often proved difficult. Nevertheless, Peggy did all in her power to secure the release of her son. The British had impressed Bowen on a voyage out of Portland. He deserted from that vessel and shipped on board a British merchantman, only to fall once more afoul of the press, this time in San Juan. His mother bemoaned the fate of her only son and begged through "tears of despair" for his release. An earlier letter from Shepherd implored her to help him return to his wife and family in the United States. He did not know which of his friends still lived and asked that his mother write a few lines to him. In response to his plea, Bowen's mother wrote not only to her son but also to a number of officials requesting a duplicate protection. She also gathered several documents from her church that would attest to Shepherd's connections to the community.[11]

The knowledge of the impressment of a child, particularly an only son, proved a difficult burden for mothers to bear, and such circumstances could often lead to unforeseen complications. The letters mothers wrote to their offspring reflect agitation and bewilderment and, not infrequently, contained tragic or disturbing news. Sarah Anderson had the sorrowful duty of informing her son John of the death of his father. Due to the absence of her son, Sarah had since lived with her brother, who had taken control of the family's estate. Despite her grief, she had worked assiduously to gather a number of documents, including a triplicate of her son's protection, a statutory declaration providing the details of his place of birth and place of baptism, a letter from the Rector of the Swedish church to which his family belonged, a letter of support from an uncle, and a separate letter from that gentleman assuring his nephew of his best efforts to deliver John from "bondage."[12]

If bondage had only entailed the traditional interpretation as the limitation of movement, then perhaps these women would not have received the news of their sons' impressment with such acute distress. Unfortunately, the conditions experienced by some at sea proved quite brutal. Rough discipline had always marked the service, especially in British naval vessels, although the public of the time mainly accepted the acute physical nature of punishment. Generally, most officers and many civilians held the view that a "thousand men on a floating area of two hundred feet by fifty-five, requires some different government from that which may suit a mixed population of little more than two hundred in a square mile." Unfortunately, one 17-year-old American newly pressed into HMS *Hussar* felt unable to face such conditions and attempted to escape by jumping over the side. Upon recapture, and despite the prisoner's plea for mercy, the captain placed the lad in leg irons before ordering him whipped before the crew. He appeared to faint in the midst of his lashing, but the captain, suspecting the youth of faking, ordered him tied with a rope and heaved overboard three times. A surgeon later bled the boy as he groaned pitiably for his mother.[13]

The violent uprooting from family or fellow shipmates and the subsequent transfer into a British man-of-war completely devastated some men, especially those not yet hardened by any significant time at sea. While mothers could hope that no American master of a ship would thus treat a son, the lack of any up-to-date information and the infrequent letters and visits home made the waiting all the more intolerable. There exists no evidence as to how long this young man fared on board the vessel or if he even survived, but some men, still reasonably young in years, returned home almost unrecognizable due to the length of their absences and the trials they had suffered.

Most American journals and newspapers carried reports of such abuse, whether real or exaggerated, and war-hawk politicians used these incidents to buttress their own political agendas. For the mothers of seafaring men, each article detailing yet another appalling tale of abduction, unjust impressment, and ill treatment sent a chilling reminder that no American was immune from such a hazard, for at one time the British even impressed the great-nephew of George Washington. While these mothers had no control over the elements, the common accidents of shipboard life, or the affairs of men that so frequently resulted in war, they could at least play an active role in agitating for the release of their sons by working assiduously and diligently to do what little they could.[14]

Unfortunately, statements made by a number of these mothers before officials bear witness to their illiteracy via the marks made beside their names. One should consider how much more fraught the process must have been for these women, for this deficiency too frequently suggests lowly circumstances, such as the case with the family of seaman Joseph Hill, whose parents "were living in obscurity." Hill had run away to sea in 1802, and not hearing from him for seven years, all thought him dead. In fact, the British had impressed the young man from an American vessel. Eventually escaping, he had the great misfortune to be captured on a French ship and imprisoned as a deserter. This young man's future looked bleak, indeed, for his parents had not entered his birth in the town records, nor had they had their son baptized, which meant that there existed no official proof to support his claim to American citizenship. Neither does his file contain a duplicate protection. It does contain a letter of appeal written on behalf of the family and a number of sworn statements, including one by his mother, Catherine, who had not seen her son for the last seven years. Despite that fact, she still recalled the places on his body that carried scars, but his light complexion, light hair, and blue eyes could have easily applied to thousands of men at sea and would do very little to advance his case. Nevertheless, Catherine dutifully placed her mark next to her name, undoubtedly leaving the office of the Justice of the Peace holding little hope for the speedy return of a much-cherished child.[15]

Understandably, it proved almost impossible for some mothers to provide accurate descriptions of their sons. Many had gone to sea as callow youths, and accidents or battle wounds, possible malnourishment or disease, and the natural maturation process would have made it difficult to reconcile their actual descriptions to those given by their mothers. Isaac Moore appealed to his mother for a duplicate protection, in his case after a nine-year absence. Upon leaving home, he possessed a "middling complexion." Now described as dark, Esther Moore could only surmise that "the hardships of the sea" must have altered him. Poignantly, she added a comment that perhaps only a mother would think to include: that when he laughed he formed dimples in his cheeks.[16]

Another distraught mother also wrote of the unique characteristics she hoped would prove her son's identity beyond any reasonable doubt. Apparently, Nicholas Curren had a scar on his left little finger and one on his left thigh. In addition, he had four sets of initials—G. C., O. B., N. C., and H. G.—tattooed on his arms below either elbow. In many instances, tattoos proved of some use in determining the identity of a seaman, but certain words, phrases, and images were too common to be of much assistance in differentiating one person from another. Indeed, a young man may have left his hometown at 16 or 17 with a protection stating that he had fair skin with no apparent marks, which would correspond with his mother's memory; however, within a year or two, he may have grown considerably, his skin would almost invariably have darkened, and he may have a number of tattoos on various parts of his body. Essentially, a man would have replaced the son, and in many more ways than just the physical.[17]

Joseph Clisby's mother had not seen her son for 14 years, and one can only imagine the difference in appearance time must have wrought. She had initially rejoiced to learn that he had finally found happiness in his travels. Writing in 1801, he had described his good fortune in England, appraising her that he had met "with one" whom he hoped would bring him lifelong joy. In all likelihood, it appeared that he planned to marry a British woman. Impressed into the Royal Navy in 1803, he remained in that service until at least 1809, when he wrote a letter of appeal describing his circumstances. If he had married a citizen of Britain, any hope for release would prove unfounded, for such a union would automatically make him a British subject by default, and no amount of applications for release by his mother would garner a positive outcome.[18]

If the appearance and circumstances of sons altered over time, so, too, did personal situations and states of health of their mothers. Impressed American John Siters received a heartfelt letter from his mother, Sarah, who had gathered a number of documents as per his request, including his birth certificate. She admonished him to "remember that I am now advancing in life and that you would at this time be a great comfort to me and that you could be a father to your brothers and sisters. I am at this time only in a middling state of health." In a separate letter to Siters, a cousin remarked that "nothing has been wanting on the part of your mother to obtain everything that could be thought necessary, no pains nor expense has she spared to obtain your release, on the part of your mother her health is not very good at the present but she has lost no time on that account." Receiving such an appeal from his mother must have tugged at Siters's heartstrings at any normal time, but given his impressed state, he surely had reason to disparage his British officers with even more invective.[19]

In their anguished state, mothers could give vent to the same level of anger voiced by their sons over incidents of unjust impressment. The manner in which some mothers expressed themselves belies the assumption that respectable females of this era always sought to conduct themselves in a genteel manner, whatever the circumstances. Ignoring the dictums that governed womanly behavior, Jane Burk railed bitterly to her son Thomas against those who had kept him "like a slave in the height of your bloom." She remained indignant that two previously dispatched sets of documents had not achieved their purpose in obtaining the release of her favorite child. While imploring him to remain patient, she also heartily prayed for his return, as she could "get no comfort" from any of his brothers.[20]

Naomi Jackson had no family whom she could call on for help, unlike Jane Burk who had sons, even if they did appear shiftless. Naomi had not seen her boy Henry in 11 years, and in that time she had lost both her husband and another son. In this case, Naomi relied on others to craft a petition for his release. Mothers frequently enlisted the help of male friends and relatives when appealing cases of impressment for a variety of reasons. Those women who could not read or write had little choice, but it appears that even those perfectly capable of crafting their own petition often sought the assistance of a man to assume such a task. Perhaps they did not have confidence in their own abilities to enter a sphere of society in which they had no experience. Some may have believed that an appeal written by a man would carry more weight, and it seems reasonable to assume that men would have had more opportunity to cultivate helpful connections that could now be put to good use.[21]

Rebecca Bouldin also relied on the generosity of a male acquaintance to organize and forward all the necessary paperwork required for an examination of the case of her impressed son, Edwin. Nevertheless, Bouldin still wrote personally to Secretary of State James Monroe in order to support Edwin's claim to citizenship and to confirm that all the relevant correspondence had arrived. Benjamin Roberts's widowed mother, Sarah, also took an active role in the process when she made a deposition attesting to the fact that she had given birth to her son in Boston and that he now had a wife and child waiting for his return to that city. She concluded, "Your petitioner therefore humbly prays your Honor to take such means as the Laws of the United States point out, or your wisdom may suggest, that her poor unhappy son may be released from his confinement . . . and restored to his friends, his Country & his aged mother."[22]

Although the reference to Bouldin's aged mother implies some degree of infirmity requiring attention, sailors often found themselves in worse physical conditions than those at home. Spencer Hopkins wrote to his mother pleading for help after his impressment by the British. Suffering from a prolonged illness, the captain had removed Hopkins from his ship and put the ailing man ashore in the Sandwich Islands, where he stayed for seven months. After recovering, Hopkins sought the best way home to America. He originally intended to work on a British vessel but quickly changed his mind when told that he would undoubtedly fall foul of another press if he sailed to England. He consequently shipped on board a Spanish ship but again found himself impressed despite all his precautions. In his letter, he encouraged his mother to work as quickly as she could, for the money he received while a captive proved completely insufficient for his needs.[23]

Thomas Jervey sailed as mate on the schooner *Galliot* bound for Gibraltar. Two days into the voyage, a violent gale resulted in the death of three crewmen. The remaining six survived by holding onto the vessel's bottom and eating a few dead rats that had floated to the surface. The desperate men retrieved a keg of water and three putrid hams by diving to the bottom but otherwise had nothing to sustain them. Fortunately, Captain Waddell of the brig *Apollo* rescued the hapless sailors and reportedly treated them with great kindness. Yet disaster would soon strike again. A press party from the British ship *Edgar*, commanded by Captain John M'Dougal, boarded the *Apollo* with the intention of finding seamen for their own vessel. As all the survivors of the *Galliot* had lost their protections at sea, they offered an easy target for the *Apollo*'s gang, which took every one of them. Writing on behalf of Jervey's family, Thomas Hill described the boy's mother as "reduced to such a state of wretchedness on his account, that beggars description." Hill closed by asking his friend to "restore a valuable and brave young citizen to his country."[24]

In the matter of impressment, the American government found itself just as incapable as its individual citizens in forcing Britain to any type of action. The Royal Navy ruled the seas, and many in the kingdom's government still viewed those living in the United States as their inferiors. Complaints regarding the impressment of American mariners continued to escalate during the Napoleonic Wars, which coincided with a heightened need for manpower. With Britain fighting for its survival, its primary concern did not rest with determining irrefutably the nationality of those the navy impressed, although ministers of the Crown did make well-intentioned attempts to placate the rising ire of American elected officials and the populace.

In reality, the US government understood its inability to force any action on the part of the British. How helpless, then, must the mothers of these men have felt when even their own government proved impotent in such matters? It appears that their American-born sons frequently became involuntary combatants in a war between two continental powers: France, which aimed to take the freedom of as many nations as it could, and Britain, which worked for the liberation of those already conquered and for the protection of those still threatened. In such cataclysmic times, the fate of the individual is inevitably subsumed to the greater good, although that liberation from the dictatorship of Napoleon could be purchased through the abduction and "enslavement" of their sons must have proven a cruel and bitter irony to these women, especially since the United States had worked diligently to stay removed from the conflict. While the American government may not have realistically had any option open to it other than to protest formally each new outrage, it did have in its power the ability to provide some basic level of support to the families of these victims of empire; yet the government passed no acts for their relief or established any agency, however small or temporary, charged with their care.

Inevitably, the bonds of affection between American sailors and their mothers transgressed the boundaries of time and space, and indeed, such distance may have increased the sense of attachment between mothers and sons, whether through distorted sentimentality or the clarity of the memory of happier times. Unfortunately, neither the government's nor the public's rage over impressment ever surpassed the level of private grief so long endured by mothers personally affected by this practice. These women never reconciled themselves to their individual sacrifice, despite their sons' collective symbolism as the public embodiment of the independence of the nation. While the suffering of its sailors rallied the country during a time of war, the situation caused little but misery for the mothers of those men to whom they were so intimately attached, while yet remaining so anonymous to all who used them for political currency.

## Notes

1. "Cases of Impressment," *Niles' Weekly Register*, supplement to vol. 8, April 18, 1812, 137–45.
2. Gary Nash, *Urban Crucible: Social Change, Political Consciousness, and the Origins of the American Revolution* (Cambridge, MA: Harvard University Press, 1979), 16; Brian DeToy, "The Impressment of

American Seamen during the Napoleonic Wars," in *The Consortium on Revolutionary Europe 1750–1850: Selected Papers*, ed. Donald D. Horward (Gainesville: Florida State University Press, 1998), 499.
3. Jesse Lemisch, "The American Revolution from the Bottom Up," in *Towards a New Past: Dissenting Essays in American History*, ed. Barton J. Bernstein (New York: Pantheon, 1968), 24.
4. Leonard Johnson to unknown, May 16, 1806, Department of State, Miscellaneous Lists and Papers Regarding Impressed Seamen, 1793–1815, Microcopy M1839, Roll 1, Record Group 59, National Archives and Record Administration (hereafter ISL).
5. Isaac Clark to his wife, October 28, 1811, ISL.
6. Alexander Boyd to his wife, January 5, 1807, ISL; Alexander Boyd to his wife, December 30, 1807, ISL.
7. James Williams to Polly Williams, n.d., ISL; Hugh Irwin to his mother, n.d., ISL; Peyton Page to his mother, July 1, 1812, ISL.
8. John Picken to Sarah Knowles, January 22, 1815, ISL.
9. Hannah Brimblecom to Monroe, March 2, 1812, ISL; Office of the American Consul in London to Hannah Brimblecom, December 23, 1811, ISL; "Protection Certificate of Philip Brimblecom," September 12, 1803, ISL. This protection was issued to Brimblecom when he was 16 years of age.
10. J. Alden to Isaiah Green, February 6, 1813, ISL.
11. Shepherd Bowen to his mother, January 12, 1812, ISL; Bowen to Mager [sic] Couzens, n.d., ISL.
12. Sarah Anderson to John Anderson, December 22, 1813, ISL.
13. "Review of Reviews," *Christian Observer*, July 1825.
14. B. Washington to unknown, January 12, 1812, ISL.
15. Aaron Hill to Robert Smith, May 2, 1809, ISL; "Deposition of Catherine Hill and Aaron Hill," April 29, 1809, ISL; Leonard House to Mr. McCulloch, n.d., ISL.
16. "Statement of Esther Moore," January 18, 1806, ISL.
17. "Statement of Olive Curien," November 7, 1808, ISL.
18. Joseph Clisby to his mother, January 18, 1801, ISL.
19. Mother to John Siters, April 27, 1812, ISL; [illegible] to John Siters, April 27, 1812, ISL.
20. Jane Burk to Thomas Burk, February 22, 1812, ISL.
21. "Deposition of Naomi Jackson," August 26, 1806, ISL.
22. Rebecca Bouldin to Monroe, January 6, 1812, ISL; "Deposition of Sarah Roberts," August 1800, ISL.
23. Spencer Hopkins to his mother, June 11, 1808, ISL.
24. Thomas Hall to Jacob Read, May 30, 1799, ISL.

## Selected Bibliography

Armitage, David. *The Ideological Origins of the British Empire.* Cambridge: Cambridge University Press, 2000.

Auchinleck, Gilbert. *A History of the War between Great Britain and the United States of America during the Years 1812, 1813, & 1814.* Toronto: Arms and Armour, 1855.

Borneman, Walter R. *1812: The War That Forged a Nation.* New York: Harper Collins, 2004.

Caffrey, Kate. *The Lion and the Union: The Anglo-American War, 1812–1815.* London: Andre Deutsch, 1978.

Coles, Harry L. *The War of 1812.* Chicago: University of Chicago Press, 1965.

DeToy, Brian. "The Impressment of American Seamen during the Napoleonic Wars." *Consortium on Revolutionary Europe 1750–1850: Selected Papers* (January 1998): 492–501.

Drake, Kelly S. "The Seaman's Protection Certificate as Proof of American Citizenship for Black Sailors." *The Log of Mystic Seaport* 50, no. 1 (Summer 1998): 11–14.

Heidler, David, and Jeanne Heidler. *The War of 1812.* Westport, CT: Greenwood, 2002.

Horsman, Reginald. *The Causes of the War of 1812.* Philadelphia: University of Pennsylvania Press, 1962.

———. *The War of 1812.* Philadelphia: University of Pennsylvania Press, 1962.

Labaree, Benjamin, et al. *America and the Sea: A Maritime History.* Mystic, CT: Mystic Seaport Museum, 1998.

Lavery, Brian. *Shipboard Life and Organization, 1731–1815.* Aldershot: Ashgate, 1998.

Lemisch, Jesse. "The American Revolution from the Bottom Up." In *Towards a New Past: Dissenting Essays in American History*, edited by Barton J. Bernstein, 3–45. New York: Pantheon, 1968.

Nash, Gary. *Urban Crucible: Social Change, Political Consciousness, and the Origins of the American Revolution.* Cambridge, MA: Harvard University Press, 1979.

Paullin, Charles Oscar. "Naval Administration under the Secretaries of the Navy Smith, Hamilton, and Jones, 1801–1814." *United States Naval Proceedings* 32 (1906): 1289–328.

Perkins, Bradford. *The Causes of the War of 1812: National Honor or National Interest?* New York: Holt, Rinehart, and Winston, 1962.

Selement, George. "Impressment & the American Merchant Marine 1782–1812." *The Mariner's Mirror* 59, no. 4 (1973): 409–18.

Snook, George, and Ira Dye. "An Episode of the War of 1812; The Seamen's Protective Certificate." *Manuscripts* 52, no. 2 (Spring 2000): 111–17.

Stagg, J. C. A. *Mr. Madison's War: Politics, Diplomacy, and Warfare in the Early American Republic.* Princeton: Princeton University Press, 1983.

Steel, Anthony. "Anthony Merry and the Anglo-American Dispute about Impressment, 1803–1806." *Cambridge Historical Journal* 9, no. 3 (1949): 331–51.

———. "Impressment in the Monroe-Pinkney Negotiation, 1806–1807." *The American Historical Review* 57, no. 2 (January 1952): 352–69.

# Chapter 4

## *Las Madres Guerreras*
### Testimonial Writing on Militant Motherhood in Latin America

*Tracy Crowe Morey and Cristina Santos*

In *Women's Activism in Latin America and the Caribbean: Engendering Social Justice, Democratizing Citizenship,* Elizabeth Maier argues that "[o]ne of the most distinctive characteristics of Latin America over the past four decades has been the increasing visibility of women as collective actors in the public domain of politics." Historically relegated to the private sphere of Latin American society, women's entrance into the public arena of politics took place primarily under the military-authoritarian governments during the second half of the twentieth century. Among those who became involved in the public arena were "[e]ducated, middle-class feminists, female guerrilla fighters, activist Mothers, and militant urban homemakers from class-oriented, grassroots organizations." This new female representation of political mobilization accounts for a heterogeneous and complex scope of individual experiences regarding women's contributions to the revolutionary movements of the 1960s through to the 1990s in Latin America.[1]

Scholars have begun to account for the diverse political nature of female participation in the various Latin American revolutionary movements. The majority of these studies have tended to focus on the activism and mobilization of mothers in human rights groups, such as the Mothers of Plaza de Mayo, largely due to their reception and promotion from international solidarity organizations. However, Latin

American mothers also participated in revolutionary movements, such as Nicaragua's FSLN (Sandinista National Liberation Front), Chile's MIR (Revolutionary Left Movement), and Argentina's *Montoneros*. Analyses of these mothers who played more logistical and/or combat roles in the leftist movements have received considerably less attention and public acknowledgement. As journalist Cherie Zalaquett argues in *Chilenas en armas* (*Chilean Women in Arms*), women are not regarded as political actors but rather as victims of human rights violations. Furthermore, where leftist movements provided active participation for women to serve in the public domain, democratization of revolutionary governments or democratic transition periods resulted in the return of many of these women to the private sphere.[2]

Much of Latin American women's testimonial literature directly responds to this marginalization from the political forum during these transitional periods of democratization. Testimonial writing provides a valuable resource for mining information concerning the various roles and contributions of female mobilization and militancy in Latin America. More important, testimonial literature bears witness to the motivations and strategies through which Latin American women negotiated the social obstacles between militancy and motherhood. Our interest, and the focus of this study, is on the role of the militant mother as remembered and theorized through testimony. Rather than concentrate solely on the activist or political mother searching and seeking justice for her missing/murdered child, our analysis primarily considers militant mothers who were active in the revolutionary movement and who were emotionally and/or physically absent from their children's lives.[3]

Together with several accounts of oral interviews collected by Margaret Randall in Nicaragua, Cherie Zalaquett in Chile, and Marta Diana in Argentina, the testimonies examined in this chapter include Dolores Tijerino's *Inside the Nicaraguan Revolution (As Told to Margaret Randall)*, Gioconda Belli's *The Country under My Skin: A Memoir of Love and War*, Carmen Rodríguez's *And a Body to Remember With*, Carmen Castillo's film *Calle Santa Fé*, Carmen Aguirre's *Something Fierce: Memoirs of a Revolutionary Daughter*, and Hugo de Marinis and Adriana Spahr's *Madre de Mendoza*. With the exception of Tijerino and the oral accounts published by Randall in 1981, much of this literature was written in retrospect, where it becomes evident that motherhood was one of the most complex and controversial negotiations for women of the leftist movements. In examining testimonials from Nicaragua, Chile, and Argentina, this chapter aims to highlight the differences but also, more important, the similarities of shared experiences and strategies of militancy and motherhood mapped across a diverse spectrum of Latin American revolutionary movements.

## FOREMOTHERS TO THE *MADRES GUERRERAS*

In her study on the representation and conceptualization of the figure of the female guerrilla or combat fighter, Meg Samuelson notes that "[t]wo strands of feminist thought diverge . . . one finds in war a potential realm of gendered equality and female liberation; another associates women with nurturing and life-giving qualities, linking them to an ethos of peace and pitting them and their interests against war." When placed alongside Western traditions of motherhood and war, the acceptance of the female militant becomes inherently unsettling: "'Mothering' and 'war' have often been twinned in a sort of lethal symbiosis: whether collusive or oppositional, conceptual or practical, life giving and death dealing are seen to be connected." In Latin America, there is a similar tradition of female militancy that has provided both controversy as well as sources of inspiration for revolutionaries in the latter half of the twentieth century since: "*La militancia era una especie de útero que te contenía en todos los terrenos: político, cultural, afectivo.*" The tradition of the active and positive figure of the *guerrera* or warrior woman is intrinsically aligned with the reaffirmation of the indigenous in Latin America. Instead of following the dominant European model of passive mothering as part of the private sphere of the home and characterized by female sacrifice, self-abnegation, and censure, female militancy in the Latin American contexts models the indigenous mythical and historical tradition of the *madres guerreras*.[4]

The figure of the warrior woman is best documented in Mexico, although this figure shares similar features in Central and South America. In Mexico, it has precolonial roots in such indigenous mythological figures as the Mexica Coatlicue and her descendant, Cihuacoatl (or Snake Woman). Both of these warrior goddesses represented female power and strength but also fertility of both the land and its people; in addition, Cihuacoatl was the patroness of midwives, called on by women "to help them through the battle of birth," as well as "a supreme strategist" on the battlefield. Historically speaking, both Coatlicue and Cihuacoatl were mother figures for the Mexica and ultimately foretold the ruin of their people to their leader Motechuhzoma I as mothers mourning for their children.[5]

In connection with traditional Western constructs of the splitting of the "good mother" / "bad mother," Latin America had its precedents in the fragmentation of the goddess Coatlicue into numerous descendants that exemplify this very binary opposition of motherhood: Tonantzin and Coatlopeuh the "good mothers" and Cihuacoatl and eventually La Malinche as the "bad mothers." Since La Malinche has been traditionally seen as the traitress of her people and a negative mother figure for the Mexican race, in 1531 this negative mother figure was replaced with the Virgin of Guadalupe—a *mestiza* version of the Christian figure of Mary—dark skinned and dark haired and a desexualized and passive image of a virgin mother. It is within this binary opposition that we can then situate La Llorona as the "third mother" of the Mexican race: "All three are mediators: *Guadalupe*, the virgin who has not abandoned us [Chicanos], *la Chingada* [La Malinche], the raped mother whom we have abandoned, and *La Llorona*, the mother who seeks her lost children and is a combination of the other two."[6]

The Mexican Revolution (1910–40) also introduced other female militant figures such as the *soldadera* (soldier) and even at times the *coronela* (colonel). These women fought alongside their men as well as served in the kitchen and as helpmates in war. Even so, Carlos Monsiváis is quick to point out in his foreword to *Sex in Revolution: Gender, Politics, and Power in Modern Mexico* that

> one thing is notorious: women (the gender, the groups, and the enormously dynamic individuals) mean very little in political and social terms and practically nothing when set before the deity of those times: History, an exclusively masculine territory. According to patriarchal doctrine, neither power nor violence nor indubitable valor nor historic lucidity are women's issues . . . Although women's participation in the revolution may have been influential in many ways, patriarchy is nothing if not an endless strategy of concealment. During the revolutionary stage . . . women were seen in an ahistoric light; they existed on the margin of the optics of political and social prestige and barely managed to join in "everyday rumour," the rhythm that, because it was secondary, did not form part of History.

All the same, these female warriors played a key active role in the Mexican Revolution despite the patriarchal limitations and censure placed on them. The *Adelitas*, *Valentinas*, and *Marietas* that populated many of the texts and popular songs of the time served a greater role: they replaced the "His-story" that negated them a place with the

"Her-story" in which they, as survivors, would be able to carry the memories from the battlefields or be the companion to bear witness to an honorable death. Unlike the *soldaderas*, the militant women of the revolutionary movements of the 1960s–1990s discussed here did not have to renounce their feminine condition to enter the revolutionary battlefield, but they did form part of an underrepresented "History" of their contributions and lived experiences in the revolutionary movements.[7]

In Nicaragua, for example, Doris Tijerino "shapes her own pantheon of female heroes," from naming her revolver Norita, "in honour of Nora Paiz, the Guatemalan revolutionary who was assassinated in 1967," to assuming the alias of Conchita Alday, "the name of a female revolutionary from a previous generation in Nicaragua." In her testimony, Tijerino recalls that "Conchita was in an advanced state of pregnancy, and the *gringo* soldiers slit open her belly with their bayonets to take out the fetus while she was still alive, and later they quartered her completely." Byron points out that "[t]his brutal murder lays bare how violence is gendered, but for later women, Alday becomes a symbol of strength of Nicaraguan women. She is a literal mother warrior whose very death further reinforces her maternity while it highlights man's brutality."[8]

Other examples of Latin American warrior foremothers are found in the fiction of Gioconda Belli. In her novel *The Inhabited Woman*, Belli populates a Nicaraguan past with the same Mesoamerican cultural groups of Mexico, the Nahuas (or Mexicas). While this novel can be identified as a testimonial one where Belli appears to be writing about her own participation in the Nicaraguan revolution through the protagonist Lavinia, Belli also provides her contemporary female characters struggling against the dictator Somoza with a female predecessor named Itzá, "a mythical mother of the revolution," tied together in a women's history of "militance [sic], strength, and triumph."[9]

In South America, although not providing a specific female antecedent, the testimonials of Carmen Rodríguez and Carmen Aguirre both associate the revolutionary movement with the indigenous traditions and nations of the Mapuche. Historically referred to as the Araucanians (*araucanos*) by the Spanish colonizers of South America, the Mapuche represent a warring model of struggle and resistance to oppression and injustice. In Rodríguez's *And a Body to Remember With* and Aguirre's *Something Fierce: Memoirs of a Revolutionary Daughter*, both mother and daughter describe, albeit in very different manners, female militancy dependent and linked with their indigenous *compañeros* (companions). Such examples include Aguirre's clandestine reconnaissance in the Andes as well as the nearly fatal fall, but subsequent revival, for Aguirre's mother in "Mapuche land"—described by Rodríguez in the story titled "i sing, therefore i am."[10]

Marta Diana delineates a similar *guerrera* genealogy in early Latin American history of women such as Juana Azurduy de Padilla; Josefa, La Federala; Pascuala Meneses (a.k.a. Pascual Meneses); and Juana Moro de López, to name a few. Some of the women whom Diana interviews acknowledge these female precedents for their own militancy and that of their shared sisters in Latin America: "*[L]as latinoamericanas hemos dado el ejemplo . . . Yo creo que una de las características de la mujer latinoamericana es la lucha. Me parece que nosotras no nos pasan de largo las cosas. También es así en la historia, por eso hubo mujeres en las montoneras.*" Diana also asserts that "*una cosa muy clara es que las compañeras tuvimos vidas muy duras y eso se ha ignorado.*" These militant women recognized this gendered power relation and combated it by embracing it as an intrinsic part to their militant mothering: "*[L]a fuerza que tuve en ese momento . . . y mantenerme firme en muchos otros, nacieron de mi condición femenina.*"[11]

Ultimately, the cultural and/or historical prefiguratives of these *guerreras* facilitate the active participation of militant mothers in the revolutions discussed here. This embodies not only a removal of the woman from the private and oppressive sphere of the patriarchal home but also a repositioning of the active mother figure as an intrinsic part of a "new" home—the revolutionary movement:

> *Pero nosotras estamos sí estamos vivas. Formamos parte de una cadena, vital y femenina, que se inció con las indígenas (que casi ya no existen), primitivas habitantes de estas tierras, cuyo próximo eslabón integran esas otras mujeres que un día en Europa abordaron inciertas naves para desembarcar en un destino más incierto todavía. De esa cadena, las que fueron guerrilleras argentinas (que casi ya no existen) también forman parte. Esta no es una cuestión política. Es una cuestión histórica, social, y humana. Lo que es político es el tratamiento que se ha dado al tema: heroínas o delincuentes.*

This well-established prefigurative, in turn, allowed for the evolution of this new sense of "*guerrera*" mothering that integrates an awareness of solidarity and sisterhood together with the notion of communal mothering—and this, we shall see, has been the legacy created by many of *las madres guerreras*.[12]

## Testifying Female Militancy

To begin, testimonial literature provides a subsequent history of women's contributions and types of involvement undertaken during the leftist movements. Much of the literature evidences forms of political activism as the founding of later female militancy—which during the periods of dictatorship resulted in political imprisonment and/or having to go underground or into exile. These women were often, regardless of geographical context, the youth (university students) who were involved with literacy projects, educational work, and/or labor unions. Interestingly, many oral interviews in *Sandino's Daughters* and testimonies in *Mujeres guerrilleras* reveal the difference between "legal" work and going underground: "jobs such as buying clothes, food, and other supplies for the guerrillas" were legal jobs, whereas going underground—described "as being burned"—was the result of "publicly [being] identified as a member of the FSLN" by taking part in an assault on a bank, car theft, or even kidnapping charges.[13]

From the preliminary oral interviews of revolutionary women in Nicaragua—many of whom were mothers at the time of their involvement in the FSLN—Randall documents that from every class women participated in some measure in the struggle against dictatorship: "[W]omen fought in the front lines as FSLN militants, participated in support tasks, worked undercover in government offices and were involved in every facet of the anti-Somoza opposition movement." Marta Diana reports in *Mujeres guerrilleras* that of the 8,961 disappeared, 30 percent were women, of which 10 percent were pregnant. Diana also points out that not all the disappeared were militants but also included innocent bystanders caught in the wrong place at the wrong time. Nevertheless, it is interesting to point out that 21 percent of disappeared were students, and the age group with the highest disappearance rate was 21–25 years of age at 32.62 percent.[14]

In Chile, female insurgents participated in political support tasks beginning in the late 1960s through to collaboration with the democratically elected socialist government of Allende. After the military coup in 1973, MIR members went underground or left to live in exile due to the brutal military response of arresting and often "disappearing" any political activist or supporter of Allende. Many of the exiled members returned to Chile or neighboring countries in the 1980s in a project called "The Return Plan." Rodríguez participated in this plan and her work involved support tasks such as the running of safe houses for the resistance, the transporting of supply needs such as information, weapons, and food, and overall logistical support work such as terrain mapping from bordering countries that could allow for the movement's blacklisted insurgents to cross over into Chile. Aguirre would join the Resistance after her mother when she turned of age. Her memoir *Something Fierce* describes her teenage years with her mother, sister, and stepfather in South America when her mother was directly involved in the insurgency in the 1980s.[15]

Diana's collection also provides a similar range of militant involvement in Argentina equally punctuated by a gendered work distribution in which women would be assigned mainly (in some revolutionary groups) to intelligence gathering and analysis but, upon insistence, also active (sometimes armed) participation. Despite the differing contexts of the leftist movements, if female militants were tasked with support work and logistics, the divide between armed and unarmed revolutionary work would not necessarily be so clear-cut, since for some women "logistical support occasionally involved combat, and it always involved the risk of being 'disappeared' (tortured and murdered)."[16]

## Mother/Children Legacies of Militancy

Whether engaged directly or indirectly in armed military roles, many of the testimonials shed light on women's involvement as mothers. One of the earliest testimonies to document both the political and militant roles undertaken by women and mothers in the Leftist movement in Nicaragua is Tijerino's *Inside the Nicaraguan Revolution (As Told to Margaret Randall)*. Transcribed by Margaret Randall from oral interviews that took place in Cuba between 1974 and 1975, this text bears close resemblance to what many scholars of testimony define as the urgency of the genre, in which "[t]ruth is summoned in the cause of denouncing a present situation of exploitation and oppression." The text in English begins as follows: "Doris Tijerino and I want people everywhere to know the truth about the present situation in Nicaragua, particularly the repressive measures of the dictator Somoza, and the people's reply to the dictatorship, which has been a lengthy struggle for national liberation." In this edition, the testimony creates a sort of urgency and a need to build on support for the Sandinista regime outside the country; yet the original Spanish language edition, titled *Somos millones... La vida de Doris María, combatiente nicaragüense (We Are Millions... The Life of Doris María, Nicaraguan Female Combatant)*, published one year earlier, provides evidence of the types of mass mobilization by the FSLN movement who were looking to garner support and recruitment for an effective resistance against Somoza. Representations of female combatants either nursing, pregnant, or carrying a young child in their arms became effective and empowering recruitment strategies for the revolutionary movements in Central and South America.[17]

In the case of Tijerino, Randall points out that her story "is not unique," not only in terms of the repression and suffering experienced by many Nicaraguans under the Somoza dictatorship, but also in terms of how women and mothers like Tijerino were mobilizing to fight against such oppression:

> Doris, this book remains a battle cry from all our sisters. It pays homage, as well to Arlen Siu, Claudia Chamorro, Maria Castilblanco, Julia Herrera and Mildred Abuanza—fallen in combat since this books was written. Charlotte Baltodano Egner, whose eloquent prison testimony reveals further details of Somoza's dungeons; Liana Benavides, Ruth Marcenaro, Rosa Argentina Ortiz and Maria Martha Beltran who turned their trial into a cry for justice around the world; the housewives bang their pots and pans in a coordinated nationwide effort to call attention to their country's lot; and the untold numbers of anonymous women who have joined the struggle, died in it, or continue to fight. M.R. Havana, April 1978.

As such, the testimony showcases exemplary action by politically or militantly active women, from female guerrilla combatants who had fallen to housewives who bang their pots and pans in solidarity to denounce the human rights violations under Somoza.[18]

Central to many of the testimonials examined here, mothers were critical in shaping how their militant children were able to contribute to the revolutionary movements. Finding inspiration and/or support from their own mothers was a common feature for many families across the spectrum of revolutionary movements in Latin America. Tijerino's testimony underscores that the kind of militant activity carried out by participants such as herself could not so easily have been accomplished without the support of mothers: "In Nicaragua, there are many cases—though not all, of course—in which those serving in the Front find solidarity for their militant activities in their mothers." Tijerino attributes much of her political consciousness to her mother, who first introduces a young Tijerino to Marxist literature and who was "somewhat politically active even against my papa's will." Tijerino's first contact with Sandinista guerrillas is through her mother's connections. This "first act of conspiracy" as Tijerino recalls, entailed the transportation of "boots, food and a rifle" at her mother's request.[19]

The birth of political consciousness is also a founding theme that runs through many of the testimonies discussed here. In Belli's *The Country under My Skin: A Memoir of Love and War*, for example, the introduction begins with her mother and the birthing of a revolutionary, for which she credits her own attraction "to the world of men, biological functions and domestic life." Although Belli's bourgeois mother does not approve of her daughter's leftist ideologies and participation in the movement, she does teach her "about the power of femininity"—the very source that empowers Belli "to live in a man's world." However, it is her first experience of witnessing political activism by another mother figure (her aunt Elena)—at the age of six—and Belli's subsequent love of poetry that become credited as another source of strength and "life-giving spirit" that would propel her into the Sandinista revolution.[20]

There are also many cases of mothers who become politically conscious only after their children's involvement or death in the revolution. In Nicaragua, Dona Santos, mother of Julio Buitrago, becomes an activist after the death of her revolutionary son: "When Julio died, Dona Santos survived. And not only did she survive and bear her sorrow at the death of her son, but she changed radically. Dona was a mother worthy of a Sandinist martyr. She went to the meetings, took part in the struggles to free the prisoners, went to many assemblies with the mothers of other imprisoned comrades, and helped plan popular campaigns." Another example is found with comrade Aurora Nunez, whose son was tortured, arrested (at the age of 15), and later killed after his release. Nunez was arrested along with her son "because a machine gun was found in her house." Tijerino recalls how "[w]e in the Organization called her 'the little mother' because she sometimes acted like the mother of many of the comrades." In this case, comrade Nunez was providing what Morena Herrera calls "a nurturing force that cared for the insurgency." In such capacity, civilian mothers were fulfilling support roles for the guerrilla, "feeding, hiding, and caring for wounded combatants."[21]

In *Madre de Mendoza* the reader is presented with the life story of María Isabel Figueroa, an Argentine mother who began her activism after her daughter disappeared. In this case family members admit that the mother at first did not necessarily take her daughter's militancy seriously but became involved because of her children's own personal commitment, even though she did not accept what did they did in its entirety. Figueroa admits, "*Yo no era de ningún partido realmente. Mi papá era radical, yo era radical, y mi mamá era de un partido un día y después del otro. A todos les desconfiaba.*"[22]

## Redefining Militant Mother(hood)s

Across the differing contexts of revolution throughout Latin America, testimonial writing offers a forum for women to theorize the motivations and the consequences of their roles as revolutionaries. In comparison to the restrictive space of the private sphere, the revolution and role of militant allowed many women the opportunity of a new state, both philosophical and physical, as liberated women in a public sphere. Many of the women's testimonials acknowledge that their militancy gave them an alternative to the standard, middle-class, and domestic life (such as Belli and Castillo); for others, what is highlighted is political consciousness based on the need to fight social injustice and oppression (as depicted by Tijerino, Rodríguez, and Figueroa).[23]

One of the lasting effects of mothers' participation in the revolutionary movements is evidenced throughout many of the testimonies and oral accounts, which reveal the complexities, ambivalence, and trauma of being a revolutionary and a mother. In the Chilean and Argentine testimonies considered here, the mothers discuss their choices of having to either abandon their families in a form of absent mothering or risk engaging in underground revolutionary work with their children still at home. Diana remarks on the irony of the situation: "*O perdíamos como militantes o perdíamos como madres.*" In these testimonies, there are complex negotiations at play as many of the militant mothers remember in retrospect their sacrifices and those of their now mature children. This is without ignoring the more complex and traumatic experience of some Argentine mothers who gave birth in the military prisons and concentration camps. In some cases, they were able to keep their children with them until they began to walk, then only having to trust that their child was being delivered safely to their families and not being "adopted" out to military families, as in the tragic cases experienced by many other political prisoners in Argentina.[24]

In the case of the Chilean MIR insurgents, many participants left their children in the care of others abroad, mainly in Cuba, in a program called the "*Proyecto Hogares*" (Home Project), which for some members lasted for more than ten years. For Margarita Marchi, one of the insurgents interviewed by Castillo in her film *Calle Santa Fé*, motherhood and revolution were part of every woman's human right. For

Castillo, however, motherhood and revolution had to be separated. Her daughter would remain in Havana in the "*Proyecto Hogares*" for 11 years before she returned to her mother. Castillo's film captures what Lisa Renee DiGiovanni notes as the "difficult negotiations that women have made between motherhood and political commitments in times of dictatorship and how these negotiations remained unresolved today." The film documents the mixed feelings of the now mature children, some of whom remain silent about the absence of their mothers, others who blame their mothers for having abandoned them for the revolution, and other daughters who are empathetic and active in commemorating and telling their mothers' story.[25]

Unfortunately, the same "bad mother" complex that we saw with the warrior foremothers also translates into modern times as what we would term the "cult(ure) of the absent mother"—a term that a patriarchal and middle-class perspective supersedes and equates as the "bad mother": "*La cultural oficial puede llegar a decir que era una mala madre.*" Nevertheless, it is important to point out that there also existed an ethos that these militant mothers may have been absent from their biological child's life but were actually "mothering"—in a communal sense—a new generation of children. In her testimony to Diana, Gringa explains, "*Con respecto a las mujeres y su condición de madres, que tanto se ha criticado, pienso que vale la misma aclaración, porque no es buena madre solamente la que se queda en casa con los hijos. También es buena madre la que sale a luchar para algo que va ser para ellos y para todos. Transformar una sociedad tan cruel, donde muchos de esos hijos no tienen ninguna posibilidad de subsistencia, es el mejor regalo que una madre podría tratar de brindarles.*" The idea of the "bad biological mother" who abandons her children is essentially replaced with the idea of "the good ideological mother." That is, militant mothering took on the task of educating the masses and extended this mothering to the wider community in the form of solidarity and sisterhood—sacrifices made by these militant mothers were not only for their own biological children but for all future generations. Nevertheless, this did not prevent the "ideological mother" from being depicted as a "bad mother," since she was "bad" not only because she was not present in her own child's life but also because of her militant and revolutionary ideologies. In her testimony, Negrita describes how during a torture session she began to lactate (she was still nursing her youngest when taken prisoner) and her torturer remarked, laughingly: "*El que toma de esa leche sale guerrillero*"—coinciding precisely with the concept of the solidarity motherhood developed by these militant mothers.[26]

Within the revolutionary movements there was an intrinsic feminist recognition of equality in which there was a built-in need to challenge "traditional stereotypes of women as perennial victims, perpetual peacekeepers, or embodiments of the nation that men seek to protect and defend." In essence, these women had to not only challenge the sociopolitical status quo via their revolutionary agendas but also overcome the *machista* prejudices both inside and outside their movements: "*Una de las cosas que aprendí fue elegir lo que quiero y lo que no quiero. Pienso que todos tenemos ese derecho. En estas actitudes se nota que uno no vivió igual que todos; en todos lados me llaman rebelde: en el trabajo, en la universidad. Ser rebelde es defender lo que es de uno y eso llama la atención.*" For many it became a "revolution within the revolution" since "*la mujer, además de militar 'igual que a un hombre' tenía que ocuparse sola de lo considerado 'feminino'*"—that is, not having to sacrifice their motherhood for militancy or vice versa, or preventing what Che Guevara had indicated as one of his concerns for all revolutionaries: "*que la guerra y la lucha no nos hagan perder la ternura.*"[27]

What seems to emerge from these personal revelations is a cult(ure) of guilt and sacrifice associated with the absent mother. The patriarchal and *machista* discourse dominant in the middle-class and bourgeois classes is that motherhood remains a valid reason to exclude women from active militancy in the revolutionary movement. Yet one notes that such patriarchal ideologies are unsuccessful in forcing these women to conform to the passive roles expected of them. The results are twofold: (1) the woman's partner accepts her role as an active revolutionary and mother and they form a strong parenting unit together in the process; or (2) the difference in opinion around the woman's militant and mother roles facilitates the breakdown of the family and is replaced by the single mother. In both cases a solidarity/sisterhood arises within the revolutionary movement to provide support to these militant mothers by way of childcare, financial assistance, and emotional encouragement. Frida, an Argentine militant, adds that her status as militant mother also caused a "collective catharsis" in her group because of its prevailing "ancestral machista formation."[28]

## Conclusion

As we can see, female militancy took on many different forms of involvement not limited to activities specifically associated with any particular revolutionary movement. That is, militant mothers could be (1) women who were active in the movement and had their children remain at home with them or (2) women who were forced to leave their children behind because of safety reasons and/or they were ordered to do so by their superior officers. Contrary to the *Madres de Plaza de Mayo*, for example, these mothers did not become active militants *after* the disappearance/death of their child. Moreover, in the case of Argentina, Mariana reveals that the aim in most prisons was also to "assist" the female militant to "recover" her more feminine state, yet "*ellos [los militares] estaban fascinados con nosotras. Eramos mujeres absolutamente distintas a las que eran sus esposas. Con nosotras podían hablar de política, armas, estrategia, cine o filosofía. De modo que junto con la atracción, se daba una contradicción.*" Most importantly, as Graciela Daleo reveals, the military "reprogramming" did not succeed in its objective—but still with great personal and collective sacrifices.[29]

It is evident that during the various stages of conflict, Latin American mothers took up active roles as militants or *guerreras* in each of their respective revolutionary movements. They did so while navigating not only sociocultural obstacles in their participation but also political limitations as to the extent of their active and/or armed role. Testimony became the way in which many of these women not only worked through their personal and collective trauma but also vindicated their role in history—all the while insisting that this was *their* particular response to *their* situation and not a universal response or type of mothering for *all* Latin American women. This militant mothering took on a philosophical and psychological role of women negotiating their sociopolitical reality while theorizing about what had happened and what had come out of their revolutionary commitments. In the end, these militant women mothered their biological children as well as their revolutionary children—thereby guaranteeing that their ultimate legacy would be defined *by them* and not by their partners, their revolutionary movement, nor the dominant patriarchal definition of womanhood or motherhood.

## Notes

1. Elizabeth Maier and Nathalie Lebon, eds., *Women's Activism in Latin America and the Caribbean: Engendering Social Justice, Democratizing Citizenship* (New Brunswick, NJ: Rutgers University Press, 2010), 26–27.
2. For general discussions of women's roles in Latin American revolutions, see Lorraine Bayard de Volo, "Drafting Motherhood: Maternal

Imagery and Organizations in the United States and Nicaragua," in *The Women and War Reader*, ed. Lois Ann Lorentzen and Jennifer Turpin (New York: New York University Press, 1998), 240–53; Meghan Gibbons, "Political Motherhood in the United States and Argentina," in *Mothers Who Deliver: Feminist Interventions in Public and Interpersonal Discourse*, ed. Jocelyn Fenton-Stitt and Pageen Reichert Powell (Albany: State University of New York Press, 2010), 253–78; Margaret Gonzalez-Pérez, "Guerrilleras in Latin America: Domestic and International Roles," *Journal of Peace Research* 43, no. 3 (2006): 313–29; Morena Herrera, "From Insurgency to Feminist Struggle: The Search for Social Justice, Democracy, and Equality between Women and Men," in *Women's Activism in Latin America and the Caribbean: Engendering Social Justice, Democratizing Citizenship*, ed. Elizabeth Maier and Nathalie Lebon (New Brunswick, NJ: Rutgers University Press, 2010), 291–306; Karen Kampwirth, *Women and Guerrilla Movements: Nicaragua, El Salvador, Chiapas, Cuba* (University Park: Penn State University Press, 2003); Jadwiga E. Pieper Mooney, "Militant Motherhood Re-Visited: Women's Participation and Political Power in Argentina and Chile," *History Compass* 5, no. 3 (2007): 975–94; Diana Mulinari, "Broken Dreams in Nicaragua," in *The Women and War Reader*, ed. Lois Ann Lorentzen and Jennifer Turpin (New York: New York University Press, 1998), 157–63; Margaret Randall, *Sandino's Daughters: Testimonies of Nicaraguan Women in Struggle* (New Brunswick, NJ: Rutgers University Press, 1981); Randall, *Sandino's Daughters Revisited: Feminism in Nicaragua* (New Brunswick, NJ: Rutgers University Press, 1994); and Cherie Zalaquett, *Chilenas en armas: testimonios e historia de mujeres militares y guerrilleras subversivas* (Santiago de Chile: Catalonia, 2009). In Nicaragua, the FSLN, founded in 1961, overthrew the Somoza dictatorship in 1979 with the Sandinistas establishing a revolutionary government from 1979 to 1990. They were defeated in the democratic elections by the National Opposition Union, under the leadership of the first elected female head of state in Latin America. See Randall, *Sandino's Daughters Revisited*. In Chile, the MIR formed in 1965 in the University of Concepción and exists today as a political party. With the fall of the socialist government of Allende in 1973, the organization went underground to actively overthrow the Pinochet dictatorship. Its members were largely exiled supporters and militants. See Zalaquett, *Chilenas en armas*. In Argentina, there were several leftist movements that organized in the 1960s, including the Montoneros; all were defeated during Argentina's Dirty War. See Marta Diana, *Mujeres guerrilleras: sus testimonios en la militancia de los setenta*, 3rd ed. (Buenos Aires: Booket, 2011).

3. Testimonial literature (*testimonio* in Spanish) encompasses autobiographical narratives that present evidence of first-person accounts of human rights abuses, violence and war, and/or life under conditions

of social oppression. See John Beverly, "The Margin at the Centre: On *Testimonio* (Testimonial Narrative)," in *The Real Thing: Testimonial Discourses and Latin America*, ed. George M. Gugelberger (Durham, NC: Duke University Press, 1996), 24. It is generally understood that testimony may include different categories considered conventional literature such as autobiography, memoir, oral history, or short story.

4. Meg Samuelson, "The Disfigured Body of the Female Guerrilla: (De)Militarization, Sexual Violence, and Redomestication in Zoë Wicomb's *David's Story*," in *War and Terror: Feminist Perspectives*, ed. Karen Alexander and Mary Hawkesworth (Chicago: University of Chicago Press, 2008), 89; Irene Matthews, "Daughtering in War: Two 'Case Studies' from Mexico and Guatemala," in *Gendering War Talk*, ed. Miriam Cooke and Angela Woollacott (Princeton, NJ: Princeton University Press, 1993), 148; Diana, *Mujeres guerrilleras*, 273. The Spanish-language quote translates as "Militancy was a type of uterus that enveloped you from all sides: political, cultural and affective" (translations ours).

5. Kay Almere Read and Jason J. González, *Mesoamerican Mythology: A Guide to the Gods, Heroes, Rituals and Beliefs of Mexico and Central America* (New York: Oxford University Press, 2000), 147–49. The term *Mexica* refers to the "Nahuatl-speaking group based in Central Mexico that dominated a significant portion of Mesoamerica from about 1350 until 1521" (309). One of the first sightings of these women depicts her dressed in white and appearing to Motechuhzoma I in 1452 and in 1502; it is said the Cihuacoatl also appeared in the Aztec city of Tenochtitlan, dressed in white and crying out, "Dear children, soon I am going to abandon you! We are going to leave."—a wail that is said to have prophesized the fall of the indigenous people to the Spanish conquest (149).

6. Tonantzin is also known as Tonantsi, both Nahuatl for "Our Honourable Mother." The site dedicated to this goddess was the same location that the Virgin of Guadalupe first appeared in 1531 to Juan Diego (a Christian convert); see Gloria Anzaldúa, *Borderlands/Frontera: The New Mestiza* (San Francisco: Aunt Lute, 1999) 49–50. It is precisely the cultural paradigm of the "good" mother found in the Virgin Mary that activist mother groups such as the Mothers of Plaza de Mayo regularly evoked as a strategic means through which to garner public acceptance and international support for their cause. As Meghan Gibbons argues, "The Argentine mothers played on the cultural paradigm of *marianismo*, a Catholic model of ideal womanhood based on the Latin American cult of the Virgin Mary . . . In her image, good, Catholic Argentine women were constructed as pious, self-sacrificing, obedient, and devoted to their families. Most importantly, women/mothers were morally superior to men, and spiritually stronger, praying patiently for the redemption of their men from sinful natures"

(255). Octavio Paz refers to La Malinche using this defamatory term drawing attention to her as the sexually violated and exploited object at the hands of Hernán Cortés. *La Chingada* is "the Mother forcibly opened, violated." Paz explains further that the verb *chingar* exists in a sexually violent relationship between man and woman centered around the man's aggressiveness and power and the woman's defenselessness: "[T]he *chingón* is the *macho*, the male; he rips open the *chingada*, the female, who is pure passivity, defenseless against the exterior world." See Octavio Paz, *The Labyrinth of Solitude: Life and Thought in Mexico*, trans. Lysander Kemp (New York: Grove, 1961), 76, 79. Irene Lara goes further to emphasize that a full recovery of an entirely racially representative positive mother figure would be the Tonantzin-Guadalupe configuration—thereby reflecting a more "human" mother and not just the "impossible ideal of virgin mother." See Irene Lara, "Goddess of the Américas in the Decolonial Imaginary: Beyond the Virtuous Virgen/Pagan Puta Dichotomy," *Feminist Studies* 34, no. 1/2 (Spring/Summer 2008): 104. The quote comes from Anzaldúa, *Borderlands*, 52.

7. Carlos Monsiváis, "Foreword. When Gender Can't Be Seen amid the Symbols: Women and the Mexican Revolution," in *Sex in Revolution: Gender, Politics, and Power in Modern Mexico*, ed. Jocelyn Olcott, Mary Kay Vaughan and Gabriela Cano (Durham, NC: Duke University Press, 2006), 4–7.

8. Kristine Byron, "Doris Tijerino: Revolution, Writing, and Resistance in Nicaragua," *NWSA Journal* 18, no. 3 (2006): 109.

9. It is interesting to note here that Belli depicts Lavinia as childless by choice, which ultimately enables her to participate in the revolutionary movement without having to experience the anguish of "absent" mothering—that is, having to leave her children in the care of others—a feature with which Belli appears to struggle in her own testimony. See Laura Barbas Rhoden, "The Quest for the Mother in the Novels of Gioconda Belli," *Letras femeninas* 26, no. 1/2 (2000): 87, 89.

10. Carmen Aguirre, *Something Fierce: Memoirs of a Revolutionary Daughter* (Vancouver: Douglas and McIntyre, 2012), 182, 249; Carmen Rodríguez, *And a Body to Remember With* (Vancouver: Arsenal Pulp, 1997), 51.

11. The first line reads, "Latin American women have given the example . . . I believe that one of the characteristics of the Latin American woman is the struggle. I think we don't let things go by. And history is like that too, that is why we had women in the Montonera movement." The second reads, "the one thing that is very clear is that we [women revolutionaries] had very difficult lives and that has been ignored." The third translates as "[T]he strength I had in that moment . . . and that kept me strong in many other situations, was born out of my

feminine condition." All translations are ours. Diana, *Mujeres guerrilleras*, 37, 63, 228, 414.
12. The blockquote translates as "But we are here alive. We form part of a chain, vital and feminine, that began with the indigenous peoples (who hardly exist anymore), primitive residents of these lands, whose next link in the chain includes those women who boarded those ships in Europe for unknown lands to embark on an even more uncertain destiny. The Argentine guerrillas (who hardly exist anymore) also belonged to this chain. This is not a question of politics. It is a historic, social, and human question. What is political is the treatment that has been given to this topic: heroine or delinquent." Ibid., 280, 444.
13. Randall, *Sandino's Daughters*, 46, 130; Diana, *Mujeres guerrilleras*, 110, 168, 374–76.
14. Randall, *Sandino's Daughters*, iv; Diana, *Mujeres guerrilleras*, 440. The quote comes from Randall and translates as "By the final offensive, women made up 30 percent of the Sandinist army and held important leadership positions."
15. See Aguirre, *Something Fierce*; Rodríguez, *And a Body to Remember With*; and Zalaquett, *Chilenas en armas*.
16. Diana, *Mujeres guerrilleras*, 101, 173; Kampwirth, *Women and Guerrilla Movements*, 36.
17. George Yúdice, "Testimonio and Postmodernism," in *The Real Thing: Testimonial Discourses and Latin America*, ed. George M. Gugelberger (Durham, NC: Duke University Press), 44; Doris Tijerino, *Inside the Nicaraguan Revolution (As Told to Margaret Randall)*, trans. Elinor Randall (Vancouver: New Star, 1978), 7. All citations from this text reflect the spelling preference of Spanish names as utilized in the translation. Bayard de Volo points out that "[t]his representation of motherhood gave the message that combat, especially in the name of one's children, did not conflict with traditional notions of motherhood." See Bayard de Volo, "Drafting Motherhood," 246. See also Kampwirth, *Women and Guerrilla Movements*; Maxine Molyneux, "Mobilization without Emancipation? Women's Interests, the State, and Revolution in Nicaragua," *Feminist Studies* 11, no. 2 (1985): 227–54.
18. Tijerino, *Inside the Nicaraguan Revolution*, 12, 14. Although, in her return to the story with *Sandino's Daughters Revisited: Feminism in Nicaragua*, Randall does acknowledge that when the revolutionary government took power in 1979, Tijerino was "the only woman to have achieved the rank of full commander in the Sandinista army." See Randall, *Sandino's Daughters Revisited*, 209.
19. Tijerino, *Inside the Nicaraguan Revolution*, 24–25, 46, 111. For many mothers participating in revolutionary activity, there is a general acceptance that they were limited without family support. As one Sandinista feminist declares, "They can say what they want, they can write what they want, but we know women are equal until they get pregnant, or

women are equal to men after they have made the decision of leaving their children with their relatives in order to continue their political praxis. Because in revolutionary Nicaragua, fathers do not leave their children, it is the mother who abandons them for the struggle." See Diana Mulinari, "Broken Dreams in Nicaragua," in *The Women and War Reader*, ed. Lois Ann Lorentzen and Jennifer Turpin (New York: New York University Press, 1998), 159.

20. Gioconda Belli, *The Country under My Skin: A Memoir of Love and War*, trans. Kristina Cordero (New York: Random House, 2003), ix, 18, 32.
21. Randall, *Sandino's Daughters*, 186; Tijerino, *Inside the Nicaraguan Revolution*, 117, 120, 195; Herrera, "From Insurgency to Feminist Struggle," 295. Randall remarks that not only mothers but grandmothers as well "of mostly very young and totally involved sons and daughters often followed their children's example and became courageous and trustworthy political activists." See Randall, *Sandino's Daughters Revisited*, 18. She makes special note of a similar scenario where "[o]ne mother discovered that her daughter was involved and the daughter realized the same of the mother only when they came upon one another, blindfolded and handcuffed, in the dictator's own personal dungeon—beneath a dining room where statesmen and their cronies nightly sipped expensive wines." See Randall, *Sandino's Daughters Revisited*, 21.
22. Hugo De Marinis and Adriana Spahr, *Madre de Mendoza: vida de María Isabel Figuero* (Buenos Aires: Corregidor, 2013), 76–77, 80, 92. The quote translates as "I didn't really belong to any particular party. My father was a radical, I was a radical, and my mother belonged to one party one day and to another party the following day. We didn't trust any of them" (translation ours).
23. See De Marinis and Spahr, *Madre de Mendoza*.
24. Diana, *Mujeres guerrilleras*, 19, 352. In many cases, the testimonies allow these women to think back on their sacrifices, including that of absent mothering, only after the political defeat of the revolutionary movements. Due to the period in which she was interviewed, Tijerino never makes mention in her testimony of ambivalent feelings toward the sacrifices mothers like herself must make with regard to her own children. Moreover, both the Madres and Abuelas (Mothers and Grandmothers) of Plaza de Mayo have been working with the children of the disappeared (HIJOS; Sons and Daughters for Identity and Justice Against Oblivion and Silence) to reunite the adopted children with their biological families. The quote translates to "We either lost as militants or we lost as mothers" (translation ours).
25. Zalaquett, *Chilenas en armas*, 158; Lisa Renee DiGiovanni, "Memories of Motherhood and Militancy in Chile: Gender and Nostalgia in *Calle Santa Fe* by Carmen Castillo," *Journal of Latin American*

*Cultural Studies* 21, no. 1 (2012): 25, 28. In a different scenario, Aguirre's mother, who could have also chosen to leave her children with the Proyecto Hogares, decided instead to take them with her to Bolivia and Argentina to be a mother and a revolutionary—demonstrating a similar sentiment of equality that is revealed by Marchi in *Calle Santa Fé*.

26. Diana, *Mujeres guerrilleras*, 177, 187, 189. The passages translate as "The official culture can ultimately label her as a bad mother"; "The one that drinks of that milk becomes a guerilla fighter"; and "With respect to women and their condition as mothers, which has been much criticized, I think it is important to clarify, the 'good mother' isn't only the one that stays at home to care for her children. The 'good mother' is also the one who leaves the home to fight for something that is for them and for everyone. Transforming such a cruel society, where many of those children have no possibility of sustenance, is the best gift a mother could give them." All translations are ours.

27. Karen Alexander and Mary E. Hawkesworth, eds., *War and Terror: Feminist Perspectives* (Chicago: University of Chicago Press, 2008), 5; Diana, *Mujeres guerrilleras*, 101, 159, 185, 283, 341. "Revolution within the revolution" is a term used by Rodolfo Walsh to refer to the contribution made by the Argentine women militants. See Diana, *Mujeres guerrilleras*, 390. The passages translate as "One of the things I learned was to choose what I wanted and what I didn't want. I think each of us has that right. In these attitudes one notes that one didn't live the same as everyone else; everywhere they can be a rebel: at work, at the university. To be a rebel is to defend what belongs to oneself and that catches people's attention; "the woman, in addition to being militant 'just like a man' also had to worry about, on her own, all that was considered 'feminine'"; and "may war and the struggle not make us lose our tenderness." All translations are ours.

28. Diana, *Mujeres guerrilleras*, 61–62.

29. Ibid., 151, 270. The passage translates as "they [the military] were fascinated with us. We were completely different women from their wives. With us they could talk about politics, arms, strategy, film and philosophy. Such that in the attraction there also existed a contradiction" (translation ours).

## Selected Bibliography

Adams, Jacqueline. "Gender and Social Movement Decline: Shantytown Women and the Pro-democracy Movement in Pinochet's Chile." *Journal of Contemporary Ethnography* 31, no. 3 (June 2002): 285–322.

Aguirre, Carmen. *Something Fierce: Memoirs of a Revolutionary Daughter*. Vancouver: Douglas and McIntyre, 2012.

Alexander, Karen, and Mary E. Hawkesworth, eds. *War and Terror: Feminist Perspectives*. Chicago: University of Chicago Press, 2008.

Anzaldúa, Gloria. *Borderlands/Frontera: The New Mestiza*. San Francisco: Aunt Lute, 1999.

Barbas Rhoden, Laura. "The Quest for the Mother in the Novels of Gioconda Belli." *Letras femeninas* 26, no. 1/2 (2000): 81–97.

Bayard de Volo, Lorraine. "Drafting Motherhood: Maternal Imagery and Organizations in the United States and Nicaragua." In *The Women and War Reader*, edited by Lois Ann Lorentzen and Jennifer Turpin, 240–53. New York: New York University Press, 1998.

Belli, Gioconda. *The Country under My Skin: A Memoir of Love and War*. Translated by Kristina Cordero. New York: Random House, 2003.

Beverly, John. "The Margin at the Centre: On *Testimonio* (Testimonial Narrative)." In *The Real Thing: Testimonial Discourses and Latin America*, edited by George M. Gugelberger, 23–41. Durham, NC: Duke University Press, 1996.

Byron, Kristine. "Doris Tijerino: Revolution, Writing, and Resistance in Nicaragua." *NWSA Journal* 18, no. 3 (2006): 104–21.

Cooke, Miriam, and Angela Woollacott, eds. *Gendering War Talk*. Princeton: Princeton University Press, 1993.

De Marinis, Hugo, and Adriana Spahr. *Madre de Mendoza: vida de María Isabel Figueroa*. Buenos Aires: Corregidor, 2013.

Diana, Marta. *Mujeres guerrilleras: sus testimonios en la militancia de los setenta*. 3rd ed. Buenos Aires: Booket, 2011.

DiGiovanni, Lisa Renee. "Memories of Motherhood and Militancy in Chile: Gender and Nostalgia in *Calle Santa Fe* by Carmen Castillo." *Journal of Latin American Cultural Studies* 21, no. 1 (2012): 15–36.

Fenton-Stiff, Jocelyn, and Pageen Reichert Powell, eds. *Mothers Who Deliver: Feminist Interventions in Public and Interpersonal Discourse*. Albany: State University of New York Press, 2010.

Gibbons, Meghan. "Political Motherhood in the United States and Argentina." In *Mothers Who Deliver: Feminist Interventions in Public and Interpersonal Discourse*, edited by Jocelyn Fenton-Stitt and Pageen Reichert Powell, 253–78. Albany: State University of New York Press, 2010.

Gonzalez-Pérez, Margaret. "Guerrilleras in Latin America: Domestic and International Roles." *Journal of Peace Research* 43, no. 3 (2006): 313–29.

Gugelberger, George M., ed. *The Real Thing: Testimonial Discourses and Latin America*. Durham, NC: Duke University Press, 1996.

Herrera, Morena. "From Insurgency to Feminist Struggle: The Search for Social Justice, Democracy, and Equality between Women and Men." In *Women's Activism in Latin America and the Caribbean: Engendering Social Justice, Democratizing Citizenship*, edited by Elizabeth Maier and Nathalie Lebon, 291–306. New Brunswick, NJ: Rutgers University Press, 2010.

Kampwirth, Karen. *Women and Guerrilla Movements: Nicaragua, El Salvador, Chiapas, Cuba*. University Park: Pennsylvania State University Press, 2003.
Lara, Irene. "Goddess of the Américas in the Decolonial Imaginary: Beyond the Virtuous Virgen/Pagan Puta Dichotomy." *Feminist Studies* 34, no. 1/2 (Spring/Summer 2008): 99–127.
Lorentzen, Louis Ann, and Jennifer Turpin, eds. *The Women and War Reader*. New York: New York University Press, 1998.
Maier, Elizabeth, and Nathalie Lebon, eds. *Women's Activism in Latin America and the Caribbean: Engendering Social Justice, Democratizing Citizenship*. New Brunswick, NJ: Rutgers University Press, 2010.
Matthews, Irene. "Daughtering in War: Two 'Case Studies' from Mexico and Guatemala." In *Gendering War Talk*, edited by Miriam Cooke and Angela Woollacott, 148–76. Princeton: Princeton University Press, 1993.
Molyneux, Maxine. "Mobilization without Emancipation? Women's Interests, the State, and Revolution in Nicaragua." *Feminist Studies* 11, no. 2 (1985): 227–54.
Monsiváis, Carlos. "Foreword: When Gender Can't Be Seen amid the Symbols: Women and the Mexican Revolution." In *Sex in Revolution: Gender, Politics, and Power in Modern Mexico*, edited by Jocelyn Olcott, Mary Kay Vaughan, and Gabriela Cano, 1–20. Durham, NC: Duke University Press, 2006.
Mulinari, Diana. "Broken Dreams in Nicaragua." In *The Women and War Reader*, edited by Lois Ann Lorentzen and Jennifer Turpin, 157–63. New York: New York University Press, 1998.
Olcott, Mary Kay Vaughan, and Gabriela Cano, eds. *Sex in Revolution: Gender, Politics, and Power in Modern Mexico*. Durham, NC: Duke University Press, 2006.
Paz, Octavio. *The Labyrinth of Solitude: Life and Thought in Mexico*. Translated by Lysander Kemp. New York: Grove, 1961.
Pieper Mooney, Jadwiga E. "Militant Motherhood Re-Visited: Women's Participation and Political Power in Argentina and Chile." *History Compass* 5, no. 3 (2007): 975–94.
Randall, Margaret. *Sandino's Daughters: Testimonies of Nicaraguan Women in Struggle*. New Brunswick, NJ: Rutgers University Press, 1981.
———. *Sandino's Daughters Revisited: Feminism in Nicaragua*. New Brunswick, NJ: Rutgers University Press, 1994.
Read, Kay Almere, and Jason J. González. *Mesoamerican Mythology: A Guide to the Gods, Heroes, Rituals and Beliefs of Mexico and Central America*. New York: Oxford University Press, 2000.
Rodríguez, Carmen. *And a Body to Remember With*. Vancouver: Arsenal Pulp Press, 1997.
Samuelson, Meg. "The Disfigured Body of the Female Guerrilla: (De)Militarization, Sexual Violence, and Redomestication in Zoë Wicomb's *David's Story*." In *War and Terror: Feminist Perspectives*, edited by Karen Alexander

and Mary Hawkesworth, 89–112. Chicago: University of Chicago Press, 2008.

Tijerino, Doris. *Inside the Nicaraguan Revolution (As Told to Margaret Randall)*. Translated by Elinor Randall. Vancouver: New Star, 1978.

Yúdice, George. "Testimonio and Postmodernism." In *The Real Thing: Testimonial Discourses and Latin America*, edited by George M. Gugelberger, 42–57. Durham, NC: Duke University Press, 1996.

Zalaquett, Cherie. *Chilenas en armas: testimonios e historia de mujeres militares y guerrilleras subversivas*. Santiago de Chile: Catalonia, 2009.

## Chapter 5

### The Women's Resistance Movement in Argentina
#### *Las Madres de Plaza de Mayo*

*Elena Shabliy*

Argentine women have always been part of the historical process. Civil wars in the nineteenth century and military dictatorship in the twentieth century compelled them to become active participants of this process, which ultimately led them to a self-realization as historical agents, despite the fact that volatile governments often suppressed their activism by all means and rarely listened to their demands for justice.[1] As in most developing countries, the Argentinian women's movement is a discursive phenomenon.[2] It had its roots in the nineteenth century, and its origin is undoubtedly linked to the European women's movement.[3] The Argentinian women's suffrage movement culminated in 1947 when, under the leadership of María Eva Duarte de Perón, the Peronista Women's Party (*El Partido Peronista Femenino*) was created. Feminist groups as well as feminist philosophies have never been welcomed by the military, which praised the conventional roles of women.

Latin America is well known for its reverence to the traditional figure of the mother. At the same time, the Argentinian cultural paradigm emphasizes male authority, making patent the dichotomy of *marianismo* and *machismo*.[4] *Marianismo* presupposes such feminine virtues as submissiveness, purity, devotion to children, and moral strength, whereas *machismo* suggests first and foremost the supremacy of men over women. *Marianismo* can be traced back to the principles of the early Christian Church, where women are first obedient to God and then to man. *Marianismo* links females to the figure of the Virgin Mary and implies women's apolitical nature. This ideology has been predominant in Argentina since its independence. It has been argued by some scholars that dictators saw themselves as absolute authorities and thus expected all men and women to submit.[5] Interestingly, during the time of the dictatorship, the image of the mother was widely used in the mass media, mostly to promote women's traditional roles, propagandize the nuclear family formation, and encourage an increase in birthrates. The junta presented itself as the defender of "tradition, family, and property."[6]

Nearly forty years ago, Argentinian women united as a group and formed the Association of the Mothers of Plaza de Mayo to find their children who disappeared during the so-called Dirty War. Today the mothers are sorrowful grandmothers who still march every Thursday as they have done since 1977. Political scientist Marguerite Guzman Bouvard writes, "[T]o meet the Mothers of the Plaza de Mayo is to understand the inner transformation that they herald as the prior condition of a new political way."[7] The inner transformation is also documented in the poetry and testimonials written by these women. Chandra Mohanty convincingly argues in *Feminism without Boarders: Decolonizing Theory, Practicing Solidarity* (2003), "Writing is itself an activity marked by class and ethnic position. However, testimonials, life stories and oral histories are a significant mode of remembering and recording experience and struggles. Written texts are not produced in a vacuum."[8] Argentinian women's texts are full of pain, struggle, and hope. Before the disappearances of their children, these women also shared characteristics of *marianismo*, but their loss transformed their identities completely and irretrievably. As feminist philosopher Sara Ruddick put it, "[W]hen children are assaulted by social evils that could be prevented, though a mother herself may be helpless to prevent them, mothering becomes cruel and bitter work. In many societies, the ideology of motherhood is oppressive to women."[9]

None of the Mothers had any prior political experience before the military coup of 1976. Their first meeting took place on April 30, 1977, but tragically the founder of the Association of the Mothers of Plaza de Mayo, Azucena Villaflor, along with 12 other women, also disappeared. The place where the Mothers assemble—the Plaza de Mayo—is historically symbolic for Argentina, as it faces the president's office and is surrounded by government buildings. Women turned this plaza into their own space where they could share their pain, feel solidarity, and protest. In 1986 the original group of the Mothers split into two branches. Both groups have managed to create an international presence, which exerts more pressure on the government. Men were excluded from the organization for many reasons, but principally because the group felt that women presented as less confrontational to the government. Nonmothers and young women were also excluded because of safety concerns stemming from the incidents of women protestors being raped in Argentina and El Salvador.

Many Latin American countries experienced similar military coups along with campaigns of violence and terror. Groups of mothers united in Chile in 1974 and in El Salvador in 1981.[10] More than 30,000 people disappeared during the military dictatorship in Argentina (1976–83), and their bodies were either burned or disfigured so that they could not be traced.[11] In 1977 in El Salvador, women founded an organization similar to the Association of the Mothers of Plaza de Mayo, named CoMadres. Salvadoran women were mostly peasant rural workers in contrast to women in Argentina. Argentinian mothers may have continued to accept their subordinate position in society if not disappearance of their sons and daughters. They used their history of silence to protest in a unique way. They walked through the streets holding pictures of their children and wearing white kerchiefs on their heads that were marked with the names of their children and the dates when they disappeared. Police cars often followed after the women as they marched around the plaza.

The experience of women in Argentina during the "Dirty War" proves that grief not only unites people but can also completely transform their social roles and identities. The Mothers of Plaza de Mayo challenged the traditional perceptions of maternity and defied the myth of women's apoliticism in Argentina. These women used their authority as mothers to speak out in public, thus shifting their essential maternal identities into collective political subjects. Their collective maternal image attracted the public's attention also because it is associated with spirituality and tenderness. The Mothers emphasized their biological "instinctive" love for missing children. Women had no choice but to position themselves as political subjects during the time of the "Dirty War," as they spoke not only for themselves but for their children. Tellingly, they considered themselves as mothers of *all* those who had disappeared. Despite the fact that most women did not have any formal higher education, they learned fast, as "they were the only group that dared to confront a repressive military government."[12] As Sara Ruddick notes, "Women's peacefulness is at least as mythical as men's violence. Women have never absented themselves from war. Wherever battles are fought and justified, whether in the vilest or noblest of causes, women on both sides of the battle lines support the military engagements of their sons, lovers, friends, and mates. Increasingly, women are proud to fight alongside their brothers and as fiercely, in whatever battles their state or cause enlists them."[13]

The administration of Isabel Perón from 1974 to 1976 prepared the ground for the "Dirty War" and the chaos that subsequently reigned. On March 24, 1976, the military seized power. Human rights activist Rita Arditti writes of this period, "This was not just one more coup; the bloodiest and most shameful period in Argentine history was about to begin, during which Argentina became infamous for the atrocities of its government and its striking similarities with the Nazi regime."[14]

During the process of National Reorganization (*El Proceso*), when the military gave itself the power to exercise judicial, legislative, and executive powers, young people (from 16 to 35) were kidnapped off the street in broad daylight, taken to clandestine detention centers, tortured, and eventually killed. Among the victims were the lawyers who defended political prisoners and their psychiatrists.[15] These young people were seen as dissidents by the state. At that time anyone who did not adhere to Christian virtue and military rule was seen as an adversary by the junta.[16] Disappearances and kidnappings became a systematic practice "designed to neutralize the political and social mobilization of citizens against repressive dictatorships."[17]

Pregnant women were also detained until the moment they gave birth. Their children were ultimately removed and adopted by high-ranking people and friends of the regime. The women that were kidnapped by the military were perceived as evil, and since they crossed the threshold of domesticity they were shown no mercy.[18] Alicia Elena Alfonsín de Cabandie, a 16-year-old girl, was seven months pregnant when she was abducted. Placed in a room with other pregnant women, she witnessed how each of them was separated from their babies after giving birth. Her child was also taken away.

The controlled press was at first "strangely silent" and then represented the Mothers looking for their children as "*locas*" or mad women.[19] But this line between normal and abnormal, especially during the wartime, is subtle. An accusation of mental instability was also a technique used by the Soviets to discredit dissident personalities: "It [is] a strategy regularly used in wars to taint the women who were considered deviant and disobedient. They had lost their status as 'good' mothers and were viewed as 'subversive whores.'"[20] The sorrow of Argentinian women made them numb to public opinion, and little by little they found compassion not only in their country but internationally. The Argentinian press, on the other hand, was afraid to speak out: 84 journalists were killed in that year alone.[21] *La Prensa* only published the names of those missing twice, in 1978 and in 1980, although it was declared by the military that no one was actually missing. The junta only acknowledged "unregistered deaths" or insisted that those who had disappeared simply went abroad.

Neither the police nor the Catholic Church offered the Mothers any assistance, despite Argentina being predominately Catholic. The Mothers emphasized their Catholic identities when they protested and when they prayed in public or gathered in churches. They addressed their prayers to the figure of the Virgin Mary, traditionally the embodiment of female virtues in Catholicism. Women tried to reach out to the Catholic Church, counting on its influence in the military. In 1978, in a letter to Pope Paul VI, the Mothers compared themselves with Mary and underlined their humble role as obedient Catholics. In 1980, women wrote a letter to the Bishops Council and later expressed their anger at the Church's indifference in a letter to the Archbishop of Buenos Aires, Cardinal Juan Carlos Aramburu. It is known, however, that between 1974 and 1983, 19 ordained Catholic priests (including two bishops) were murdered or abducted, and about one hundred members belonging to religious orders suffered torture or were exiled or detained.[22]

Without the support of the Catholic Church and police, there was little alternative but to become independent investigators. The Mothers acknowledged that they were "members of a group confronting the same nightmare."[23] Motherist activism thus formed a social movement. Collective actions are the part of normal political process of every country. A social movement usually occurs when a feeling of dissatisfaction takes place and government is not able to respond adequately. The capacity for mobilization depends on two important factors: the availability of material resources such as work, money, benefits, and services as well as nonmaterial resources such as authority, faith, solidarity, moral engagement, and friendship.[24] Argentinian women mostly could rely on nonmaterial sources.[25] The Mothers emphasized that they always had this feeling of solidarity in their group, especially when they walked together around the plaza in full silence. As the political scientist Marguerite Guzman Bouvard points out, "What brings these strong individuals together are their determination and their political convictions: there are thousands of mothers of *disappeared* young adults but, now, only a few hundred of Mothers de Plaza de Mayo. Although each Mother does not consider her own suffering as more important than that of the other

Mothers, each welcomes opportunities to talk about her child because to do so gives her child a social presence and helps to combat the terrible intent of *disappearances*—to annihilate the memory as well as the person."[26]

Only after the fall of the military regime could the Mothers openly resume their search for children. One can argue that Argentinian women and motherist activism played an important role in building democracy in Argentina.[27] In 1980, members of the European Parliament nominated the Mothers of Plaza de Mayo for the Nobel Peace Prize, drawing world attention to their plight.[28] The new democratic government of President Raul Alfonsín allowed the Mothers to establish the Argentine National Commission for the Disappeared (CONADEP). Ernesto Sábato, an Argentinian writer, headed the CONADEP commission and examined the situation. However, one of the founders of the Association of the Mothers of Plazo de Mayo, Hebe Bonafini, criticized CONADEP and its chair, writer Ernesto Sábato, since he had once been supportive of General Jorge Rafael Videla's regime.[29]

Estela Barnes de Carlotto, a human rights activist, is the current president of the Association of the Grandmothers of Plaza de Mayo, an organization that aims to find the stolen babies. In July 2012, two former dictators, Jorge Rafel Videla and Reynaldo Benito Bignone, were found guilty by an Argentinian court of stealing dozen of babies and were sentenced to 50 and 25 years in prison, respectively. Only a few grandmothers have ever been reunited with their grandchildren. Rita Arditti notes, "Since most grandmothers have not yet been able to identify their grandchildren, those who have been found are very special to them. The presence of these children reminds them of their successes, reassures them that their work is not a hopeless dream, and gives them confidence that other children will also be found. The youngsters seemed very much aware of that role as they moved among the various Grandmothers, asking about their work and their families, reflecting the intimate knowledge and bonds that exists among them."[30]

According to a philosopher M. M. Bakhtin, no horizon exists for *the dialogic context*: "There is no first or last discourse, and dialogical context knows no limits (it disappears into an unlimited past and in our unlimited future)."[31] Two Elizabethtown College professors, John Rohrkemper and James Haines, created an opera about the Mothers of Plaza de Mayo, thus continuing the dialogue about Argentinian victims through art. The Mothers created a communal discourse via their testimonials and poems. In their accounts, women speak of themselves as "we," emphasizing the collective nature of their actions. They desperately wanted to make the public aware of their tragedy. Eventually, they forced the dictatorship to respond. In 1977, in *La Prensa*, General Jorge Rafael Videla acknowledged that the disappearance of some people was, indeed, a consequence of the "Dirty War." He placed the blame, however, on those who had disappeared. The ambiguous status of the *disappeared* children gave women hope that there was a possibility that they may yet be alive. The women could not bury those who were neither dead nor alive, and Mothers refused to recognize the death of their daughters and sons without proof and begged for answers. The continuation of the dialogue about these women is important because it contributes to breaking the silence that poisoned Argentinian politics and society for so many years. Rita Arditti writes, "The Grandmothers want the past to be remembered and speak often about the importance of collective memory. However, their focus is on the future. They believe that for a *true* national reconciliation to take place, those guilty of atrocities must admit their crimes and accept punishment. Only then will Argentine society have a chance to become fertile ground on which true democracy may flourish."[32]

Although the male sex has traditionally been associated with violence, women, too, have fluid identities and adjust to given circumstances accordingly: "Even peace-loving women, like most men, support organized violence, at least in 'emergences.'" Although mothers can support the military policies of the state, "maternal thinking and practices are still important resources for developing peace politics."[33] This resistance movement demonstrates the effectiveness of individual and collective action against a tragic episode in Argentine history. The (Grand)Mothers of Plaza de Mayo resisted the brutality of the dictatorship and provided a future moral leadership.[34] According to Cynthia L. Bejarano, "Utilizing the roles of motherhood as forms of resistance was extremely important in their successes."[35] Argentinian women proved with their lives that if there is no justice, it does not mean that justice does not exist at all. The imprisonment of former dictators is a symbol of their victory. The Mothers became "the moral conscience of the country and gained a space in the political arena, challenging the notion of women as powerless and subservient to family and state."[36]

## Notes

1. According to Donald Meyer, in the nineteenth century, "women [began] thinking about themselves in new ways" and realized themselves as historical agents. See Donald B. Meyer, *Sex and Power: The Rise of Women in America, Russia, Sweden, and Italy* (Middletown, CT: Wesleyan University Press, 1987), xiv.
2. The debate on whether feminism is a global phenomenon is still ongoing. It is interesting to note that some scholars reject the term *feminism*. They prefer to use the term *womanist* instead, since they define feminism through class, race, religion, etc. See Chandra Mohanty, *Feminism without Borders: Decolonizing Theory, Practicing Solidarity* (Durham, NC: Duke University Press, 2003).
3. One of the forms of the movement was philanthropic activity that was usually performed by upper- and middle-class women, which played a crucial role in women's social engagement in Argentina as anywhere else in Europe.
4. Meghan K. Gibbons gives a comprehensive historical analysis of *marianismo* and *machismo* in *Essentially Powerful: Political Motherhood in the United States and Argentina* (PhD diss., University of Maryland, College Park, 2007).
5. In the *Nunca Más* (Never Again) report, people who tortured the prisoners refer to themselves as God: "We are everything for you." "We are justice." "We are God." See *Nunca Más: The Report of the Argentine National Commission on the Disappeared* (New York: Farrar, Straus, Giroux, 1986), 25.
6. Rita Arditti, *Searching for Life: The Grandmothers of the Plaza de Mayo and the Disappeared Children of Argentina* (Berkeley: University of California Press, 1999), 8.
7. Marguerite Guzman Bouvard, *Revolutionizing Motherhood: The Mothers of the Plaza de Mayo* (Wilmington, DE: Scholarly Resources, 1994), 5.
8. Mohanty, *Feminism without Borders*, 238.
9. Sara Ruddick, *Maternal Thinking: Toward a Politics of Peace* (Boston: Beacon, 1989), 29.
10. Marjorie Agosín, *Mothers of Plaza de Mayo (Linea Fundadora): The Story of Renée Epelbaum, 1976–1985* (Trenton, NJ: Red Sea, 1990), 14.
11. Many Jews suffered from the junta. It is hard to estimate the number of disappeared Jewish people, but some scholars argue that it is about 10 percent.
12. Bouvard, *Revolutionizing Motherhood*, 1.
13. Ruddick, *Maternal Thinking*, 154.
14. Arditti, *Searching for Life*, 7.

15. Jerry W. Knudson, "Veil of Silence: The Argentine Press and the Dirty War, 1976–1983," *Latin American Perspectives* 24, no. 6 (Nov. 1997): 94.
16. Arditti, *Searching for Life*, 9.
17. Agosín, *Mothers of Plaza de Mayo*, 13.
18. There were also pregnant adolescent girls who disappeared without a trace: Laura Beatriz Segarra, 18 years old, eight months pregnant; Inés Beatriz Ortega de Fossati, who gave birth to a child in Police Station No. 5 of La Plata; Nidia Beatriz Muñoz, 18 years old, four months pregnant; Noemí Josefina Jansenson de Arcuschin, aged 18, and three months pregnant. See *Nunca más*, 286.
19. Knudson, "Veil of Silence," 94.
20. Cynthia L. Bejarano, "Las Super Madres de Latino America: Transforming Motherhood by Challenging Violence in Mexico, Argentina, and El Salvador," *Frontiers: A Journal of Women Studies* 23, no. 1 (2002): 137.
21. *Nunca más*, 372–74. Foreign journalists also disappeared during the "Dirty War." See Bouvard, *Revolutionizing Motherhood*, 31.
22. Arditti, *Searching for Life*, 28.
23. Bejarano, "Las Super Madres de Latino America," 132.
24. See Donatella Della Porta and Mario Diani, *Social Movements: An Introduction* (Oxford: Blackwell, 1999).
25. Bouvard, *Revolutionizing Motherhood*, 137.
26. Ibid., 12.
27. While the role of women's movements in Latin America played a crucial critical role in establishing democratic politics, in the Eastern Europe, on the contrary, in the process of transition women's mobilization was almost invisible. Georgina Waylen explains it by the nature of previous regimes and civil society. See Georgina Waylen, "Women and Democratization: Conceptualizing Gender Relations in Transition Politics," *World Politics* 46, no. 3 (April 1994): 327–54.
28. Arditti, *Searching for Life*, 39.
29. Ibid., 52.
30. Ibid., 4.
31. Tzvetan Todorov, *Mikhail Bakhtin: The Dialogical Principle* (Minneapolis: University of Minnesota Press, 1984), 110.
32. Arditti, *Searching for Life*, 6.
33. Ruddick, *Maternal Thinking*, 12.
34. Arditti, *Searching for Life*, 2.
35. Bejarano, "Las Super Madres de Latino America," 131.
36. Arditti, *Searching for Life*, 37.

## Selected Bibliography

Agosín, Marjorie. *Mothers of Plaza de Mayo (Linea Fundadora): The Story of Renée Epelbaum, 1976–1985*. Trenton, NJ: Red Sea, 1990.

Arditti, Rita. *Searching for Life: The Grandmothers of the Plaza de Mayo and the Disappeared Children of Argentina*. Berkeley: University of California Press, 1999.

Argentine National Commission on the Disappeared. *Nunca Más: The Report of the Argentine National Commission on the Disappeared*. With an introduction by Ronald Dworkin. New York: Farrar, Straus, Giroux, 1986.

Bejarano, Cynthia L. "Las Super Madres de Latino America: Transforming Motherhood by Challenging Violence in Mexico, Argentina, and El Salvador." *Frontiers: A Journal of Women Studies* 23, no. 1 (2002): 126–50.

Bouvard, Marguerite Guzman. *Revolutionizing Motherhood: The Mothers of the Plaza de Mayo*. Wilmington, DE: Scholarly Resources, 1994.

Della Porta, Donatella, and Mario Diani. *Social Movements: An Introduction*. Oxford: Blackwell, 1999.

Gibbons, Meghan K. *Essentially Powerful: Political Motherhood in the United States and Argentina*. PhD dissertation, University of Maryland, College Park, 2007.

Knudson, Jerry W. "Veil of Silence: The Argentine Press and the Dirty War, 1976–1983." *Latin American Perspectives* 24, no. 6 (November 1997): 93–112.

Meyer, Donald B. *Sex and Power: The Rise of Women in America, Russia, Sweden, and Italy*. Middletown, CT: Wesleyan University Press, 1987.

Mohanty, Chandra. *Feminism without Borders: Decolonizing Theory, Practicing Solidarity*. Durham, NC: Duke University Press, 2003.

Ruddick, Sara. *Maternal Thinking: Toward a Politics of Peace*. Boston: Beacon, 1989.

Todorov, Tzvetan. *Mikhail Bakhtin: The Dialogical Principle*. Minneapolis: University of Minnesota Press, 1984.

Waylen, Georgina. "Women and Democratization: Conceptualizing Gender Relations in Transition Politics." *World Politics* 46, no. 3 (April 1994): 327–54.

# Chapter 6

## Japanese Mothers and Rural Settlement in Wartime Manchukuo
### Gendered Reflections of Labor and Productivity in *Manshû Gurafu* (Manchuria Graph), 1936–43[1]

*Annika A. Culver*

## Introduction

Japan's involvement in what would become World War II began as early as 1931, when Japanese Kantô Army troops invaded Manchuria, or northeast China, and helped engineer the 1932 creation of the nominally independent state of Manchukuo after occupying the area. Beginning in the thirties, Manchukuo's Japanese handlers and its Chinese collaborators intended for the nation to serve as a model utopia for Japanese developmental aims. Following the 1937 Japanese invasion of China south of the Great Wall, the wartime goals of the imperial Japanese government began to suffuse all aspects of public and private spheres as propaganda efforts intensified both domestically and throughout Japan's empire during a time of total war—including in Manchukuo. Women, and especially mothers, became the targets of these endeavors as well as serving as active participants in the war effort, through their labor as both workers and child bearers. Propaganda media such as magazines and pictorials linked domestic Japan with its empire and touted desirable behaviors for all Japanese subjects where women raised future soldiers, supported their men as they went to war, and took their places at work in both urban and rural locales.

From the 1930s into the 1940s, the frenzied media portrayal of Manchukuo's "empty" lands and its ability to relieve rural pressures in domestic Japan was no exception. This flurry of Manchuria-related media supporting state propaganda aims also extended to advertisements and commercial publications, as Japanese companies took advantage of growing public interest in Japan's development of "frontier" areas in occupied northeast China. Even the Shiseidô Corporation, which produced high-quality cosmetics for urban Japanese women, featured a rural pioneer woman (*kaitaku-sha*) on the November 1938 cover of its *Hanatsubaki* (Camellia) magazine.[2] With her white headscarf, straw basket carrying sheaves of grain, simply patterned indigo cotton kimono, and no-nonsense tied-back sleeves, the young woman serves as an unmistakable icon of the new, developing rural Manchukuo. Her contented smile and rosy plump cheeks reveal her potential fertility and suitability to hard work outdoors.

Beginning in the midthirties and intensifying in the early forties, Japanese farmers in distressed areas like Nagano prefecture were encouraged to migrate to Manchukuo. To support this policy initiative of the imperial Japanese government, propaganda pictorials published in Japanese and English by the South Manchuria Railway Company (SMRC) like *Manshû gurafu* (*Manchuria Graph*, 1933–44) portrayed the region as a fertile utopia for rural Japanese families—ensuring prosperity, elevated productivity of crops, and future generations. For example, a montage of scenes from an August 1936 edition shows women performing various tasks like plowing alongside men, building seed beds, weeding rows of corn, and tending cattle, with the Japanese caption touting, "Settling the great lands of Manchuria at the Self-Defense Village" and, in English, stating, "Breaking up the virgin soil of Manchoukuo—at the 'Railway Guards' settlements."[3] None of the pictured women yet carry babies on their backs, but the images imply an imminent fertility of the soil and its settlers.

In the late thirties, young women began to arrive in larger numbers from the Japanese archipelago to serve as "continental brides" (*tairiku hanayome*) for male rural settlers of Manchukuo. In *Manshû gurafu* and other media, they were depicted accompanying their new grooms in mass marriage ceremonies at the numerous Shintô shrines dotting Japanese settlements in northern Manchuria. As opposed to (usually) urban Japanese women who had already been living in Manchukuo for several years, an "imported" wife from the Japanese mainland was believed to have maintained proper levels of

"Japaneseness" as a *Yamato-nadeshiko* (true Japanese maiden) uninfluenced by the harsh, frontier environment and its often crude, masculine ways. Upon arrival, their duty was first and foremost to serve as mothers and productive helpmates.

A spread in the August 1936 issue captioned "Japanese Lullabies Over Desolate Manchurian Plains" shows two women modestly looking down while carrying infants on their backs bundled in quilts. The English caption elaborates on their important role in settling the areas surrounding the railways and peopling the region with offspring while maintaining the stability (and security) of crucial areas:

> In close cooperation with the near-by [sic] Manchoukuoan farmers, the Japanese settlers of the "railway guards" settlements shoulder a weighty and noble duty of being life-long [sic] guards of the railways. Consequently, they are all married, well-built young men with a strong will to settle in Manchuria. As the safety of the railways enhances [sic] day by day, and as the cultivation of the settlers continues year after year, the number of the offsprings [sic] of the settlers increases, and today, just as in the peaceful villages of Japan, soothing melodies of Japanese lullabies can be heard over the virgin soil of Manchoukuo.[4]

The newly married women displayed in the photographs within *Manshû gurafu*'s pages hoisting sheaves of grain while carrying smiling babies on their backs reflected the pronatalist stance of the government, which exhorted settlement of the region. A December 1936 cover image shows a woman in a padded winter kimono in trousers with the proverbial plump infant bundled against her back boasting a cute hand-knit wool hat with a pompon.[5] Such recurrent scenes in this pictorial of mothers at work in productive rural villages revealed government preoccupations with the appropriate roles for women. Moreover, by the early forties, advertisements for various patent medicines improving women's reproductive health and boosting men's virility appeared alongside enthusiastic articles touting the extraordinary production potential and fertility of the land under Japanese auspices. Propaganda magazines such as this one reflected imperial Japanese ambitions to create a utopian paradise as a template for occupied regions in China, and after 1940, Southeast Asia.

The October 1, 1940, edition of *Manchuria* opines that these farming communities represent a quaint but respectable vision of virtue, and that if one grasps the conditions in this microcosm, Manchukuo as a whole can be understood:

The farmers who compose rural villages are but poorly educated, but they respect their honor and their credit just as much as the intelligent class . . . Peace and order is generally well kept in the village . . . . Anyway, it is an urgent duty to permeate the national policy through every nook and corner of the land by taking full consideration of farming villages and their inhabitants, so that their merits may be made much of and their demerits removed. For this purpose, the Japanese residents in this country would do well to inspect them on the spot, and surely they will find much to amuse them and benefit them. Real knowledge of Manchoukuo begins with the study of farming communities; that is my advice.[6]

Though Manchukuo's political atmosphere remained largely peaceful into the 1940s, the region also served as an important frontier buffer zone against the Soviet Union and a base for Japanese operations in China and Southeast Asia.

Rural Japanese women's wartime contributions to the war effort through their support of colonization and settlement activities in Manchukuo is a long-neglected topic in English-language scholarship and an issue that has received only scant attention by Japanese scholars.[7] However, in Manchukuo, Japanese women as mothers would play a special role as efficient producers of both children and crops to showcase the success of Japan and its empire during a critical time. As propaganda, these images with their accompanying captions elide Japanese military aggression in China and on the continent but leave an important record in the gendered legacy of Japan's total war in these largely unrecognized female actors.

## The Historical Context of Images of Japanese Settlers in a Rural Utopia

The images of Japanese settlers in *Manshû gurafu* appear against the backdrop of Japan's deepening imperialistic war on the continent, begun first with the military maneuvers of the Kantô Army in Manchuria after 1931 and then, following the 1933 Tangu Truce, with tensions in the demilitarized zone between Manchukuo and China proper from 1933 to 1937.[8] Small-scale skirmishes finally erupted into the Second Sino-Japanese War by July 1937, which resulted in the costly "China quagmire" (1938–45). Amid a climate of ever-increasing operations in China south of the Great Wall, the Japanese government's rhetoric focused on the need for greater involvement in the affairs of other East Asian nations. By 1940, this culminated in plans for the "Greater East Asia Co-Prosperity Sphere." However, as early as 1938, diplomat and foreign ministry spokesman Tatsuo Kawai (1889–1965) argued, "The objective of Japanese expansion is neither the attainment of capitalistic supremacy nor the acquisition of colonies, but the realization of harmony and concord among the nations of East Asia and their common happiness and prosperity."[9]

"Harmony" and "concord," or *kyôwa*, were ideals first articulated in Manchukuo by proponents of a right-wing version of socialism (like that of Colonel Ishiwara Kanji, who masterminded the 1931 Manchurian Incident), in which capitalism took a backseat to the aims of a utopian, Confucian-inspired paternalistic government. In 1940, the Greater East Asia concept developed from Foreign Minister Arita Hachirô's (1884–1965) proposal, whereby Japan would guide East Asia's nations based on the lessons of the Manchurian experiment. An editorial titled "The New Morality" from the October 1, 1940, edition of *Manchuria* notes the "social renovations" sweeping East Asia through the New Order:

> A healthy sign in these crucial days is the new, spontaneous movement towards simpler life and more spiritual living. War is a mighty purger: it cleanses the dross of life that accumulates through long years of peace. A life of sobriety and thrift is now being held up as a pattern . . . But the current reform which personally affects the average resident of Manchuria or Japan is the waves of social renovations now sweeping the whole of East Asia. All the Occidental frivolity and foibles, that were recklessly imported, for several decades, largely through alien agents for their commercial gain, are drastically discarded or remodeled one by one.[10]

Arita's successor, Matsuoka Yôsuke, a former president of SMRC, would soon coin the term "Greater East Asian Co-Prosperity Sphere." In April 1943, Shigemitsu Mamoru (1881–1957) proclaimed the liberation of East Asia as Japan's primary war objective. If we view the images of the rural pioneers against this background of rising conflict along with exhortations for a new spiritual order celebrating the exact type of values found in rural locales, we can finally grasp the important role the Japanese settlers played in the geopolitics of East Asia.

The photographs of the *kaitaku-sha* thus serve as examples of the intrepid Japanese settler who developed the northern Manchurian frontier amid Japan's deepening conflicts on the continent. By the early 1940s, Manchukuo was lauded by Japanese officialdom as a template for the Southeast Asian nations into which the imperial army "advanced" in order to help "liberate" them from Western colonial rule. In *Manshû gurafu*, emphasis on labor and productivity in the rural and urban spaces of Manchukuo remained a constant theme throughout its roughly 11 years of existence. An evident evolution of themes can be seen in three historical phases of images featured in the years from 1933 to 1937, 1937 to 1940, and 1941 to 1944. These stages parallel political developments in Japan and the Empire as well as the eruption of the war in China (1937) and the Pacific (1941); 1937 was also the concluding year of the first five-year plan for Manchukuo, while 1942 was the concluding year for the second. Thus, in *Manshû gurafu*, the placement of certain recurring images like those of mothers at work in rural areas is important in terms of how they are framed and juxtaposed with events taking place in the Japanese Empire.

## The "Reproducibility" of Japanese Rural Settlements in Manchuria, 1936–40

Early images of the *kaitaku-sha* appearing the year of *Manshû gurafu*'s 1933 inception communicated the area's vast potential for settlement, while later editions focused almost exclusively on the northern Manchurian Japanese pioneers or military operations in north China. From 1936 onward, individual editions were more likely to feature Japanese *kaitaku-sha*, but they were just one of many topics related to Manchuria. From the late 1930s onward, individual editions increasingly devoted more spreads to these farmers, while a December 1940 special edition titled "*Kaitaku-chi wo meguru*" ("Touring the Rural Development Areas") was the first to focus exclusively on their efforts.

Naturally, it was a huge undertaking for the governments of Manchukuo and Imperial Japan to attract the settlers and to convince them to immigrate, in accordance with state aims, from 1933 to 1936. Therefore, all media in charge of propaganda in both countries, including the SMRC-funded *Manshû gurafu*, were mobilized. In the two years following the Manchurian Incident, the Japanese public consumed songs, images, and myriads of mass culture products (including war songs, film melodramas, "human bullet" candy, and even odd Manchurian-themed restaurant menus) induced by a climate of "war fever" and soon developed a voracious appetite for news with a Manchurian theme.[11] In addition, printed materials related to Manchuria also took off during this time, fortuitously jump-starting a flagging Japanese publishing industry. An industry yearbook even happily declares that "brisk sales of books on Manchuria have breathed new life into an utterly stagnated publishing industry."[12] Nonetheless, prospective Japanese farming families had to be convinced that the area was fertile as well as safe, and that it presented them with a better life than in the cramped and resource-poor archipelago.

Thus scenes such as in the December 1936 edition captioned "The Image of Peaceful Living" in Japanese, and "Peaceful Life at a Settlement" in English, feature bucolic images that reveal women (with the requisite baby on their backs) walking on a path between wide vistas of land sown with grain and interspersed with streams boasting families of ducks tending numerous ducklings.[13] Here, empty lands appear illuminated by the sun, clear streams flow full of ducks and fish, and the ever-present woman works productively in the fields with an infant carried in a sling on her back.[14] According to Michael Baskett, this image of "real" women in the Manchurian space was also very common in films of the era, such as the 1937 Japanese-German coproduction *Atarashiki tsuchi* (*New Earth*).[15] The message emphasizes that both people and animals in the region will prosper while abundantly producing offspring in the new rural utopia.

The path toward planning for the colonization of northern Manchuria was formulated in the early to mid-1930s in both Tokyo and Shinkyô, the capital of the new nation. In Manchukuo, Shinkyô hosted a colonization conference in November 1934 for a group of fifty experts and interested parties to discuss the settlement of this part of the region by Japanese farmers.[16] In December 1935, in the same city, the Manchuria Colonial Development Company was organized with start-up capital of 15 million yen.[17] It assisted settlers in acquiring suitable land; supervised and distributed that land; and provisioned financial aid, equipment, and facilities: "One-third of the authorized capital was provided by the Manchukuo government, one-third by the South Manchuria Railway Company, and one-third by the general public in Japan."[18] Interestingly, this joint venture represented the fascistic corporatism of Manchukuo in its even division of responsibility for the endeavor among the new state's government, SMRC (as long-term developer of the region), and the Japanese people. SMRC's *Fifth Report on Progress in Manchuria to 1936* notes, "In April, 1936, it [the Manchuria Colonial Development Company] decided to settle 20,000 Japanese farming families in ten years and 1,500 families during 1936, and the Department of Colonial Affairs in Tokyo placed at the disposal of the Company 1,135,000 yen and the Manchoukuo Government the necessary land. The settlements will take place in Pinkiang Province."[19] The area in question was located in northeastern-most Manchuria a hundred miles away from the Russian-influenced city of Harbin—a land of harsh climatic contrasts and frontier character close to the Soviet Union.

Instant success was not guaranteed during the shaky first wave of settlement in 1933–36, when five groups of five hundred farmsteads attempted colonization. The message conveyed in *Manshû gurafu* seemed to be that colonization was hard work and required *gaman*, or endurance, but that in the end a uniquely Japanese perseverance would prevail. Despite the best efforts of the Manchuria Colonial Development Company, the December 1936 special edition of *Manshû gurafu* titled *Nihon yimin no sôbô* (*The Faces of Japanese Settlers*) notes that 40 percent left the settlements, either "dying of illness [or] quitting their new land owing to some unavoidable circumstances."[20] Whatever these "unavoidable circumstances" were is never explained, but in northern Manchuria, Chinese landlords often hired local mercenary militias consisting of young Han Chinese peasant men who would cultivate the land during the growing season and defend their territory (and raid other areas) in the fallow season and in severe winters.[21] Not surprisingly, if Chinese gentry failed to be properly compensated for their land, these informal militias would come to rectify matters. Such mercenary-armed Chinese peasants were characterized as "bandits" by the Japanese settlers, who, as a result, supported an increased Kantô Army presence (in collusion with SMRC, whose tracks they were ordered to patrol) and also armed their own young men. This lent a militaristic character to these isolated villages, which were connected only by a growing railway network built by SMRC.

By November 1938, captions in *Manshû gurafu* insistently focus on security and "peace," much of it provided courtesy of SMRC. This hints at the fact that personal safety might have been a very relevant concern for the growing numbers of settlers: "In addition, immigrants in the South Manchuria Railway Company's Self-Protective Villages, free immigrants encouraged by various prefectures, and immigrant groups of religious and social organizations will [sic], shortly settle in Manchuria. These groups are expecting to build up peaceful farm communities within their respective settlements and will strive to develop agriculture, advance culture, and maintain peace and order."[22] The caption continues with a hopeful description of some of the paternalistic, Confucian-inspired slogans of the new state, which are intended to ease tension in the locals: "No doubt, the native inhabitants will receive much benefit from the newcomers, and the two will effect a strong, cordial relationship full of inter-racial harmony and peace in the new born [sic] land, Manchoukuo."[23] The repetition of words such as "peace," "harmony," and "cordiality" appearing in the pictorial's pages in the late 1930s ring hollow to the contemporary reader, who benefits from hindsight.

In addition to a less-than-welcoming reception by the local Han Chinese population, the Japanese settlers also had to deal with the powerful presence of the Soviet Union, which loomed as an ever-present threat to the Japanese rural settlements in northern Manchukuo. Even if fear of the Russians and Chinese bandits could be overcome, the Siberian winter challenged even the hardiest Japanese recruits from mountainous regions in Nakano.[24] Moreover, pregnancy, childbirth, and the rearing of infants were negatively affected by a harsher and drier climate conducive to respiratory ailments. The food as well would have taken much getting used to, since northern rivers only provided muddy-tasting fish that could not be eaten raw, and cabbages and other vegetables tasted coarse to the Japanese palate. Added to this, rice was not one of the staples; these were millet porridge and wheat flour for buns and noodles.[25]

Nevertheless, the cover of the December 1936 special edition of *Manshû gurafu* shows a heartening image of robust young women in *monpe* (loose work trousers), with adorable babies in knit caps strapped to their backs, harvesting wheat or millet (no doubt this photograph was shot at the beginning of autumn rather than in winter).[26] Inside, a spread titled "A Day in the Settlements" juxtaposes a gendered division of labor in images on the page's left-hand side: a homestead appears at the top, over the scene of a gateway framing schoolchildren, above the snapshot of a midwife on her way to a birth, with a newborn being bathed at the bottom, while on the opposite side male teachers lead children into a school, a medical clinic is being built, a man fishes by a stream, and a hunter aims into the horizon.[27] The magazine clearly indicates that it is indeed possible to raise a family in rural Manchukuo among all the requisite elements of Japanese civilization (proper dwellings, schools, hospitals, and medical care), and that "even" women can easily perform the necessary farm work alongside their men despite their duties as mothers.[28]

Along with these hopeful images, an article in the same edition on "The Utopia of Japanese Settlers in North Manchuria" reflects on the pioneering efforts of the volunteer Youth Corps, who preceded these immigrants, and encouragingly notes, "The remaining 60 percent, the picked youths, however, has [sic] conquered every difficulty and has proved the possibility of Japanese emigration to Manchuria."[29] The fact that mere youths laid the groundwork for these Japanese families highlights the rugged nature of the "Japanese race" or *Yamato minzoku*, which could even flourish in the wide, open plains of

Manchuria. To the left, the article also features a circular insert of a Japanese shrine built by settlers and, at the bottom, a map of rail-linked settlements in Sanjiang Province, currently part of China's Heilongjiang Province, with Tieli City (Tetsuryô, a former training center for the Youth Corps) as its county seat. Tetsuryô's Shintô shrine, of course, serves as the spiritual nerve center of the community, as a place where marriages are conducted and subsequent offspring are blessed and receive their names. Traditional Japanese values, thus reproduced in the rural Manchurian space, are coupled with modern communications and transportation networks.

The pictorial highlights the modernity of the settlements by stressing the fact that all of them are (or will be) connected via telephone, road, and rail access courtesy of SMRC. The photographers portray the settlements as well organized, with the Japanese farmers using mechanized McCormick-Deering tractors purchased from the United States, and villages are peopled with well-fed families in which no woman past adolescence appears without a plump infant strapped to her back. Hence the scenes emphasize the fertility both of the land and of its new immigrants and thus the potential reproducibility of the entire rural development scheme on a large scale.

After the mid-1930s, Japan's colonization schemes in northern Manchuria began to accelerate, with the government aiming for the mass migration of Japanese farmers into Manchukuo who would then flourish and populate the region with their own offspring. This is made clear in the November 1938 edition of *Manshû gurafu*, whose cover shows two robust young Japanese women smiling and holding plump infant sons, with a young toddler in the foreground.[30] As on a similar cover featured two years earlier, the women and children depicted create a picture of well-fed good health. A further spread features scenes of uniformed girls and boys attending school and mothers attending a mass meeting with their infants, framing the top of a large image of children in western clothing gleefully walking down a country path carrying their siblings, with the accompanying caption, "Children who grow on the new land, the 'good earth.'"[31] The caption title references contemporary popular culture through the popular Japanese/German coproduced feature film *New Earth* released in 1937 as well as Pearl S. Buck's bestselling novel *The Good Earth*, which received a Nobel Prize in Literature in 1938.

An essay within the magazine's same issue also discusses official settlement attempts: "The Japanese government completed recently a plan calling for the immigration of a million families or a total of 5,000,000 individuals within 20 years, but at the present time the

First Stage Five Year Program which aims at the sending of 500,000 people is being pushed."[32] In prose and images, the pictorial elucidates much of this plan, which was developed during the intensification of the government's efforts to exhort settlement amid a global political climate in which Japan's Axis ally, Nazi Germany, favored extended *Lebensraum* (living space) for its ethnic population.[33] A caption emphasizes the archipelago's need for more land for its burgeoning population: "The average area of land available for farming in Japan is about 1 *chobu* per household. In comparison to other countries this average is about 1/60 of the United States, 1/90 of Canada, 1/7 of Germany, and approximately 1/16 of Denmark. To make matters worse, Japan is being pressed with an annual increase of 900,000 in population, which make [sic] living more difficult for the people who are already stricken with poverty."[34]

The following two-page spread, with the English title "Japanese Immigrant Settlements in North Manchuria," is underlined by the Japanese caption *"Hirake'iku shojô-chi"* ("Tilling Virgin Land") spread in white lettering over a photo of two strong young Japanese men from the Tetsuryô Youth Training Camp. In a few years, they too will be ready for marriage and will wait for the arrival of brides from domestic Japan. According to the essay, "7,000 families have settled in 50 localities so far under governmental sponsorship (total for April, 1939), but besides this total, the Young Men's Training Camp capable of accommodating 30,000 boys from Japan will be established in North Manchuria within this year."[35] The photo illustrating this phenomenon appears on a diagonal, with one-half of the land remaining as prairie and the other half having been ploughed into rows with the metal fingers of a tiller pulled by an American Caterpillar tractor—in an image reminiscent of John Steinbeck's *East of Eden* and the American West.[36] Through the recurring juxtaposition of symbols evocative of what Alan Tansman terms the "fascist moment,"[37] which highlights the productivity of both land and family, readers are constantly regaled with the potentially high fertility of northern Manchuria's soil and its settlers.

Since 1938, when squadrons of youth labor corps pioneers like the two young men in the *Tilling Virgin Land* image were sent over, writings of all kinds and even literature about the intrepid Japanese pioneers and settlers began to proliferate. In a similar vein as the now-defunct 1920s proletarian literature movement, these stories propagated an antibourgeois right-wing version of socialism, or what I call "right-wing proletarianism," whose spirit is also captured in the photographs examined before. Of course, Italian fascism, which the Manchukuo example most closely resembles, was indeed a right-wing version of socialism. The influence of "right-wing proletarianism," where a paternalistic state safeguards the rights of farmers and workers, also suffuses the Manchukuo-related works of the now politically converted Japanese proletarian writers Nogawa Takashi (1901–44) and Yamada Seizaburô (1896–1987). Like Shimaki Kensaku (1903–45) and Yamada, who began the trend of writing about the rural pioneers in 1939–40, formerly proletarian authors like Nogawa and even Tokunaga Sunao (1899–1958) also published works dedicated to this topic. For example, Tokunaga's 1939 novel *Sengentai* (*The Pioneers*) focuses on the youth labor corps and contains scenes of young Japanese teenagers astounded at the labor productivity of Han Chinese coolies hired for the settlements.[38] Japanese readers avidly consumed these visions of empire with their compatriots flourishing in newly developed areas overseas.

## Productivity and Reproduction during Wartime, 1941–43

After 1941, *Manshû gurafu* began to change its focus, seemingly evincing a less artistic inclination in favor of the new orientation of the Manchukuo regime as a base for Japanese military operations in China proper and Southeast Asia. However, one of the continuities with earlier editions of *Manshû gurafu* is an obvious intensification of the obsession with production from the early forties to 1944. Large spreads of women at work—many of them mothers tending to their babies while engaged in agricultural labor—replacing the men also become more frequent. For example, in the December 1940 special edition on the rural settlers, a photo essay and article on "Women of the Rural Development Areas" ("*Kaitaku-chi no jôsei*") shows women carrying enormous sheaves of grain on their backs, tending sheep, preparing a meal, and walking through the fields with their children or with infants on their backs.[39] They appear as strong, capable individuals cheerfully going about their daily work, both in the household and out in the fields.

Intriguingly, images of men become less and less frequent, and the December 1943 special edition on "Grain Storehouse Manchuria" features a woman in a curiously similar pose to the November 1938 *Hanatsubaki* cover. Broadly smiling amid the rays of benevolent summer sunshine, she proudly holds a sheaf of grain, doing her patriotic duty to supply the Japanese troops fighting in China and Southeast Asia with much-needed rations as food in domestic Japan becomes scarce. At this point in the Asian and Pacific conflicts, Manchukuo served an important role as Imperial Japan's grain storehouse, cultivated largely by the nation's Japanese women.

Nevertheless, despite the "disappearance" of men and food supplies amid the darkening wartime climate, agricultural productivity and the creation of large families remain an all-consuming idée fixe for both the Manchukuo state and its propaganda organizations. Similar equivocal messages appear in the *Manshû gurafu* shots of the Japanese *kaitaku-sha*, but with a different political import. The latter show that frenzied agricultural production in the rural space proceeds in an efficient and scientific manner, with the land being worked by self-consciously smiling Japanese families (usually women and their offspring) who eagerly produce a bounty of both agricultural products and children—helpful in repopulating the ranks of soldiers killed amid the intensifying Sino-Japanese conflict, the burgeoning war in the Pacific, and extended operations in Southeast Asia.

In a rather rare late-1943 image of the archetypal pioneer family in the same "Grain Storehouse Manchuria" edition, a husband holds his son while his wife carries a hoe.[40] With the inset of the family overshadowed by unrealistically large wheat or millet plants, the couple smiles in broad grins as the barefoot child toddler looks at the camera with some trepidation. Accompanying nationalistic poetry lauds the power of agricultural production, where even one grain and one bean can move the Japanese toward total victory. The rays of the sun illuminate this archetypal settler family of Manchuria wearing summer clothing, which is somewhat ironic since the edition was released at the beginning of a harsh, Siberian winter.

Further articles such as "The Agricultural Production and Resources of Manchuria as a Military Base," which contain helpful statistics, illustrate the fact that Manchuria now unabashedly serves Imperial Japan's war efforts. The 1943 special edition contains more specific examples from certain locales, such as the one featured in "Touring an 'Increasing Battle Power' County: Map of Siping County." Complete with a map, towns appear on the map with the corn, beans, and millet that they specialize in, while railroad lines provided by the South Manchuria Railway Company connect these tiny hamlets.

However, the frenzied pace of labor depicted in *Manshû gurafu* begs the question of how the Japanese settlers (and the readers of the periodical), both young and old men not at the front, children, and women of all ages, are supposed to sustain the level of energy required to produce the proper yields of crops and children emphasized by the pronatalist state? In addition, the government slogan exhorted by Imperial Japan, *Umeyo fuyaseyo* (Give birth and multiply), also clearly was in full force to urge the growth of large families in Manchukuo. Even the advertisements featured in the pictorial in the 1940s emphasize productivity on behalf of the Manchukuo regime. For example, patent medicine ads targeting Japanese men and women liberally pepper these later editions, promising to increase their labor power and virility or femininity (thus ensuring the production of more crops as well as children). The emphasis on efficient production is reinforced in ads for medicines ranging from the energy promoter Vitamin B to several strangely named *horumon* (hormone) concoctions, one for each gender, which supposedly boosted the sex hormones.

To address these two concerns, Japanese pharmaceutical companies produced supplements in the form of over-the-counter patent medicines like Neo-paranutolin, based on Vitamin B1, which promised to increase one's strength in an easily digestible form, and Purehormone, which allegedly improved the functioning of both the male and female reproductive organs. For those who desired similar supplements in easily consumable pill form, Metabolin touted that it would boost strength in men due to its Vitamin B compounds, while Oivestin promised menstrual regularity and normal reproductive ability for women through the addition of estrogen. The graphics of the advertisements emphasize the name of the product in blocky *katakana* script used for foreign or scientific words, with its purported uses in smaller type in the middle.

In fact, in the early 1940s, an obsession with birth and breeding of all kinds, whether of humans or livestock, appeared in mass-consumed propaganda films as well as in more highbrow forms of art. For instance, in the short documentary titled *Manchukuo: The Newborn Empire*, the commentator discusses initiatives focusing on the cross-breeding of native Manchurian sheep with varieties from Japan to increase the production of wool.[41] After leafing through numerous editions of these later volumes, the reader keenly notices that this fixation becomes increasingly ominous, as it indicates that Imperial Japan is losing its overextended war. This theme of high productivity of both crops and children in the Manchurian space even permeated fine art. Consider, for example, the avant-garde artist Asai Kan'emon's (1901–83) striking 1943 painting featuring a Madonna-like Japanese mother (complete with wispy, halo-like clouds near her head) dressed in blue, with her red-kimono-attired toddler son, in an image titled *Hôshû (Homare no kazoku)* (*Abundant Harvest [Family of Distinction]*).[42] The promised "abundant harvest" appears to be the production of one blessed child, who looks toward the viewer, while his mother modestly casts her gaze downward at the child's jacket, which he will later wear at his first *shichi-go-san* shrine visit.[43] At the *monpe*-clad mother's feet rests a teapot, while a dog resembling a red fox, or *kitsune*, in the lower right corner portentously gazes at the matriarchal family. In Japanese folk wisdom, the red fox is a trickster, and his presence casts an ironic shadow over this family that is missing its traditional head, the absent father likely having been called to war. The peaceful scene of maternal harmony is disrupted by the flame-like ochre of the soil and the turbulence of the rolling clouds in the background. Though these two media forms both illustrate the importance of the reproducibility of the Japanese settler communities in very different ways, they still reveal the growing vacuum of men called to the front—a phenomenon that pushes women to the forefront by compelling them to serve as the heads of their families as well as the Empire's leading productive units.

## Conclusion

In conclusion, Japanese mothers were an integral part of the Manchukuo experiment during wartime. Their efforts were praised as part of Imperial Japan's government-sponsored *ryôsai kenbô* (Good wife, wise mother) philosophy dating since the Meiji period (1868–1912). However, during wartime, this model of virtuous behavior praised by the state intensified, when pronatalism became part of national policy. The positive aspects of the birth of children who would in turn become soldiers or mothers were reflected in media throughout the Empire, and especially in Manchukuo, which became an important base for Japanese operations in Southeast Asia after 1942.

From the late 1930s into the early 1940s, Japanese handlers of occupied northeast China attempted to portray the new state of Manchukuo as a utopian "paradise" for rural Japanese settlers and their families. Mothers served as the cornerstones of these families and were placed in charge of reproducing the ideologies of empire along with children. Such immigration efforts into northern Manchuria would help relieve pressures on domestic rural localities and provide an overseas base for the production of food and manpower for maintaining the war effort. Numerous propaganda publications, including *Manshû gurafu* (*Manchuria Graph*) published by the South Manchuria Railway Company, touted the region as fertile and productive, with ample opportunities to raise numerous healthy children in the wide-open spaces and salubrious climate. The pictorial displayed scenes of a model rural populace settling the region, where men were productive laborers but women supported the dual role of producing and raising children as well as crops. Magazine covers feature seasonal depictions in which the settlers are shown happily cultivating or harvesting crops (with babies on the backs of women).

Images such as these promoted an ideal of peaceful, rural areas as a depository for Japanese values that were to be translated elsewhere— that is, newly conquered multiethnic areas in Southeast Asia. In addition, they showed both Japanese and Western audiences the success of the Manchukuo experiment through these intrepid pioneers flourishing in their new environment. However, as Japan's war effort bogged down in China and intensified in Southeast Asia and the Pacific, women became increasingly important for the Empire in their childbearing and rearing capabilities while still maintaining labor productivity. Revisiting long-neglected propaganda images such as these is fascinating, because they elide the violence of wartime and portray what I term a "right-wing proletarian" utopia desired by Japanese framers of the fascist state—representing ideals they were unable to realize in domestic Japan.

## Notes

1. Portions of this text are reprinted with permission of the publisher from *Glorify the Empire* by Annika Culver © University of British Colombia Press 2013. All rights reserved by the publisher.
2. Kazumasa Nagai and Yusuke Kaji, eds., *Creative Works of Shiseidô* (Tokyo: Kyuryudo Art, 1985), chronological collage of *Hanatsubaki* covers, 1937–56, unpaginated rear photo materials.
3. *Manshû gurafu* [*Manchuria Graph*] vol. 4, no. 8 (number 25) (Tokyo: Yumani shobô, 2008), reprint, 147.
4. Ibid., 148.
5. *Manshû gurafu* [*Manchuria Graph*] vol. 4, no. 12 (number 29) (Tokyo: Yumani shobô, 2008), reprint, 223.
6. *Manchuria*, October 1, 1940, 488.
7. Most Japanese sources focus on the policies involved in the rural settlement of Manchukuo, though some discussions of women appear imbedded in the text. Recent sources include the following: Fukuda K, *Onna to sensô (Kindai jôsei bunken shiryô gyosho)* [*Women and War—Volume 8 (Modern Women's Text and Resource Collection 8)*] (Tokyo: Oozora-sha, 1992); Iida-Shi rekishi kenkyûsho [Iida City Historical Research Institute], *Manshû imin—Iida Shimo Ina kara no messeiji* [*Manchurian Immigrants—A Message from the Ina Valley in Iida*] (Tokyo: Gendai shiryo shuppan, 2007); Munekage Tadashi, *Kaitakumin—kokusaku ni honrô sareta nômin* [Immigrant Settlers—Farmers at

JAPANESE MOTHERS AND RURAL SETTLEMENT 111

the Mercy of Government Policy] (Tokyo: Kôbunken, 2012). Sources focusing on memories and oral history include the following: Nishida Masaru, Sun Chiwu, and Zheng Min, eds. *Chûgoku nômin ga akashisu "Manshû kaitaku"* no jissô [*Chinese Peasants Witnessing the True Face of "Manchurian Development"*] (Tokyo: Shogakukan, 2007); Nozoe Kanji, ed., *Manmô kaitaku no shuki—Nagano-ken jin no kiroku* [*Memoirs of Settlement in Manchuria and Mongolia—Memories of People from Nagano Province*] (Tokyo: Nihon hosô shuppan kyôkai, 1979).

8. Named for a location near Shanhaiguan where the Great Wall of China meets the sea, the Tangu Truce was decided on by both the Chinese nationalists under Chiang Kai-Shek and the Japanese to provide a buffer zone between China and Manchukuo and to limit the hostilities of the Kantô Army from penetrating further into China proper by sacrificing the northeast.

9. From Tatsuo Kawai, *The Goal of Japanese Expansion* (Westport, CT: Greenwood, 1973 [1938]), 67. Quoted in Zeljko Cipris, "The Responsibility of Intellectuals: Kobayashi Hideo on Japan at War," *Japan Focus*, 1, http://old.japanfocus.org/products/topdf/1625, accessed on August 4, 2010.

10. *Manchuria*, October 1, 1940, 488.

11. See Louise Young, *Japan's Total Empire: Manchuria and the Culture of Wartime Imperialism* (Berkeley: University of California Press, 1998), 69–78.

12. *Sôgô shuppan nenkan* [*General publishing yearbook*] (Tokyo: Tosho kenkyûkai, 1932), 963. Quoted in Young, *Japan's Total Empire*, 70.

13. *Manshû gurafu* [*Manchuria Graph*] vol. 4, no. 12 (number 29) (Tokyo: Yumani shobô, 2008), reprint, 234–35.

14. Ibid., 235.

15. Michael Baskett, *The Attractive Empire: Transnational Film Culture in Imperial Japan* (Honolulu: University of Hawaii Press, 2008), 127–28. Cesar Franck headed the German side of the production, while Amakasu Masahiko (1891–1945) of Man'ei [Manchurian Film Association] directed the shooting in Manchukuo.

16. South Manchuria Railway Company, *Fifth Report on Progress in Manchuria to 1936* (Dairen: South Manchuria Railway Company, 1936), 132.

17. Ibid.

18. Ibid.

19. Ibid. The publication is referring to Binjiang Province, located in the area near Harbin in what is now Heilongjiang Province in the People's Republic of China.

20. *Manshû gurafu* [*Manchuria Graph*] vol. 4, no. 12 (number 29) (Tokyo: Yumani shobô, 2008), reprint, 226.

21. This was corroborated in my conversations with Liu Yong, whose grandfather Liu Shan-Zheng was the son of a landlord family in

Qing'an (Qingcheng, or Keijô, prior to the 1949 liberation) near the Tieli Japanese development area in northern Manchuria. In Japanese maps from 1938, the Liu family estate, or Liu Yuan-zi, can be found equidistant between Tieli (Tetsuryô) and Qing'an (Qingcheng, or Keijô).

22. *Manshû gurafu* [*Manchuria Graph*], vol. 6, no. 11 (number 52) (Tokyo: Yumani shobô, 2008), reprint, 244.
23. Ibid.
24. For more on the villages from which these rural Japanese settlers came, with the majority coming from the Nakano area, see Iida-shi rekishi kenkyûsho-hen [Historical Research Institute of Iida City], ed., *Manshû imin: Iida Shimo Ina kara no messeji* [*Manchurian Immigrants: A message from Iida City in the Ina Valley*] (Tokyo: Gendai shiryô shuppan, 2007).
25. Other than the ever-present tofu also consumed by Han Chinese, Japanese settlers would have had to accustom themselves to the heavy meat of local main dishes (a high-protein diet being necessary to overcome the cold). Impoverished Chinese made do with a diet of millet porridge, wilted cabbage, pickled vegetables, and frozen tofu.
26. *Manshû gurafu* [*Manchuria Graph*] vol. 4, no. 12 (number 29) (Tokyo: Yumani shobô, 2008), reprint, 223.
27. Ibid., 232.
28. Preceding these immigrant families were the volunteer Youth Corps, consisting of young teenage boys who began to cultivate the land in camps that were ruled by harsh military discipline. For more on the Youth Corps, see Ronald Suleski, "Reconstructing Life in the Youth Corps Camps of Manchuria, 1938–1945: Resistance to Conformity," *East Asian History* 30 (2005): 67–90.
29. *Manshû gurafu* [*Manchuria Graph*] vol. 4, no. 12 (number 29) (Tokyo: Yumani shobô, 2008), reprint, 226.
30. *Manshû gurafu* [*Manchuria Graph*] vol. 6, no. 11 (number 52) (Tokyo: Yumani shobô, 2008), reprint, 243.
31. Ibid., 255.
32. Ibid., 244.
33. At the same time, in Nazi Germany, Adolph Hitler clamored for more *Lebensraum* (living space) for the ethnic German population, using this as an excuse to expand into neighboring regions/countries harboring large German-speaking populations, like the Sudetenland and Austria. This edition came out a few months following the 1938 Munich Conference, at which the League of Nations countries appeased Hitler in the hopes that he would be satisfied with the territory he had so far acquired.
34. *Manshû gurafu* [*Manchuria Graph*] vol. 6, no. 11 (number 52) (Tokyo: Yumani shobô, 2008), reprint, 244.
35. Ibid.
36. Ibid.

37. Alan Tansman's concept of the "fascist moment," or a moment "in which the individual is depicted as merging with, or is called on to merge imaginatively with, a greater whole," evolved from Christopher Bollas's "fascist state of mind," or "an inclination to thoughts, feelings, and acts of binding that purge the mind of the messy diversity of contradictory views and fills the gap left by that purging with 'material icons.'" See Alan Tansman, *The Aesthetics of Japanese Fascism* (Berkeley: University of California Press, 2009), 18–21.
38. Tokunaga Sunao, *Sengentai* [*The Pioneers*] (Tokyo: Kaizô-sha, 1939).
39. *Manshû gurafu* [*Manchuria Graph*] vol. 8 no. 12 (number 77) (Tokyo: Yumani shobô, 2008), reprint, 119–20.
40. *Manshû gurafu* [*Manchuria Graph*] vol. 11 no. 12 (number 113) (Tokyo: Yumani shobô, 2008), reprint, n.p.
41. The images of the sheep even resemble Terashima's pictorialist photos. See http://www.youtube.com/watch?v=AlyKKLKsBqQ, or contact Prelinger Archives, San Francisco, at http://www.prelinger.com.
42. Otani Shôgo, ed., *Chiheisen no yume: Shôwa 10 nendai no gensô kaiga* [*Dreams of the Horizon: Fantastic Paintings in Japan, 1935–1945*] (Tokyo: Tokyo National Museum of Modern Art, 2003), 92.
43. In Japan, even today, parents bring children attired in their best clothing to the local shine on their third, fifth, and seventh birthdays for a blessing.

## Selected Bibliography

Baskett, Michael. *The Attractive Empire: Transnational Film Culture in Imperial Japan*. Honolulu: University of Hawaii Press, 2008.

Iida-shi rekishi kenkyûsho-hen [Historical Research Institute of Iida City], ed. *Manshû imin: Iida Shimo Ina kara no messeji* [*Manchurian Immigrants: A Message from Iida City in the Ina Valley*]. Tokyo: Gendai shiryô shuppan, 2007.

Kawai, Tatsuo. *The Goal of Japanese Expansion*. Westport, CT: Greenwood, 1973. First published in 1938.

Nagai, Kazumasa, and Yusuke Kaji, eds. *Creative Works of Shiseidô*. Tokyo: Kyuryudo Art, 1985.

Shôgo, Otani, ed. *Chiheisen no yume: Shôwa 10 nendai no gensô kaiga* [*Dreams of the Horizon: Fantastic Paintings in Japan, 1935–1945*]. Tokyo: Tokyo National Museum of Modern Art, 2003.

Suleski, Ronald. "Reconstructing Life in the Youth Corps Camps of Manchuria, 1938–1945: Resistance to Conformity." *East Asian History* 30 (December 2005): 67–90.

Sunao, Tokunaga. *Sengentai* [*The Pioneers*]. Tokyo: Kaizô-sha, 1939.

Tansman, Alan. *The Aesthetics of Japanese Fascism*. Berkeley: University of California Press, 2009.

Young, Louise. *Japan's Total Empire: Manchuria and the Culture of Wartime Imperialism*. Berkeley: University of California Press, 1998.

# CHAPTER 7

## DEAR OKĀSAN...
## AN ANALYSIS OF FAREWELL LETTERS FROM KAMIKAZE PILOTS TO THEIR MOTHERS

### Salvador Jimenez Murguia and Benjamin A. Peters

### INTRODUCTION

Official narratives often emerge sanitized and in some cases void of any realistic or even factual content. Indeed, the horrors of war can be reduced to revisionist rhetoric that somehow sugarcoats tragic notions of pain and suffering, neatly packaging a much more benign account of events for history books intended for general audiences. Toward the close of World War II, the Japanese military used the now infamous kamikaze strategy of flying suicide missions into Western Allied warships, taking the lives of nearly 4,000 pilots. Although official narratives may interpret the actions of these pilots as acts of ultimate sacrifice for the nation, such an interpretation only seems to reinforce stereotypical imaginings of the Japanese sense of honor and pride bound to nationalism. For example, one rather common Western view of the kamikaze is that these soldiers were somehow lacking in rationality, independent volition, and even civility. David C. Earhart has noted that the term *kamikaze* "entered colloquial English as an adjective synonymous with senseless actions of desperate, crazed fanatics," adding that such a bias "attests to Westerners' antipathy toward suicidal tactics and belies ignorance of the Japanese experience of the war."[1] This misinterpretation aside, there may be a much more accurate account of kamikaze actions that is tied directly to a commitment to one's family, specifically one's mother, rather than one's nation.

There is no doubt that Japanese soldiers were willing to sacrifice others and themselves at the command of the Japanese state during the imperial era. During World War II alone, the Japanese military killed 5,964,000 civilians throughout the Asia-Pacific region.[2] An additional 2,700,000 Japanese soldiers and civilians died in the war.[3] The question at hand, however, is how Japanese soldiers who sacrificed their lives, in particular kamikaze pilots, justified their deaths to themselves and others. In other words, this chapter is an inquiry into the object of sacrifice for suicide pilots. Did they sacrifice their lives for the Emperor, the sacred embodiment of the nation, or did they sacrifice for others—namely, their mothers—in an effort to protect and honor them as well as refrain from bringing shame on them?

To answer this question, it is important first to note the difference between the personal bonds of a family (mother, father, siblings, etc.) and how state-level actors attempted to co-opt and manipulate these relationships. To be sure, there is evidence that governmental agencies tried to appropriate the role of the mother in order to sustain and bolster the war effort. In addition to Japan's Cabinet Information Bureau (CIB)—the branch of government charged with coordinating all information used as war propaganda—the government instituted the Educational Kamishibai[4] Federation, which generated illustrated storyboards targeting young children, encouraging them to embrace the war. One 1943 *kamishibai* titled *Mother of a Warrior-God* actually depicted a real soldier bidding farewell to his mother, inclusive of an illustration after his suicide and a posthumous communiqué that read, "Mother, please be happy. We did it."[5] Such instances of state-generated propaganda aside, our focus will be on what actual kamikaze pilots thought of and wrote about their mothers prior to their suicide missions. In this brief survey of farewell letters, poems, and other statements from the kamikaze, we provide some evidence for a different view about the object of sacrifice. Specifically, we suggest that mothers may have been the central objects toward which many kamikaze, supposed exemplars of sacrifice-unto-death for the nation, committed their sacrificial actions.

## The Political Cultivation of the Will to Sacrifice

The 1868 Meiji Restoration marked the emergence of Japan as a modern state and nation. Meiji-era leaders had the dual goals of catching up with and surpassing competitor states, especially Western states that had forced Japan to abandon centuries of isolationism, and neutralizing and incorporating domestic rivals intent on preserving the feudal arrangements of the Edo era (1603–1868). They accomplished their aims through a modernizing strategy of state formation (*kokka keisei*) and nation making (*kokumin keisei*). Successful state formation depended on establishing a centralized administrative capacity that could monopolize coercion and extraction, and successful nation making depended on the development of a national collective identity centered on the Emperor.

State formation and nation making converged in Meiji political leaders' attempts to inculcate the will to sacrifice in their subjects. Nowhere was this more evident than in the prescriptions of the Imperial Rescript to Soldiers (1882) and the Imperial Rescript on Education (1890).[6] The Meiji government established Japan's first military establishment based on universal conscription and its first universally compulsory school system, and the Rescripts prescribed the desired attitudes and behaviors of their members.

Military conscription began in 1873, marking the end of the distinct class privileges of the samurai. A new sense of loyalty to the state and its military was not, however, immediately forthcoming. Many peasants viewed military conscription suspiciously, since it was possible for those of means to void their son's "compulsory" service through the payment of a fee.[7] In fact, Sims notes, "popular objections to conscription were so great that 82 percent of twenty-year-olds took advantage of the various means of gaining exemptions in 1876."[8] Nevertheless, the national army's ability to quell an uprising of tens of thousands of ex-samurai during the Satsuma Rebellion of 1877 demonstrated the state's growing coercive potential. The rebellion itself, however, was a lesson to the Emperor and his government of their need for subjects' loyalty. The Imperial Rescript to Soldiers operationalized that loyalty and pointed the way to sacrificing on behalf of the Emperor.

The Emperor delivered the Imperial Rescript to Soldiers to Japanese Imperial Army commander Yamagata Aritomo (1838–1922) in 1882, and it remained in force until 1945. The Rescript, memorized and recited by soldiers, established a central moral code for combatants. While it outlined virtues such as faithfulness, valor, and simplicity, its core principle was unwavering loyalty to the Emperor. Establishing the soldier's subordinate relationship to the Emperor as "the 'Grand Way' of Heaven and earth and the universal law of humanity," the

Rescript elevated peasant conscripts to samurai-like status and with it the imperative of self-sacrifice.[9]

Like the Imperial Rescript to Soldiers, the Imperial Rescript on Education of 1890 alluded to the martial ethics of the samurai and posited the Emperor as the center of the nation and the object of self-sacrifice. Posted, memorized, and recited in all Japanese schools from its promulgation until 1945, the Rescript established loyalty and filial piety to the Emperor as the quintessence of morality.[10] In other words, in reciting the Rescript, students pledged their loyalty to the Emperor over and above all others—their neighbors, their teachers, and even their own families. It was through the daily recitation of the Rescript that students understood the relationship between the Emperor and his subject as "the essence of the nation" (*kokutai*) and the necessity of offering oneself to the state in times of national emergency.[11] As with the Imperial Rescript to Soldiers, it pointed to the will to sacrifice as the foundation of the nation and the key to its vitality.

The centering of the will to sacrifice for the Emperor as the embodiment of the nation was conveyed in the *kokutai* or "national essence" ideology. In short, *kokutai* as concept was the cipher of national identity, joining loyal subjects to their sovereign, the former an impersonal unit, the latter the source of all authority and embodiment of the eternal nation, a relationship premised on the former's willingness to sacrifice to the death for the latter.

Educators were the primary propagators of the *kokutai* ideology, and the Ministry of Education published *Cardinal Principles of the National Essence* (*Kokutai no Hongi*) for students in 1937. The text explained to students that the nation's vitality depended on subjects' willingness to die for the Emperor: "[O]ffering our lives for the sake of the Emperor does not mean so-called sacrifice but the casting aside of our little selves to live under his august grace and the enhancing of the genuine life of the people of the state."[12] Part of the wider political culture of the times, in schools the *kokutai* ideology reinforced the imperatives of sacrifice and loyalty to the Emperor set out in the Meiji-era Rescript on Education. Together, they posited and prescribed the will to sacrifice as the sustenance of the nation with the Emperor as its source.

The nationalist propagandist Tanaka Chigaku promoted the *kokutai* ideology as a means to preserve the nation and clarified the role of the will to sacrifice. In his popular text *What Is Nippon Kokutai*, Tanaka views *kokutai* in biological and immutable terms as that instinctive essence "running through the veins of the race, and . . . never chang[ing] since the days of the gods."[13] Promoting a view of the relationship between the nation and the will to sacrifice as one that was mutually constitutive and reinforcing, Tanaka argued, "In a national emergency, our patriotic sentiment becomes suddenly more vigorous and when dying on the battlefield we call, 'Long live the Emperor!' and gladly meet our end without hesitation. Judging from this fact, you can understand that in the real heart and blood of the people is latent the *Kokutai* sense."[14] According to Tanaka, Japanese soldiers and any other subjects who sacrificed themselves for the Emperor embodied the *kokutai* and could not act otherwise.

## AN ALTERNATIVE VIEW OF SACRIFICE

Despite attempts by the Japanese government—from ministry-level officials to school teachers—to cultivate the will to sacrifice through both political institutions and the "official" political culture, evidence suggests an alternative view of soldiers' loyalties, especially in terms of willingness to kill themselves.

One scholar in particular, Tanaka Yuki, has developed a number of different interpretations of sacrifice as executed by the kamikaze. Analyzing private records of the kamikaze, Tanaka outlined five "psychological themes" that contributed to the acceptance of a suicide mission. Among these themes was a "belief that to die for the 'country' was [to] show filial piety to one's own parents, particularly one's mother."[15] According to Tanaka, the final farewell letters from many pilots conveyed apologies to their parents for their impending suicides and for any future grief their premature deaths may cause. Accompanying these apologies, however, were suggestions that committing to one's mission also meant committing to fulfilling the demands of filial piety. Tanaka notes, "Filial piety ('koo') to parents became identical with loyalty ('chu') to parents and then to 'country.' Their loyalty to the emperor invariably emerges as a logical extension of loyalty to parents and hometown, rather than the reverse."[16] Tanaka's interpretation herein discerns the differences in loyalty in conjunction with an abstract model for prioritizing allegiance. Emphasizing the priority of the family relative to the Emperor marks a symbolic point of departure away from a commitment to dying for the nation, diverting it toward sacrifice for the community—or, more particularly, the family. Moreover, this priority of the family highlighted the relationship between mothers and their kamikaze sons. Tanaka adds, "To defend one's mother in one's hometown was thus the most basic, almost instinctive, element in rationalizing a cadet's death as a kamikaze pilot . . . The majority of cadets viewed their unavoidable duty as defending their mothers no matter how corrupt the society and politics. The strong emotional attachment to mothers is overwhelmingly clear in their private records, a phenomenon perhaps related to the fact that the majority of these youth were not yet involved in sustainable relationships."[17] In this way, mothers may be viewed as the ultimate objects of sacrifice. Indeed, this interpretation becomes quite clear after viewing some of the letters written by soldiers as they anticipated sacrificing themselves in war.

In 1949, the Japan Memorial Society for Students Killed in the War compiled content from various farewell letters, diaries, poems, and other correspondences between Japanese soldiers and their friends and families. This collection resulted in a book titled *Listen to the Voices from the Sea*, showcasing a vast collection of literature produced by soldiers anticipating their deaths. For the purposes of this chapter, this collection provides a wealth of information about soldiers' personal explanations of their motivations to sacrifice and of their objects of sacrifice. In particular, we see the central role of mothers as objects of their sons' sacrifices. To be clear, the soldiers' letters make reference to a host of individuals who the soldiers wished to address before their deaths, ranging from family members and friends to community members and teachers. Yet the majority of the young soldiers' letters contain content about the authors' mothers. In comparison, only a fraction of the letters mention the Emperor or the nation, and even in those cases, the Emperor or the nation are secondary objects of sacrifice in relation to mothers and other family members.

In terms of the contents of soldiers' letters written directly to their mothers, and letters that reflect on the soldiers' relationships with their mothers and families, there are several recurrent themes. The first is soldiers' sense of guilt over dying and an accompanying plea to their mothers for forgiveness. A letter written by Army Captain Uehara Ryōji (1922–45) exemplifies this motif: "It pains my heart that my time will come before I can return, or try to return, any of these favors I received. But in Japan, where loyalty to the Emperor and filial piety are considered one and the same thing, and total loyalty to the nation is a fulfillment of filial piety, I am confident of your forgiveness."[18] Uehara's missive seems to express a sense of ambiguity about his impending sacrifice. On one hand, he is full of regret for filial obligations that he will be unable to meet due to his approaching and inevitable death. On the other hand, he sounds a note of certainty—perhaps to reassure his mother—justifying his future death by premising his loyalty to the Emperor on his loyalty to family. There seems no doubt in either instance, however, that the object of his sacrifice is, at base, his mother. This is made all the more clear by his plea for forgiveness. Uehara emphasizes that obligation which will go unfulfilled over and against the one that he will fulfill. His mother occupies place of privilege as the object for whom he sacrifices and as the only one who can forgive his failure to fulfill his obligations. Despite his reassurance that "loyalty to the Emperor and filial piety are considered one and the same thing," he seems to reveal his belief that in sacrificing himself in war, he is, in fact, transgressing against his mother—a transgression that sacrificing for the Emperor alone could never absolve.

A letter written by junior army officer Hirai Kyoshi echoes the themes of Uehara's letter. In a letter written to his mother and reflecting on his relationship with her, Hirai appears to be grappling with the inevitability of his death and the anticipated sense of disappointment he believes his mother will experience after his death:

> I wept in my heart and joined my hands in veneration, but I had to wear a smile on the outside when dealing with my loving mother's appeals and entreaties. What a contradiction and what a dilemma to be in. I wept with pain in my heart because of this struggle between two souls in conflict, and ended up crying out loud ... Mother I really do understand how you feel, dear mother, but the times we live in and the education that I have received do not allow me to go along with your wishes. Please, please forgive me for the great impiety of dying before your own time has come.[19]

Hirai expresses a fatalistic notion of his role in the war and suggests that he cannot do otherwise than to sacrifice his life in battle. This sense of inevitability, however, is not enough to convince his mother—or himself—that his sacrifice for the cause is the ultimate sacrifice, for if it were, there would be nothing impious about it and there would be no need for forgiveness. Like Uehara's letter, Hirai's letter also reveals the author's sense of transgression against a higher source of moral obligation than the nation. Simply put, his main concern is justifying his course of action to his mother and pleading for her endorsement-through-absolution.

Apart from such pleas for forgiveness, another common theme of soldiers' letters is gratitude to their mothers, especially for their efforts in raising them. In a letter written by Army Lieutenant Sanada Daihō (1917–43), the author recounts his memories of his mother's kindness, understanding, and encouragement throughout his upbringing. While the main theme is gratitude, feelings of guilt and shame again reveal the centrality of a sense of moral obligations to one's mother. In this case, the author harbors a sense of guilt for failing to reciprocate the love and affection he received from his mother:

> Oh, what a huge and bottomless love and benevolence! What thoughtfulness far beyond what I could ever deserve! Oh the mother's love and trust that were and are shining over me! How could I ever dream of living without making things better? A mother who accepts all of her children's pleasure and happiness as if it were her own, and what a terrible act of impiety it is to betray this parental love! From now on, for sure, I am resolved to put an end to this shallow life, and to be reborn into a stronger existence. Mother—the only one in the whole world for me—I hope that you will take good care of yourself.[20]

Sanada's letter is notable both for the extent to which he expresses his gratitude to his mother and for his relative lack of focus on his impending death. The author's description of his mother's love is such that his adoration for her eclipses the significance—the very mention—of the author's relationship to the Emperor or nation. While Sanada does sound the theme of impiety and betrayal as a way to imply his eventual self-sacrifice, he does so indirectly, almost implying that he will continue living. His letter seems to portray his mother as the very source and sustenance of his life, as the antithesis of war and its imperatives of death.

Sanada's emphasis on his mother's love as a source of sustenance points to another common theme in the young soldiers' letters—the juxtaposition of mothers as a source of security and peace against the uncertainties and dangers of war. While it is not always clear whether the image of one's mother and home represents a fleeting desire to escape from the terrible conditions of war or rather a force of benevolence and love that actually stands as a counterweight to and possible symbolic negation of war, some of the young soldiers' writings suggest an explicit apposition of their mothers and war. One example is a simple poem penned by Army Corporal Nagata Kazuo (1916–44). After writing of hearing the sounds of gunfire in battle, Nagata's letter immediately turns toward thoughts of his mother, family, and community:

> Suddenly I think of home.
> I wonder how my mother is.
> I wonder how my younger brothers are doing.
> And I wonder what my friends are doing now.[21]

Nagata's letter, especially the mention of his mother just after recounting the sound of gunfire, suggests the centrality of his relationship with his mother along with the other intimate relationships in his life. It is as if thoughts of these intimate relationships are a salve to the fear induced by proximity to the battlefield and a model of human relationships that negates the social dislocation of war.

Perhaps the farewell letter written by Hayashi Ichizō (1922–45) epitomizes much of this sentiment surrounding the mother as the central object of sacrifice. Reciting a poem from a celebrated Tokugawa intellectual, Hayashi begins

> My dear Mother:
>
> The time has finally come for me to write a very sad letter. How will the parents' loving hearts, even exceeding the love of a child for its parents, hear of the news today?
>
> (The last farewell poem of Yoshida Shōin, 1830–59)

With Yoshida's words establishing the tone, Ichizō breaks into an emotional farewell to his mother. Avowing his regrets and asking for forgiveness for his "selfish behavior," Hayashi then seems to somehow rectify what he views as his personal shortcomings by making mention of the service he has been selected to execute: "I am pleased to have the honor of having been chosen as a member of a Special Attack Force that is on its way into battle, but I cannot help crying when I think of you, Mom." Despite the sense of honor Hayashi feels, he again focuses on his mother, lamenting the fact that she will never again know the joy of watching him grow and mature: "When I reflect on the hopes you had for my future, Mom, and how you brought me up as though it were a matter of life and death, I feel so sad that I am going to die without doing anything to bring you joy or to relieve your worries."[22] Finally, in only the way a son can return the bonds of affection, Hayashi bids farewell: "The realization that I shall be dying very soon feels like something that is happening to someone else. I mean that somehow I feel as though I can get to see you whenever I wish, probably because it is too sad to think that I will never see you again."[23]

## CONCLUSION

The view that kamikaze were ultranationalists who selflessly laid down their lives for Emperor and nation remains one of the prevalent, popular images of the Pacific War. It is a mythic view, however, that conceals the complex motivations and priority of loyalties of the suicide pilots themselves. While the political institutions and "official" political culture of Imperial Japan attempted to cultivate the will to sacrifice among young men, especially soldiers, by promoting imaginings of a transcendent national essence or *kokutai*, an examination of the last written words and intimate thoughts of soldiers before their impending deaths reveals an alternative object of sacrifice to the nation—namely, the young soldiers' mothers.

In this survey of farewell letters, poems, and other statements from the kamikaze, we have provided evidence for a different view of the object of sacrifice in war. In particular, the contents of this survey suggest that there was, if nothing else, a strong emotional and affectionate bond between the kamikaze and their mothers. While on the surface, highlighting this bond may come as no surprise to our readers—especially for those who have experienced the depths of such familial bonds themselves—complicating the notion of this bond by questioning the object of sacrifice may serve to discern a difference between sacrificing oneself for one's family versus one's nation. Moreover, the writings of the kamikaze preparing to sacrifice themselves in battle reveal a complex but recurrent set of thoughts and feelings regarding the centrality of their mothers as ultimate objects of sacrifice and moral exemplars. As these excerpts suggest, soldiers thought that sacrificing their lives for the Emperor and nation was not enough to absolve them of their unfulfilled filial obligations, especially to their mothers. In other words, the Emperor and nation could not suffice as ultimate objects of sacrifice; otherwise, there would be no question about the young soldiers' absolution. Mothers, then, may be viewed as the ultimate objects of sacrifice.

Stemming from the soldiers' sense of unfulfilled obligations were their feelings of guilt over dying and their pleas to their mothers for forgiveness. Again, their guilt revealed a sense that their transgressions could only be absolved by their mothers—not by their acts of sacrifice on behalf of the Emperor and nation. This reveals the notion that they considered their mothers as a higher source of moral obligation than the nation. It can be argued that the young soldiers, in fact, viewed their mothers as moral exemplars—the source and symbol of ultimate values. This is further evidenced by the deep sense of gratitude that the kamikaze pilots had for the mothers, especially for their mothers' efforts in bringing them up.

Perhaps the most significant image of mothers portrayed by the suicide pilots, if only implicitly, is of mothers as the ultimate source of love and sustenance. While this is a straightforward and perhaps unsurprising assertion, its significance lies in the contrast between mothers, as a source of peace and safety, and the terror of war. Soldiers' reflections on their mothers, family members, and friends precisely at the moment of battle seem to indicate a sense of longing for the deepest of human relationships, which negate the rending of the social fabric by the brutality of war.

Although our interpretation runs contrary to some narratives, inclusive of those that would hold that the kamikaze committed their acts of suicide in direct allegiance to the Emperor or the nation, we believe questioning the object of sacrifice furthers the discussion underpinning the personal realities of war and altruistic suicide. In this way, we are not arriving at definitive conclusions about psychological, social, or even political motivations but are instead attempting to broaden the parameters of scholarly discussion on this subject.

## NOTES

1. David C. Earhart, "All Ready to Die: Kamikazefication and Japan's Wartime Ideology," *Critical Asian Studies* 37, no. 4 (2005): 570.
2. R. J. Rummel, *Death by Government* (New Brunswick, NJ: Transaction, 1994), 143.
3. See John W. Dower, *War without Mercy* (New York: Pantheon, 1986).
4. The term *kamishibai* refers to a popular form of street theatre using paper panels and storytellers to educate children.
5. Earhart, "All Ready to Die," 574–75.
6. *Gunjin Chokuyu* and *Kyōiku ni Kansuru Chokugo*, respectively.
7. Mikiso Hane, *Japan, A Short History* (Oxford: Oneworld, 2000), 96.
8. Richard Sims, *Japanese Political History since the Meiji Renovation* (New York: Palgrave Macmillan, 2001), 41.
9. Ryusaku Tsunoda, Wm. Theodore De Bary, and Donald Keene, eds., *Sources of Japanese Tradition, Vol. II* (New York: Columbia University Press, 1958), 194.
10. Yoshimitsu Khan, *Japanese Moral Education Past and Present* (Cranbury, NJ: Associate University Presses, 1997), 69.
11. Ibid., 71.
12. Compilation Committee, Bureau of Educational Reform of the Ministry of Education, *Kokutai no Hongi*, trans. John Owen Gauntlett (Cambridge, MA: Harvard University Press, 1949), 80.
13. Chigaku Tanaka, *What Is Nippon Kokutai?*, trans. Kishio Satomi (Tokyo: Shishio Bunko, 1937), 95.
14. Ibid., 99.

15. Yuki Tanaka, "Japan's Kamikaze Pilots and Contemporary Suicide Bombers: War and Terror," *The Asia Pacific Journal: Japan Focus* (2005), http://www.japanfocus.org/-yuki-tanaka/1606.
16. Ibid.
17. Ibid.
18. Japan Memorial Society for the Students Killed in the War—Wadatsumi Society (Nihon Senbotsu Gakusei Kinen-Kai). *Listen to the Voices from the Sea (Kike Wadatsumi no Koe): Writings of the Fallen Japanese Students*, trans. Midori Yamanouchi and Joseph L. Quinn (Scranton, PA: University of Scranton Press, 2000), 236.
19. Ibid., 112–13.
20. Ibid., 83–85.
21. Ibid., 190.
22. Ibid, 216.
23. Ibid., 218.

## Selected Bibliography

Bureau of Educational Reform of the Ministry of Education, Compilation Committee. *Kokutai no Hongi*. Translated by John Owen Gauntlett. Cambridge, MA: Harvard University Press, 1949.

Dower, John W. *War without Mercy*. New York: Pantheon, 1986.

Earhart, David C. "All Ready to Die: Kamikazefication and Japan's Wartime Ideology." *Critical Asian Studies* 37, no. 4 (2005): 569–96.

Hane, Mikiso. *Japan: A Short History*. Oxford: Oneworld, 2000.

Japan Memorial Society for the Students Killed in the War—Wadatsumi Society (Nihon Senbotsu Gakusei Kinen-Kai). *Listen to the Voices from the Sea (Kike Wadatsumi no Koe): Writings of the Fallen Japanese Students*. Translated by Midori Yamanouchi and Joseph L. Quinn. Scranton, PA: University of Scranton Press, 2000.

Khan, Yoshimitsu. *Japanese Moral Education Past and Present*. Cranbury, NJ: Associate University Presses, 1997.

Rummel, R. J. *Death by Government*. New Brunswick, NJ: Transaction, 1994.

Sims, Richard. *Japanese Political History since the Meiji Renovation*. New York: Palgrave Macmillan, 2001.

Tanaka, Chigaku. *What Is Nippon Kokutai?* Translated by Kishio Satomi. Tokyo: Shishio Bunko, 1937.

Tanaka, Yuki. "Japan's Kamikaze Pilots and Contemporary Suicide Bombers: War and Terror." *The Asia Pacific Journal: Japan Focus* (2005). http://www.japanfocus.org/-yuki-tanaka/1606.

Tsunoda, Ryusaku, Wm. Theodore De Bary, and Donald Keene, eds. *Sources of Japanese Tradition, Vol. II*. New York: Columbia University Press, 1958.

CHAPTER 8

SOCIAL TRAUMA AND MOTHERHOOD
IN POSTWAR SPAIN

*Lorraine Ryan*

The Spanish Second Republic (1931–36), in keeping with its liberal and progressive ethos, created optimum conditions for women's advancement in society. The Constitution of 1931 not only granted women the right to maternity insurance and legalized civil marriage, but it also sought to eradicate discrimination in the workplace by legislating profeminist labor laws. Women's reproductive freedom was safeguarded by the legalization of contraception and abortion, and women also began to participate in political life. Not surprisingly, such emancipatory measures created a situation in which an enormous amount of women's organizations flourished. Innovative measures, such as divorce by mutual consent and a lack of legislative differentiation between legitimate and illegitimate children, ensured that the Second Republic was, in the words of Daniéle Bussy Genevois, "in the forefront of the parliamentary democracies of Europe in granting women their rights." However, the Republic's secular left-wing inclinations were anathema to right-wing groups such as the Church and entrepreneurs, as they perceived a serious threat to their omnipotence in the Second Republic's progressive policies. On July 17, 1936, the Spanish Civil War began with an uprising in Melilla. The Right, unified under the leadership of General Francisco Franco, emerged victorious following an internecine civil war that claimed the lives of more than 600,000 Spaniards.[1]

Following General Franco's victory in 1939, the notion of the "anti-España" (against Spain), which vilified all forms of otherness such as socialism, communism, and liberalism, was established. The Republicans were excoriated as an intolerable "other," whose covetousness of Nationalist property, amorality, and general baseness had culminated in the civil war. This traumatic schism between the "real Spain" and the "anti-Spain" engendered a collective trauma that can be defined as "when members of a collectivity feel they have been subjected to horrendous events that leave indelible marks upon the group's consciousness, marking their memories forever and changing their future identity in fundamental and irrevocable ways." Bruno Charbonneau and Geneviève Parent argue that while trauma is experienced individually, it is overcome socially and communally. Concurring with this conceptualization of trauma at the interface between individual suffering and the wider social context, E. Ann Kaplan maintains that trauma can only be understood "with reference to cultural norms and the organization of the community." Claire Stocks qualifies this scholarly caveat by decrying the tendency to group trauma survivors into a homogeneous whole, which leads to the overlooking of significant gender, ethnic, class, and cultural differentials. In Francoist Spain, femininity and the issue of women's sexuality, specifically their maternal experiences, were extirpated from their personal control and swept into the vortex of the regime's social policies and the perpetuation of the trauma of the Civil War. This being so, this essay will explore how the public and the private merged in post–civil war Spain—that is, how motherhood was converted into a hegemonic tool, and how the trauma of the civil war was perpetuated in the continuing ostracism of the Republican mother and the vilification of her figure. The reaction of the Republican mother will be assessed in order to ascertain the degree to which she managed to resist in the private sphere the public onslaught against her and the transformation of her maternal role in this traumatic situation. Comparison, where appropriate, will be occasionally made with the Nationalist mother.[2]

Upon assuming power, the Franco regime effectively abrogated the advances made under the liberal Second Republic (1931–36). Further instigated by their alliance with the Catholic Church, they implemented legislation that can only be described as inimical to women's progress on a social, economic, and personal level. Indeed, Lidia Falcón goes as far as to say that the "suppression and exploitation of women was intensified on all levels during the Francoist regime." The repression of women manifested itself in the *Ley de Derechos Politicos, Profesionales y Laborales de la mujer y el niño*, which stipulated that a married woman could not work without her husband's consent. The woman who dared to work required *una licencia marital*, which proved that she had the necessary permission of her husband. Laws such as the 1938 *Fuero del Trabajo*, which stated its main objective as being "to liberate the married woman from the factory," consolidated this patriarchal domination. Thus an essentialist polarized conception of gender relations pervaded Spanish life, and motherhood was designated as the unique contribution of women to Spanish society. The prototype of Francoist womanhood was docile and asexual, compliant with her husband's wishes, and possessed of an endless capacity for self-abnegation. The regime implemented a pronatalist policy, which comprised both incentive and prohibitive measures. "*Premios de Natalidad*" (Birth Prizes) were awarded to large families. Rewards for large families were gradated: families with 4 to 7 children were placed in Category 1; families with more than 7 were placed in Category 2; while families with more than 12 children were honored with a special audience with *El Caudillo*, Franco. The awarding of these prizes was widely publicized in the media, thus further glorifying the large family.[3]

Ensuring the reproduction of Francoist values, ascriptive motherhood was, in fact, essential to the consolidation of the Franco regime. Jacques Donzelot asserts that the state will entrust the family with the task of ensuring that their children conform to the dominant ideology. It is the mother who is given the task of socializing the children in these values, embodying as she does culture within the private sphere. Therefore the mother's power is considerable, as "she exemplifies in one person religion, social conscience and nationalism." The corollary to this was that Republican mothers who had subscribed to the liberal values of the Second Republic were considered highly subversive, as they personified antithetical values and the possibility of the transmission of, in the words of the Francoist psychiatrist Antonio Vallejo Nágera, "the Marxist virus to her children," which could give rise to future sedition. Thus, while the Nationalist mothers were extolled as "the angel of the house," Republican mothers were an object of scorn and contempt, excoriated as "viragos, sluts, monsters and bloodsuckers." Republican women's engagement in a wide range of activities during the Second Republic and the Civil War "othered" them, and promiscuity and baseness were imputed to them during the Franco period. In fact, Vallejo Nágera posited that it was precisely their deviation from the prescribed womanly trajectory during 1931–39 that had warped their moralities. Since "good mothers" were submissive, docile, and asexual, their sexualization justified their exclusion from the canon of "good mothers." Concomitant with this vilificatory process was both a punitory system that forced Republican women to carry out the cleaning of the streets and churches and a process of public humiliation that including drinking castor oil and hair shaving. The readoption of their children into pro-Francoist families frequently meant that Republican women were even deprived of the exercising of motherhood, while the vicious assaults to which they were subjected sometimes left them infertile. Such strategies of defeminization aimed to enact a retrospective punishment on those who had transgressed what the Francoist held to be immutable gender norms and cemented their exclusion from their communities.[4]

The fact that Republican mothers did not incarnate the prescribed attributes of Francoist motherhood did not mean that they were exempt from the New State's insistence on the maternal inculcation of its religious and patriotic values. The Republican mother's reaction to the imposition of the rigid Francoist model of motherhood brings us to the following two categories:

1. Acquiescent: Republican mothers who outwardly complied with this model.
2. Dissenting: Republican mothers who rejected this model and consequently suffered imprisonment.

The memory of these Republican mothers can be categorized as what Michel Foucault terms "a counter memory," which is the memory of the repressed. In Spain, Republican countermemory corresponded to "local, fragmented and fugitive memories that barely survived silence and fear in the interstices of the hegemonic versions of the Nationalist victory." The recuperation of Republican countermemory, therefore, is an arduous task, as invariably "the wish to know the voices and feel the passions of a cast of hitherto silent actors creates a powerful tension between the desire to know and the availability of materials." In short, available historical sources reflect the views and experiences of the powerful, which problematizes the recovery of countermemory. The invisibility of the repressed is compounded in this case by the fact that women were for so long consigned to a subordinate position in Spain and were consequently excluded by official historical discourse until well into the 1980s. As Gallego Méndez so astutely realizes, "they were not part of history nor did they make history." The corollary to their marginalization is that the scholar must recur to other sources to obtain an insight into the countermemory of Republican mothers. Hence, in this essay, I will attempt to uncover the effect of the traumatic social reconfiguration of Spain on the emotional state of Republican mothers and their experience of the maternal role of by using survivors' testimonials, which have been gathered as part of the recent effort to recuperate Republican memory in contemporary Spain, as well as autobiographical texts. Some of these testimonials are based on interviews with their now octonogenerian children, as there is a dearth of mothers' narratives due to their advanced age (over ninety years of age) and the failure to collect their testimonies in an earlier period, which can be attributed to the lack of focus on the history of the private sphere.[5]

## Acquiescent Republican Mothers

The model of ascriptive motherhood imposed by the Franco regime can be defined as a role with low flexibility, according to the definition by Teresa Del Valle: "Low flexibility roles have many obligatory rules and very little possibilities of improvisation." Mothering in Spain, therefore, was transformed from a private nurturing function to a publicly vigilated role with very specific and exacting criteria judging the performance of the mother. In some cases, this had a stifling effect on the Republican mother, who sacrificed herself in order to ensure the survival of her family in the postwar period. For the Republican mother, the degree of self-sacrifice required exceeded that of the Nationalist mother, as many were widowed and had no financial support. Moreover, as they were not granted *salvaconductos* (a license to work) because of their political adhesions, they frequently had to resort to illegal activities. Lidia Falcón recalls the story of her cultured and staunchly Republican mother, who she says, euphemistically, "traded on her looks" after being rejected for countless jobs. The change in her status and the belittlement to which she was subject changed her personality: "It was an awful experience for her. The terrible memories of that time remained with her all her life, as well as a certain grudge towards my grandmother, who calmly accepted the money without asking any questions." Her mother lived in constant fear, so much so that she constantly repeated the motto "Be Quiet and Forget" to her children: the severity of her expression, Falcón writes, reinforced the necessity of obedience to this order. Despite her penury and the hardship of her life, the mother invented ways to circumvent the regime's dictates and to transmit her secular, oppositional values to the children: she arranged for Lidia not to make her First Holy Communion, she turned off the radio when the National anthem was played, and she did not go to mass. Therefore she rejected, as much as possible, the role assigned to her by the regime—that of an inculcator of values—and only conveyed to her children the need to conceal these values in the public sphere. Significantly, she did not, at any time, impart a negative opinion of these same values, a silence which is symptomatic of the reluctance to adopt a recusant stance in the postwar period.[6]

Her miniscule acts of defiance can be classified as what James C. Scott terms "hidden transcripts"—oppositional acts carried out in independent autonomous fora that allow the subjugated to express their separate identities. Theorists concur that identity is a performative act, whose validation is contingent both on the continual narrativization and articulation of its tenets and on temporal continuity; the forcible excision of the past from one's life story both causes and exacerbates trauma, as it simmers inwardly and is denied resolution. This being so, hidden transcripts allowed the Republican mother to mitigate the effect of the social trauma by articulating her identity in the private sphere. They constituted a defiatory act that permitted her to obtain the aforementioned prerequisites of a sustainable identity: narrativization and temporal continuity.[7]

Given the disjunction between the public performance of obedience and private dissent, one can also conclude that the Republican mother utilized the private sphere as a locus in which to preserve her own values, a manipulation of space that effectively subverted the Francoist regime's intended symbiosis of the public and private spheres. In fact, the private sphere acted as a refuge for the Republicans, and the Republican mother would be crucial in preserving its qualities as an inviolate sanctum. For thirty years following the Francoist victory, Manuel Cortés was a *topo*, a Republican who hid in his own house for fear of potential reprisals from the regime. In order to protect him, his wife Juliana forbade their daughter, María, from bringing friends home and also reiterated the need for silence. María was grateful to her mother for preserving the family unit but was saddened by the enforced secrecy and consequent inability to refer to her father in school. Therefore the Republican mother intimated their dissension to the children and effectively subverted the intense indoctrination to which the children were subject in school by separating their world into the real world of affective values (the home) and the artificial world (the public sphere) where only a superficial obedience and no real conviction or adherence to Francoist values was required in order to survive. Some Republican mothers exceeded the parameters of hidden transcripts and clearly articulated their oppositional stance to their children by using a moral rationalization that evidenced the incoherence of the Regime's supposed Christianity. In the words of Enric Ripoll i Borrell: "When the atrocities began, my mother said that killing reds was very bad, but killing in the name of God was worse, because if those who killed did not believe in God, they were bad, of course, but those who killed in God's name were worse." It is important to note that although the Republican mother acted as a bulwark against the highly invasive encroachments of the Francoist New State, her dissidence was pacific, and in some cases, she acted as a dissuasive force against the violence and vengeance convulsing Spain. As Manuel Rabanal Taylor recalls, "My brother said, 'they killed my father and when I'm grown up, I'll get a gun and I'll avenge his death.' My mother replied, 'Don't say those kind of things, people don't have to be vengeful. God will punish them.'"[8]

As I previously mentioned, the Republican mother suffered ritual humiliation because of her political leanings. The following testimony of Cándida Ayuste Honrubia poignantly illustrates their consequent social ostracism: "When they gave you things in Auxilio Social, milk or toys, you had to queue and they insulted and humiliated you. One night before *Los Reyes Magos*, Three Kings, I queued with my daughter, Pepi, in the square where they gave out the toys: when it was my turn, they said. 'Not you, get out of the queue, you're a red.' He was a Fascist, worse than the devil."[9]

Such shaming, which usually "makes people defer to domination and inhibits their abilities to ally with others," did not have the desired effect, as Republican mothers overcame the adverse circumstances in which they found themselves by the aforementioned resistance and also an unquestioning solidarity with their families. In fact, they evince a remarkable resilience in the face of inconceivable hardship and a certain selflessness, both of which are revealed through their lack of self-pity and indeed any reference to the toll such repression exacted on them. The mother of Ceferina Calurano Delgado was tortured in prison because of her husband's political allegiance, yet her daughter remembers her as an optimistic and cheerful woman.

> Of course, my mother suffered a lot, then, but she was always very cheerful, like me. She always encouraged everybody. She used to say "Wait and see, you'll see tomorrow it won't be our turn to suffer."
>
> Even when the vans came to take the people away to prison, she'd say "Do you see that? It isn't our turn today. Well, maybe, it won't be our turn tomorrow either."[10]

In most cases, their primary concern seems to be their family, and although this is commendable, it also points to an adherence to the omnipresent Francoist discourse concerning mothering, which promoted the self-sacrificing "angel of the house" who forsook her own needs to devote herself entirely to the family. After all, these women were supposedly proponents of the progressive values fomented by the Second Republic, yet in the testimonies there is a patent paucity of any political references or indeed comments on gender relations. Neither did they enjoy reproductive freedom. As one woman comments: "I had six children and 10 miscarriages. I breastfed them for two years, and while I breastfed, I didn't get pregnant. It was afterwards. You could abort by putting parsley into yourself, but if anyone found out, you could go to prison."[11]

It is tenable to suggest that perhaps survival, a task of almost Herculean proportions, superseded all other concerns, a typical case of Maslow's hierarchy of needs. And indeed the testimony of Mariá García would seem to corroborate this supposition: "After the war, they imprisoned my husband and I was left with five children, the youngest was only fifteen days old. They wrecked the house a few times. I had to feed my children and send food to their father. I had to go on the *estraperlo* (black market) and every day, I sold bread. And one day, they took everything from me. I then had to work, to wash clothes from dusk till dawn and they only gave me five pesetas."[12]

García's entry into the public sphere, albeit into the covert black market, also showcases the other means by which the Republican mother undermined the regime's relegation of women to the public sphere—namely, by engaging in the other public sphere, the illegal black market that was a widespread social phenomenon, and using the money earned there to economically maintain their private sanctum: the home. Some mothers worked in factories and even managed to get their sons and daughters jobs there, while others cleaned houses. Ironically, the fact that the Republican mother existed outside the boundaries of prescriptive Francoist femininity afforded her a scintilla of independence and self-reliance, inconceivable for Nationalist women. In order to fully appreciate just how novel this degree of gender autonomy was in Spain of that period, it is apposite to contrast the Republican mother's situation with that of the Nationalist mother. Luce Irigaray maintains that women do not really actively participate in the community but are instead completely excluded with not even the remotest possibility of integration. Certainly, in Francoist Spain, the circumscription of women to the private sphere was rigidly enforced by a myriad of previously mentioned measures.

De Beauvoir envisaged dangerous consequences in the limitation of the mother to the private sphere and suggested that the mother must have some relationship with the community in order to retain a sense of well-being. Therefore, the Nationalist mother, who was confined to the private sphere, suffered psychosomatic symptoms, which can be attributed to dissatisfaction with her restriction to the private sphere. Given that Nationalist mothers were deprived of any chance to articulate their desires, many were transformed into the "castrated mother who suffers regression, degenerates." Their "castration" manifested itself in psychosomatic illnesses, an apathetic attitude toward life in general, and in some cases a barely concealed bitterness. Esther Tusquets remembers the disillusionment of her Nationalist bourgeois and exquisitely cultured mother, who did not find sufficient self-fulfillment in the maternal role. At antipodes to the disillusionment of the Nationalist mother is the pride of the Republican mother in her ability to maintain her family in such dire circumstances. Ana María Hernández Muñoz regarded the fact that "each of my children had a plate and a fork, and a lot of people did not have that," as an accomplishment. Ana María also emphasized her ingenuity, her ability to use the available resources to provide for her family: "I found a republican flag in the drawer. It was silk and it had been there a long time. My husband said that I should throw it out quickly lest anybody see it, but I just tore off the purple and with the red and yellow parts, I made a dress for my daughter." Moreover, their ability to maintain their family is praised and very much appreciated by their children, and there is none of the resentment toward their parents that is often evident in testimonials of children brought up in Nationalist families. As María Flores affirms, "she did everything in order to feed us." Adorno affirms that when the objective of the family is value indoctrination, it induces the child to feel a superficial closeness with the parent, which later transforms into a festering resentment. One could surmise that the Republican mother's disengagement from the constant reiteration of the edicts of the regime and her provision of a subtle counter discourse fomented trust within the family.[13]

## Dissenting Republican Mothers

By the end of the civil war, between 150 and 188 prison camps had been built, which housed 367,000 Republican prisoners. The regime was primarily concerned with the identification and containment of all those who might pose a potential threat to the New State. Staff of the concentration camps treated inmates with unmitigated cruelty, with random shootings, beatings, and meagre rations being commonplace. Indeed, the form that their mistreatment took (head-shaving, compulsory uniforms, etc.) would seem to correspond to a desire to dehumanize the enemy. Ángela Cenarro postulates that this mistreatment was motivated by a desire to "consolidate the dichotomy between those who won the war and those who had lost." Compounding the degradation of the prisoners were the overcrowded conditions; to cite just one example, the concentration camp of La Magdalena in Santander, which had been built to accommodate only 600 men, actually housed 1,600. The church entered wholeheartedly into the process of redeeming prisoners, with the Society of Jesus supplying chaplains to the prisons and women's prisons being overseen by nuns. This being so, the primary objectives of the prison system—namely, the extirpation of any ideological adherence to the Republic and the imposition of the Catholic values of the nascent state—reflected the syncretic merger of church and state. In actual fact, their aims complemented each other, as the re-Catholicization of the prisoners conveniently served to mask the political nature of their punishment. For example, although many of the putative "crimes" were political in nature, the allegations against the women prisoners were couched in judgmental, moralistic language: they were alluded to as "deviant women." Moreover, religious inculcation and proselytization were very much the order of the day: in 1941, a law was introduced that stipulated that attendance at religion classes was mandatory in order to be considered for early release; participation in choirs was favorably viewed, and mass attendance became compulsory.[14]

Unlike the acquiescent Republican mothers, who, as I have illustrated, succeeded in preserving the home as a private sanctum, dissident Republican mothers were confronted with an environment from which no reprieve could be obtained. Space, which always reflects the extant social power structure, was controlled absolutely by a hostile force that aimed to eradicate their ideological convictions. Therefore the most intimate and joyous moments of being a mother, such as spending time with the child following his or her birth, were denied to them. Nieves Waldemer Santisteban remembers how she was treated following the birth of her son: "They separated us almost immediately. I had to go down after half an hour and they put me in a cell with four sick women. I only had to eat what another prisoner gave me, two tomatoes, and that was my only meal after giving birth to my son."[15]

The exercising of the maternal function was dependent on the capriciousness of the nuns: Tomása Cuevas recalls one mother who refused to go to mass because of her child's illness. She was consequently beaten and imprisoned in a cage. As the women prisoners were rarely told the date of their execution, the forced removal of their children signified the mother's imminent demise. Interestingly, even the fear generated by this news did not reduce the mother's fear for her child's future; moreover, testimonies denote the aforementioned selflessness, for most of the mothers do not lament their own condition but concentrate exclusively on the child's future. The memoirs of Fr. Gumersindo de Estella testify to this all-consuming concern:

> Each of the two women prisoners had, in their arms, a one year old child. They were their daughters. And I asked "What are they going to do with these children?" Somebody told me that two members of the clergy had already been contacted to take them away, but taking away their children wasn't as easy a task as one might suppose. I heard frightening screams: "My daughter, don't take her away from me! I want to take her to the other world!" Another shouted: "I don't want to leave my daughter with these monsters. Kill her with me: oh, my daughter, what will become of you?"[16]

However, despite the fact that the obstacles they faced were greater, they, like the acquiescent Republican mothers, managed to enact resistance by articulating and even performing, on occasions, their dissidence. Antonio García, a prisoner in the designated "Mothers' Prison," Las Ventas, in Madrid, remembers some of their surreptitious activities:

> In Ventas, we had some secret festivals, in the gallery that you just wouldn't believe. One time, we did a play.
> María Valés acted the fascist, and she was horrible, and Angelina Vázquez was the Republic, and she was beautiful. We had costume competitions with the material they gave us for sewing, and we made funny toys. You just can't imagine the things we did in that gallery. We even acted out García Lorca's plays with beautiful costumes.[17]

Their ability to manipulate part of the space of the prison, which was in Foucauldian terms a panoptic that allows the individual no agency but instead imposes its institutional dictates, testifies to these mothers' intrepidness. The mothers manipulated not only space but also temporality by dividing the day into compliance with the institution until closure and articulation of their dissent after nine o'clock. María Salva, a prisoner in Las Ventas, explains their bifurcated day: "Our lives as people began exactly when they closed the prison doors and we were isolated from the rest. Then, we began our political, cultural artistic lives, readings and everything. We made a world within a world."[18] The measures taken to combat such resistance, such as *turismo penitenciario* (penitentiary tourism), the regular transferal of prisoners that ensured that the prisoners never remained in one prison long enough to form a resistance group, proved counterproductive, because their short stay in the prison did not impede their organization of other less savvy prisoners. To cite just one example, the highly organized women prisoners of the Las Ventas prison in Madrid introduced order and a support system into the chaotic Malága prison. Guided by a communist ethos, they ensured that each *camarade* cared for a child; they bathed the children and cut their nails; and they also read letters for the illiterate women. Therefore the mothers overcame their difficulties by female solidarity and by manipulating both space and temporality in order to express their individuality and to not allow their identities to be subsumed by the incessant repression.

## Conclusion

The testimonies of these mothers demonstrate fortitude in the face of almost insurmountable difficulties, such as repression and social control, which combined with spectacular efficacy to reduce daily life for the defeated Republicans to a never-ending spiral of hardships, social stigma, and fear in the postwar period. Their resourcefulness, as has been amply acknowledged by their children, was the determinant factor in the survival of the Republican family. Their battle to eke out a meager, subsistence-style living caused them to transcend the gender segregation of the era, as they engaged in the public sphere by working in a variety of often exploitative jobs. Neither did they cede to the oppositional Francoist ethos, but rather circumvented the onslaught of the public sphere by conserving the intimacy of the home in order to transmit their political ideals. If we consider their utilization of space in conjunction with the acquiescent Republican mother's preservation of the home as a separate space, it also indicates a gendering of space. As the Republicans suffered *exilio interior* (internal exile), which was tantamount to a total exclusion from the public sphere and their attendant disempowerment, the private sphere became their refuge. This reconfiguration of space effectively means that the public space became the inhospitable, patriarchal sphere while the private sphere, for the Republican mothers, evolved into a space that represented the feminine qualities of nurturing and caring. The Republican mother enacted this dichotomization of space even in institutions of the public sphere such as prisons, which, in their absolute and implacable control of space, could be considered nearly impermeable to resistance. Their resilience proves that maternal love, in the words of Erich Fromm, not only constitutes "the most elevated form of love" but can also serve to create an ability to withstand and survive the most traumatic of situations.[19]

## NOTES

1. Carolina Martín Carretero, *Las Mujeres Jóvenes: Empleo, Educación y Familia. Avances y Retrocesos en la Igualdad de Oportunidades* (Madrid: Instituto de la Juventud, 1999), 9; Lluís Flaquer and Julio Iglesias de Ussel, "Familia y Análisis Sociológico: El Caso de España," *Revista Española de Investigaciones Sociológicas* 61, no. 3 (1993): 60; Helen Graham, "Gender and the State: Women in the 1940s," in *Spanish Cultural Studies: an Introduction. The Struggle for Modernity*, ed. Helen Graham and Jo Labanyi (Oxford: Oxford University Press, 1995), 184; María José Gámez Fuentes, "Representaciones de lo Materno en Narrativas Literarias y Fílmicas de la Democracia Contemporánea: España, 1975–1995" (PhD diss., University of Nottingham, 1999), 14; Daniéle Bussy Genevois, "The Women of Spain from the Republic to Franco," in *A History of Women in the West V: Towards a Cultural Identity in the Twentieth Century*, ed. George Duby, Michelle Perrot, and Françoise Thébaud (Cambridge, MA: Belknap Press of Harvard, 1994), 178. Although the Second Republic conceded much freedom to women, theorists concur that this did not eradicate traditional thinking and moreover did not expedite equality in the workplace. See Mary Nash, "Pronatalismo y Maternidad en la España Franquista," in *Maternidad y Políticas de Género: La Mujer en los Estados de Bienestar Europeos, 1880–1950*, ed. Gisela Bock and Pat Thane (Valencia: Ediciones Cátedra, 1987), 282. Divorce was only availed of in traditional, left-wing cities; in Madrid, a relatively liberal city, only 8 out of every 1,000 troubled marriages ended in divorce. See Genevoise, "The Women of Spain from the Republic to Franco," 182.
2. Jeffrey Alexander, "Toward a Theory of Cultural Trauma," in *Cultural Trauma and Collective Identity*, ed. Jeffrey Alexander (Berkeley: University of California Press, 2004), 28; Bruno Chabornneau and Geneviève Parent, "Introduction: Peacebuilding, Healing, Reconciliation," in *Peacebuilding, Memory and Reconciliation: Bridging Top-Down and Bottom-Up Approaches*, ed. Chabonneau and Parent (London: Routledge, 2011), 11; E. Ann Kaplan, *Trauma Culture: The Politics of Terror and Loss in Media and Literature* (New Brunswick, NJ: Rutgers University Press, 2005), 39; Claire Stocks, "Trauma Theory and the

Singular Self: Rethinking Extreme Experiences in the Light of Cross Cultural Identity," *Textual Practice* 21, no. 1 (2007): 76.
3. Gisela Kaplan, *Contemporary Western European Feminism* (New York: New York University Press, 1992), 199; Amparo Moreno Sardá, "La Réplica de las Mujeres al Franquismo," in *El feminismo en España: Dos Siglos de Historia*, ed. Pilar Folguera (Madrid: Editorial Pablo Iglesias, 1988), 97; Rafael Abella, *La vida cotidiana en España bajo el régimen de Franco* (Madrid: Temas de Hoy, 1985), 221; Rafael Torres, *El Amor en Tiempos de Franco* (Madrid: Grupo Anaya, 2002), 126.
4. Jacques Donzelot, *La Policía de las Familias* (Valencia: Ediciones Pre-Textos, 1998), 53; Sheila Kitzinger, *Women as Mothers* (Oxford: Martin Robertson, 1978), 63; Adrienne Rich, *Of Woman Born: Motherhood as Institution and Experience* (London: Virago, 1977), 45; Antonio Vallejo Nágera, *Política Racial del Nuevo Estado* (San Sebastián: Editorial Española, 1938), 78; Genevoise, "The Women of Spain from the Republic to Franco," 191; Raquel Osborne, "Good Girls versus Bad Girls in Early Francoist Prisons: Sexuality as a Great Divide," *Sexualities* 14, no. 5 (2011): 519. Marxism was actually considered a virus during this period. A psychiatrist named Antonio Vallejo Nágera carried out experiments on Republican prisoners in order to establish the causes of Marxism. He concluded that Marxism was a hereditary virus, and consequently, he recommended extreme vigilance of the Republican family and even its dismemberment and the reconversion of the Republican child. See Lorraine Ryan, "The Sins of the Father: The Destruction of the Republican Family in Franco's Spain," *The History of the Family* 14, no. 3 (2009): 245–52. Moreover, the infertility of Republican women is a recurrent trope in contemporary Spanish literature. For example, Ángeles López's 2006 novel, *Martina, la rosa número trece*, depicts how the protagonist, a 22-year-old woman named Martina Borroso García intuits her own infertility, after having been subject to repeated assaults by a torturer named Aurelio Rodríguez.
5. Michel Foucault, *Language, Counter-Memory, Practice* (Ithaca, NY: Cornell University Press, 1980), 153; Francisco Ferrándiz, "The Intimacy of Defeat: Exhumations in Contemporary Spain," in *Unearthing Franco's Legacy: Mass Graves and the Recuperation of Historical Memory in Spain*, ed. Carlos Jerez Ferrán and Samuel Amago (Notre Dame: University of Notre Dame Press, 2010), 309; James Wilkinson, "A Choice of Fictions: Historians, Memory, and Evidence," *Publications of the Modern Language Association of America* (1996): 80–92; María Teresa Gallego Méndez, *Mujer, falange y franquismo* (Madrid: Taurus Ediciones, 1983), 143.
6. Teresa Del Valle, *Gendered Anthropology* (London: Routledge, 1993), 139; Enrique González Duro, *El miedo en la posguerra: Franco y la España derrotada: la política del exterminio* (Madrid: Oberón, 2003), 230–32. All translations are the author's own.

7. James C. Scott, *Domination and the Arts of Resistance* (New Haven: Yale University Press, 1990), 53; Paul Ricoeur, *Memory, History, Forgetting* (Chicago: University of Chicago Press, 2004), 81, 85; Ernst Van Alphen, "Symptoms of Discursivity: Experience, Memory and Trauma," in *Acts of Memory: Cultural Recall in the Present*, ed. Mieke Bal (London: University Press of New England, 1999), 27.
8. Francisco Sevillano Calero, *Exterminio: El Terror con Franco* (Madrid: Oberón, 2005), 86; Jorge M. Reverte and Socorro Tomás, *Hijos de la Guerra: Testimonios y Recuerdos* (Madrid: Temas de Hoy, 2001), 35, 41.
9. Sevillano Calero, *Exterminio*, 151. *Los Reyes Magos*, January 6, is a national holiday in Spain. Children receive presents from the Three Wise Men.
10. Temma Kaplan, "Reversing the Shame and Gendering the Memory," *Signs* 28, no. 1 (2002): 184; Reverte and Tomás, *Hijos de la Guerra*, 29.
11. Encarnación Barranquero Texeira and Lucía Prieto Borrego, *Así Sobrevivimos al Hambre: Estrategias de Supervivencia de las Mujeres en la Postguerra Española* (Málaga: Servicio de Publicaciones, Centro de Ediciones de la Diputación de Málaga, 2008), 163.
12. González Duro, *El miedo en la posguerra*, 160. Abraham Maslow's hierarchy of needs theory contends that the lowest human needs are physiological while the highest center on self-actualization. Therefore, if the basic physiological needs are not satisfied, this will impede the individual embarking on the quest for self-realization or being concerned with more elevated matters such as politics or gender equality.
13. Ibid., 272, 277; Luce Irigaray, *Le Temps de la Différence: Pour une Révolution Pacifique* (Paris: Librairie Générale Française, 1989), 23–24; Simone de Beauvoir, *The Second Sex* (London: Random House, 1949), 59, 501; Esther Tusquets, *Habíamos Ganado la Guerra* (Barcelona: Brugera, 2006), 30; Barrnaquero Texeira and Borrego, *Así Sobrevivimos al Hambre*, 184, 194, 292; Theodor W. Adorno, *The Authoritarian Personality* (New York: W. W. Norton, 1969), 338.
14. Nicolás Sartorius and Javier Alfaya, *La Memoria Insumisa: Sobre la Dictadura de Franco* (Madrid: Espasa-Calpe, 1999), 125; Angela Cenarro, "La Institucionalización del Universo Penitenciario Franquista," in *Una Inmensa Prisión: Los Campos de Concentración y las Prisiones durante la Guerra Civil y el Franquismo*, ed. Carme Molinero (Barcelona: Crítica, 2003), 152; Antonio Ontañón, *Rescatados del Olvido: Fosas Comunes del Cementerio Civil de Santander* (Santander: Universidad de Santander, 2003), 64; Ricard Vinyes, *Irredentas: Las Presas Políticas y sus Hijos en las Cárceles de Franco* (Madrid: Temas de Hoy, 2002), 40, 55, 167.
15. Tomasa Cuevas Guitiérrez, *Testimonios de mujeres en las cárceles franquistas* (Huesca: Instituto de Estudios Altoaragoneses, 2004), 91–92.

See also David Harvey, *Justice, Nature, and the Geography of Difference* (Cambridge, MA: Blackwell, 1996).
16. Cuevas Guitiérrez, *Testimonios de mujeres*, 321; Vinyes, *Irredentas*, 89.
17. Cuevas Guitiérrez, *Testimonios de mujeres*, 339.
18. Vinyes, *Irredentas*, 162.
19. Erich Fromm, *El Arte de Amar: Una Investigación sobre la Naturaleza del Amor* (Buenos Aires: Paidós, 1976), 56–57.

## Selected Bibliography

Abella, Rafael. *La vida cotidiana en España bajo el régimen de franco*. Madrid: Temas de Hoy, 1985.
Adorno, Theodor W. *The Authoritarian Personality*. New York: W. W. Norton, 1969.
Alexander, Jeffrey. "Toward a Theory of Cultural Trauma." In *Cultural Trauma and Collective Identity*, edited by Jeffrey Alexander, 1–30. Berkeley: University of California Press, 2004.
Barranquero Texeira, Encarnación, and Lucía Prieto Borrego. *Así sobrevivimos al hambre: estrategias de supervivencia de las mujeres en la postguerra española*. Malága: Servicio de Publicaciones, Centro de Ediciones de la Diputación de Malága, 2008.
Beauvoir, Simone de. *The Second Sex*. London: Random House, 1949.
Bussy Genevois, Daniéle. "The Women of Spain from the Republic to Franco." In *A History of Women in the West V: Towards a Cultural Identity in the Twentieth Century*, edited by George Duby, Michelle Perrot, and Françoise Thébaud, 177–93. Cambridge, MA: Belknap Press of Harvard University Press, 1994.
Cenarro, Angela. "La institucionalización del universo penitenciario franquista." In *Una inmensa prisión: los campos de concentración y las prisiones durante la guerra civil y el franquismo*, edited by Carme Molinero, 133–55. Barcelona: Crítica, 2003.
Chabornneau, Bruno, and Geneviéve Parent. "Introduction: Peacebuilding, Healing, Reconciliation." In *Peacebuilding, Memory, and Reconciliation: Bridging Top-Down and Bottom-Up Approaches*, edited by Bruno Charbonneau and Geneviéve Parent, 1–17. London: Routledge, 2011.
Cuevas Guitiérrez, Tomasa. *Testimonios de mujeres en las cárceles franquistas*. Huesca: Instituto de Estudios Altoaragoneses, 2004.
Del Valle, Teresa. *Gendered Anthropology*. London: Routledge, 1993.
Donzelot, Jacques. *La policía de las familias*. Valencia: Ediciones Pre-Textos, 1998.
Elordi, Carlos. *Los años difíciles: el testimonio de los protagonistas anónimos de la guerra civil y la posguerra*. Madrid: Aguilar, 2003.
Ferrándiz, Francisco. "The Intimacy of Defeat: Exhumations in Contemporary Spain." In *Unearthing Franco's Legacy: Mass Graves and the Recovery*

of *Historical Memory in Spain*, edited by Carlos Jerez Farrán and Samuel Amago, 305–32. Notre Dame: University of Notre Dame Press, 2010.

Flaquer, Lluís, and Julio Iglesias de Ussel. "Familia y análisis sociológico: el caso de España." *Revista Española de Investigaciones Sociológicas* 61, no. 3 (1993): 57–75.

Foucault, Michel. *Language, Counter-memory, Practice*. Ithaca: Cornell University Press, 1980.

Fromm, Erich. *El arte de amar: una investigación sobre la naturaleza del amor*. Buenos Aires: Paidós, 1976.

Fuentes, María José Gámez. "Representaciones de lo materno en narrativas literarias y fílmicas de la democracia contemporánea: España, 1975–1995." PhD dissertation, University of Nottingham, 1999.

Gallego Méndez, María Teresa. *Mujer, falange y franquismo*. Madrid: Taurus Ediciones, 1983.

González Duro, Enrique. *El miedo en la posguerra: Franco y la España derrotada: la política del exterminio*. Madrid: Oberón, 2003.

Graham, Helen. "Gender and the State: Women in the 1940s." In *Spanish Cultural Studies: An Introduction: The Struggle for Modernity*, edited by Helen Graham and Jo Labanyi, 182–95. Oxford: Oxford University Press, 1995.

Harvey, David. *Justice, Nature, and the Geography of Difference*. Cambridge, MA: Blackwell, 1996.

Irigaray, Luce. *Le temps de la différence: pour une révolution pacifique*. Paris: Librairie Générale Française, 1989.

Kaplan, E. Ann. *Trauma Culture: The Politics of Terror and Loss in Media and Literature*. New Brunswick, NJ: Rutgers University Press, 2005.

Kaplan, Gisela. *Contemporary Western European Feminism*. New York: New York University Press, 1992.

Kaplan, Temma. "Reversing the Shame and Gendering the Memory." *Signs* 28, no. 1 (2002): 179–99.

Kitzinger, Sheila. *Women as Mothers*. Oxford: Martin Robertson, 1978.

López, Ángeles. *Martina, la rosa número trece*. Madrid: Seix Barral, 2006.

Martín Carretero, Carolina. *Las mujeres jóvenes: empleo, educación y familia. avances y retrocesos en la igualdad de oportunidades*. Madrid: Instituto de la Juventud, 1999.

Martín Gaite, Carmen. *Retahílas*. 2nd ed. Barcelona: Ediciones Destino, 1979.

Moreno Sardá, Amparo. "La réplica de las mujeres al franquismo." In *El feminismo en España: dos siglos de historia*, edited by Pilar Folguera, 85–110. Madrid: Editorial Pablo Iglesias, 1988.

Nash, Mary. "Pronatalismo y maternidad en la España franquista." In *maternidad y políticas de género: la mujer en los estados de bienestar europeos, 1880–1950*, edited by Gisela Bock and Pat Thane, 279–307. Valencia: Ediciones Cátedra, 1987.

Ontañón, Antonio. *Rescatados del olvido: fosas comunes del cementerio civil de santander*. Santander: Universidad de Santander, 2003.

Osborne, Raquel. "Good Girls versus Bad Girls in Early Francoist Prisons: Sexuality as a Great Divide." *Sexualities* 14, no. 5 (2011): 509–25.

Reverte, Jorge M., and Socorro Tomás. *Hijos de la guerra: testimonios y recuerdos*. Madrid: Temas de Hoy, 2001.

Rich, Adrienne. *Of Woman Born: Motherhood as Institution and Experience*. London: Virago, 1977.

Ricoeur, Paul. *Memory, History, Forgetting*. Chicago: University of Chicago Press, 2004.

Ryan, Lorraine. "The Sins of the Father: The Destruction of the Republican Family in Franco's Spain." *The History of the Family* 14, no. 3 (2009): 245–52.

Sartorius, Nicolás, and Javier Alfaya. *La memoria insumisa: sobre la dictadura de franco*. Madrid: Espasa-Calpe, 1999.

Scott, James C. *Domination and the Arts of Resistance*. New Haven: Yale University Press, 1990.

Sevillano Calero, Francisco. *Exterminio: el terror con franco*. Madrid: Oberón, 2005.

Stocks, Claire. "Trauma Theory and the Singular Self: Rethinking Extreme Experiences in the Light of Cross Cultural Identity." *Textual Practice* 21, no. 1 (2007): 71–92.

Torres, Rafael. *El amor en tiempos de Franco*. Madrid: Grupo Anaya, 2002.

Tusquets, Esther. *Habíamos ganado la guerra*. Barcelona: Brugera, 2006.

Vallejo Nágera, Antonio. *Política racial del nuevo estado*. San Sebastián: Editorial Española, 1938.

Van Alphen, Ernst. "Symptoms of Discursivity: Experience, Memory and Trauma." In *Acts of Memory: Cultural Recall in the Present*, edited by Mieke Bal, 24–39. London: University Press of New England, 1999.

Vinyes, Ricard. *Irredentas: Las presas políticas y sus hijos en las cárceles de franco*. Madrid: Temas de Hoy, 2002.

Wilkinson, James. "A Choice of Fictions: Historians, Memory, and Evidence." *Publications of the Modern Language Association of America* (1996): 80–92.

# Chapter 9

## Barbara Hepworth and War

### Themes of Motherhood and Sacrifice in Hepworth's *Madonna and Child*, St. Ives Parish Church

*Lyrica Taylor*

## Introduction

After 1945, artists in Great Britain powerfully addressed the sacrifices of the British people sustained during and after the war. This paper explores an important artwork by one of the most significant postwar artists: Barbara Hepworth's *Madonna and Child* (1954, St. Ives Parish Church).[1] Through her work, Hepworth communicated the central themes of motherhood and sacrifice to create a catalyst for restoration and rebuilding, and community and wholeness, in order to help herself and the British people heal after the tragedies of war. Her artwork also suggests a renewed interest in religious art in the postwar years, brought about by the lingering horrors of World War II and the demand for new churches following the widespread destruction of property. Hepworth's artistic vision deepens an understanding of the vital role the visual arts and beauty played in shaping human experience and awareness of the sacred in an era that witnessed unprecedented devastation and personal suffering.

A preeminent British sculptor of the twentieth century and one of the few British women artists to achieve international prominence, Barbara Hepworth (1903–75) created figurative and abstract sculptures, paintings, and drawings that express the human body and spirit in the landscape. Hepworth trained in sculpture at the Leeds School of Art and at the Royal College of Art in the 1920s, and also studied in Italy during that period. She married the British artist John Skeaping in 1925, and they became leading figures in the new sculptural movement associated with direct carving and with abstraction in London in the 1920s. Hepworth and Skeaping had a son, Paul Skeaping, in 1929.

Hepworth's powerful monolithic sculptures are often biomorphic and female in appearance. The artist eloquently described the source of her inspiration and the overall purpose of her artwork in 1966:

> Whenever I am embraced by land and seascape I draw ideas for new sculptures: new forms to touch and walk round, new people to embrace, with an exactitude of form that those without sight can hold and realize. For me it is the same as the touch of a child in health, not in sickness. The feel of a loved person who is strong and fierce and not tired and bowed down. This is not an aesthetic doctrine, nor is it a mystical idea. It is essentially practical and passionate, and it is my whole life, as expressed in stone, marble, wood and bronze.[2]

## Hepworth, Motherhood, and War

A significant part of Hepworth's adult life was affected by war—both World War II and the Malayan Emergency. In the years just before the war, Hepworth lived in Hampstead in London, an area that became a vibrant center of the arts. Hepworth and Skeaping divorced in 1933. One year later, Hepworth and the painter Ben Nicholson had triplets, and they married in 1938. Together with a group of eminent European exiles who arrived in London in the mid-1930s, including Piet Mondrian, Naum Gabo, and László Moholy-Nagy, escaping oppression from the Nazis, Hepworth and other English artists became the center of a group of artists based in Hampstead committed to avant-garde ideas. Hepworth later remembered many of these artists and these years in Hampstead immediately preceding the war: "Because of the danger of totalitarianism and impending war, all of us worked the harder to lay strong foundations for the future through an understanding of the true relationship between architecture, painting, and sculpture."[3]

The years just before the outbreak of the war proved very difficult for Hepworth and Nicholson in their work as artists. Hepworth reflected,

By early 1939 the Spanish War, Munich, and the ever-increasing threat of a European war not only absorbed most people's energy, but it seemed to extinguish for a while the interest which had been growing during the previous years. From late 1938 until war was declared it became increasingly difficult to sell a painting or a sculpture and make a bare living. At the most difficult moment of this period I did the maquette for the first sculpture with color, and when I took the children to Cornwall five days before war was declared I took the maquette with me, also my hammer and a minimum of stone carving tools.[4]

At the outbreak of war, Hepworth, Nicholson, and their three young children left their home and studio in Hampstead and evacuated to St. Ives, on the Cornish coast. Hepworth communicated the effect that the conflict had on her artwork and outlook, and her continuing strong "will to live":

At that time I was reading very extensively and I became concerned as to the true relationship of the artist and society. I remember expecting the major upheaval of war to change my outlook; but it seemed as though the worse the international scene became the more determined and passionate became my desire to find a full expression of the ideas which had germinated before the war broke out, retaining freedom to do so whilst carrying out what was demanded of me as a human being. I do not think this preoccupation with abstract forms was escapism; I see it as a consolidation of faith in living values, and a completely logical way of expressing the intrinsic "will to live" as opposed to the extrinsic disaster of the war.[5]

Hepworth became focused on the unifying theme of the artist's place within the community. She turned to her local community to help her bear and overcome the difficulties and fears of modern life, which became overwhelming in the immediate postwar years, especially with regards to the Holocaust and the dropping of atomic bombs on Hiroshima and Nagasaki.[6]

During the war, Hepworth also saw the role of family as being a central part of her work as a woman artist.[7] In one of her reflections on her life and artwork, she divided her artistic career into six periods and commented on the integration of her local (and larger) community and her family: "being a woman, every daily event of home and family as well as contemporary events in the world at large have had to be related and resolved within my work."[8] Looking back on the war, Hepworth wrote in 1953 of the importance of sculpture and artwork in general as expressing social and spiritual truths in a time of war and violence: "Only a society in a state of affirmation can produce sculpture—a primitive society or one fighting for its existence . . . on the basis of active belief in both the virility of nature & the spiritual ascendancy of man."[9]

Hepworth was greatly affected by the conflict, artistically, emotionally, and spiritually. She described the great changes that the war had on her outlook: "It is hopeless to presume that I, or anybody, thinks the same as in 1936, either about Art, Philosophy or Religion. You won't have a friend who thinks the same after this war as they did before it."[10] The war most strongly affected Hepworth's view of the importance of the human body. She intentionally went to the cinema to see reportage from the Belsen concentration camp. Seeing images of the Holocaust altered Hepworth's understanding of the human body and of the role of the individual in society. She described her new approach as religious and responded to the evil in the world by wanting to create "as many good sculptures as one can before one dies" and by looking to the human figure and to public art as a means of public and private healing and restoration.

At the end of the war, and with its attendant anxieties, Hepworth demonstrated a new focus on figurative work in painting, drawing, and sculpture.[11] The family became a particularly emotional theme of Hepworth's painting and sculpture, as evidenced in her beautiful and touching sculpture, *Madonna and Child*. Hepworth's emotional stone sculpture *Madonna and Child*, created for the Lady Chapel in St. Ives Parish Church, together with her painting *Two Figures (Heroes)* (1954, Tate), served as a memorial to her oldest son, Paul Skeaping, who was killed in action while on active service with the Royal Air Force during the Malayan Emergency. The memorial is listed in the Imperial War Museum's War Memorials Archive, formerly the UK National Inventory of War Memorials (number 61404). Hepworth also created the tender and sensitive painting *Madonna and Child* (1953, private collection) in oil and graphite on panel as a preparatory painting for her carving *Madonna and Child*.

Paul Skeaping was born to Hepworth and John Skeaping (her first husband) on August 3, 1929. An aircraft designer and professional pilot, Paul was stationed in Bulawayo and RAF Butterworth in the late 1940s and early 1950s. The Malayan Emergency was fought between Commonwealth armed forces and the Malayan National Liberation Army, the military arm of the Malayan Communist Party, from 1948 to 1960, after the creation of the Federation of Malaya in 1948. Paul and his flight navigator, John Williamson, were flying a patrol over Malaya on February 13, 1953, when they crashed. Both flying officers are buried in the Protestant Cemetery in Bangkok, Thailand, and both of their names are included on the Armed Forces Memorial at the National Memorial Arboretum, Alrewas, Staffordshire. While the crash is generally considered to have been accidental, Paul's father, John Skeaping, suggested that it was the result of a terrorist bomb.[12] Like Hepworth, John Skeaping also created a memorial to Paul: a seven-foot wooden crucifix made from cedar, created by burning away the wood instead of carving it away, producing an emotional and agonizing sculpture.

Hepworth gave her memorial sculpture to the Parish Church of St. Ives. By doing so, Hepworth's private grief became a public grief shared by her community. Notably, the subject of the Madonna and Child in war memorials in Britain is quite rare. The British artist Eric Gill created the Briantspuddle War Memorial in Dorset, England, to commemorate those lost in World War I and depicted the Virgin and Child on one side and an image of Christ showing the stigmata on the other. Henry Moore also created a war memorial depicting the Madonna and Child for the parish of Claydon, Suffolk, now in Barham Church, after the war. He was commissioned to create the memorial by Sir Jasper Ridley as a tribute to Ridley's son and those in Claydon who were killed in the war.

The loss of her son influenced Hepworth artistically and emotionally, and she used the sculpture to express a great sense of grief and, simultaneously, of hope. *Madonna and Child* is an uncommon example of a direct correlation between an event in Hepworth's life and her work.[13] A close friend of Hepworth, Margaret Gardiner, recorded that Paul's death was "a lasting grief" to the artist.[14] Hepworth later related that her work often resulted from a period of crisis and adversity that created "the moral climate in which my sculpture is produced."[15] In August of 1954, Hepworth visited Greece to help recover from Paul's death. Hepworth wanted to focus on hope rather than despair throughout her life, including after Paul's death, by creating beautiful sculptures, as communicated through her words just after the end of the war: "Good things always seem concrete to me. Bad things seem amorphous."[16]

In her preparatory painting for the final sculpture, Hepworth beautifully evoked the incredible delicacy and tenderness of the Mother and Child. Multiple lines radiate around Mary's head, creating a halo. A few pencil lines precisely outline the profile of the Child's face as He embraces His Mother, creating a vulnerable and sensitive image. Hepworth preserved all focus on the Mother and Child by avoiding any hint of a background. The pure whiteness of the Mother and

Child gently contrasts with the soft golden background, maintaining the quietness of the image. Hepworth's approach to creating the light in *Madonna and Child* is particularly important because of the theme of motherhood and sacrifice, and the unity between mother and son. Hepworth later commented, "There is an inside and an outside to every form. When they are in special accord, as for instance . . . a child in the womb . . . then I am most drawn to the effect of light. Every shadow cast by the sun from an ever-varying angle reveals the harmony of the inside to outside."[17]

In her painting *Madonna and Child*, Hepworth responded visually to the long Byzantine history of religious icons. The embracing actions of the Mother and Child's arms and the unbroken contour that encloses the two figures suggest strongly that Hepworth was looking specifically to the figures of Mary and Jesus in the renowned *Virgin (Theotokos) and Child (Vladimir Virgin)* icon (late eleventh to early twelfth century). In both Hepworth's *Madonna and Child* and the *Vladimir Virgin*, the artists created tender images of Mary as the Virgin of Compassion who presses her cheek against her Son. Both images communicate a deep pathos as Mary contemplates her Son's future sacrifice. This pathos is made even more explicit on the back of the *Vladimir Virgin*, which depicts the instruments of Christ's Passion.

In turn, Hepworth created an image that evoked her own sorrow at her son's death earlier that year. Hepworth's creation of *Madonna and Child* suggests that she personally identified with Mary's tragic sorrow, as both mothers experienced the death of their firstborn sons. Her poignant work communicates the artist's direct experience of carrying a child in herself and of the separation of birth.[18] This unity and separation are embodied in *Madonna and Child*, as Mary contemplates the future death of her Son. Hepworth's sculptural assistant, David Lewis, later reflected, "[Hepworth's] sorrow over the death of her son Paul in an RAF plane crash over Thailand cast a dark shadow over all of us. Researching her early sculptures I found especially moving the semi-abstract mother and child alabasters, in which the two figures could be separated and reconfigured, yet always belong one to the other . . . In spite of her growing recognition, I have no doubt that Barbara remained deeply lonely. But her sculptures now had an inner nurturing, a quietness, and a rhythm from deep within herself."[19]

It was through witnessing and experiencing the loss of life during the war and the postwar years that Hepworth created and maintained her strong focus on sacrifice and life. This focus is evident in the subject of *Madonna and Child*, in which it is through the future sacrifice of Christ that life after death is made possible, thus giving Hepworth hope that her son's sacrifice in war was not given in vain. In an interview in 1959, Hepworth expressed her resilient "faith in life" and her triumph over fear despite "anti-human or mechanistic" forces:

> The work of the artist today springs from innate impulses towards life, towards growth—impulses whose rhythms and structures have to do with the power and insistence of life. That is how I feel it: Life will always insist on begetting life. By upholding this faith in life we strengthen those who are flagging and becoming cynical because they fear for their lives. They fear for the continuity of life. This continuity contains a tremendous and impelling force . . . That is why it is so important that we find our complete sense of continuity backwards and forwards in this new world of forms and values.[20]

Later in her life, Hepworth paid a stirring tribute to her son's skill as a pilot, her continued anguish regarding his death, and her gratitude for his brave service to his nation:

> Coming back from America after one of my visits . . . I begged permission to go into the cockpit and make a drawing of the sunrise . . . It was one of the great experiences of my life . . . But quite apart from the super-natural colors and shapes, and the sense of real flying, I think I was even more deeply impressed by the utter ease of movement by pilot and co-pilot and navigator in such incredibly restricted space.
>   To go on seemed sensible. To descend a very hard discipline. I would like to be an astronaut and go round the moon, and maybe remain in orbit for ever. But I would not like to land in case the light of the moon went out forever and all poetry die and deeper anguish descend on this anguished earth. But my son Paul once told me that there was a new aesthetic in flying and space and maybe these many brave men will guide us.[21]

On the back of Hepworth's accompanying memorial to her son, *Two Figures (Heroes)*, the artist inscribed, "dedicated to | Paul & John | pilot and navigator, killed February 13th 1953."[22] *Two Figures (Heroes)* demonstrates how throughout her postwar visual expression, Hepworth remained rooted in the human.[23] Hepworth reflected on the cohesion of the two heroes in this painting, explaining, "It is an extension of the same idea which started in November 1934, but extended gradually from within outwards; through the family group and its close knit relationship out to larger group related architecture."[24] The painting also emphasizes the significance of family connections through the image of a picture within a picture. The figure on the left-hand side of the painting seems to be holding a small picture. The imagery of this smaller picture repeats that of the main painting. Thus Hepworth suggests the inclusion of family figures who would otherwise be absent—namely, a portrait of her dead son, Paul.[25] Hepworth made a deliberate return to the figurative in both *Madonna and Child* and *Two Figures (Heroes)*.

Five years after creating *Madonna and Child*, Hepworth created another explicitly religious work that commemorated the death of Paul. *Figure (Requiem)* (1957, Aberdeen Art Gallery) refers to his death through its reference to a mass for the repose of the souls of the dead, a funeral hymn, an elegiac poem, or a more general act of remembrance. By giving her sculpture this title, Hepworth communicated not only her continued sorrow for the death of her son but also her desire for rest to be granted to his soul after suffering. This desire is also evident in a letter that Hepworth wrote regarding her determination to conquer despair and unhappiness: "My sculpture has often seemed to me like offering a prayer at moments of great unhappiness. When there has been a threat to life—like the atomic bomb dropped on Hiroshima . . . my reaction has been to swallow despair, to make something that rises up, something that will win. In another age . . . I would simply have carved cathedrals."[26]

Even before Paul's death, Hepworth communicated her compassion for those who suffered in times of war. In 1938, she created *Project (Monument to the Spanish Civil War)* (1938–39, destroyed in war), which reflected her commitment to the Republican cause. In 1952, the year before her son's death, Hepworth created her *Maquette for "The Unknown Political Prisoner"* (Tate), which was displayed in the *Unknown Political Prisoner* competition organized by the Institute of Contemporary Arts and held at Tate Britain from March 14 to April 30, 1953. The competition received 3,500 applications from 57 countries, and Hepworth received a second prize award of £750. One month before the competition opened, Hepworth's son Paul died.

*Madonna and Child* was not the last sculpture that Hepworth created in tribute to a loved one or friend who had sacrificed their life for others. In June of 1964, 11 years after Paul's death, Hepworth attended the unveiling of her monumental sculpture *Single Form* at the United Nations building in New York. This work had been commissioned in memory of Hepworth's friend, Dag Hammarskjöld, the Secretary General of the United Nations, who had been killed in 1961. Hepworth's commitment to remembering those lost while seeking international peace is strongly communicated in *Single Form*.

Hepworth's focus throughout her artistic career on the themes of motherhood and sacrifice began with her sculpture *Infant* (1929), based on her son Paul. Notably, in *Infant* Hepworth depicted her confident infant son as sitting upright, rather than lying down. By doing so, she gave the infant a sense of authority deriving from the long iconography of the Christ Child.[27] Thus Hepworth developed a close connection between herself and her son as the Madonna and Child from a very early stage of Paul's life, with the isolation of the single figure of Paul in *Infant* suggesting Christ's future sacrifice.

Hepworth wrote extensively of her own experience as a woman artist and on the themes of motherhood and sacrifice, reflecting,

The feminine point of view is a complementary one to the masculine. Perhaps in the visual arts many women have been intimidated by the false idea of competing with the masculine. There is no question of competition. The woman's approach presents a different emphasis. I think that women will contribute a great deal to this understanding through the visual arts, and perhaps especially in sculpture, for there is a whole range of formal perception belonging to feminine experience. So many ideas spring from an inside response to form; for example, if I see a woman carrying a child in her arms it is not so much what I see that affects me, but what I feel within my own body. There is an immediate transference of sensation, a response within to the rhythm of weight, balance and tension of large and small forms making an interior organic whole. The transmutation of experience is, therefore, organically controlled and contains new emphasis of forms. It may be that the *sensation* of being a woman presents yet another facet of the sculptural idea. In some respects it is a form of "being" rather than observing, which in sculpture should provide its own emotional and logical development of form.[28]

Hepworth believed that women artists were privileged, as she expressed reflecting on the experience of motherhood: "The sculptor sets out to appeal to all the senses of the spectator, in fact to his whole body, not merely to his sight and his sense of touch."[29] This sense of the privilege of being a woman artist was formed in Hepworth at an early age, and she later wrote in her autobiography, "A woman artist is not deprived by cooking and having children . . . one is in fact nourished by this rich life, provided one always does some work each day; even a single half hour, so that images grow in one's mind."[30]

While the theme of maternity was a foundational aspect of the modernist carvings of Hepworth's contemporaries Jacob Epstein and Henry Moore, who depict the figures of pregnant women as symbols of creation and nurturing, Hepworth's overall approach to the theme is more complex, depicting mother and child as unified within one sculpture and yet as distinct figures. Hepworth created both figurative and abstract sculptures approaching the theme of maternity, in which small forms are enfolded, nurtured, and protected by a larger one.[31]

Despite the great suffering Hepworth experienced throughout the war and the postwar years, most particularly the death of her son Paul, the artist communicated a great sense of hope in her sculptures, especially in *Madonna and Child*. Her sculpture is simultaneously an expression of war, community, life, hope, and, perhaps most surprisingly, praise, as she wrote in 1966 on the purpose behind her artwork being of "praising God and his universe. Every work in sculpture is, and must be, an act of praise and an awareness of man in his landscape."[32] In a sculpture that powerfully communicates the importance of the human, the individual, and the incarnational, Hepworth focused on life and made hope visible, both an individual and a worldwide hope, in a triumph of life over death.

Hepworth expressively articulated this hope in 1966, writing, "A sculptor's landscape embraces all things that grow and live . . . the shape of the buds already formed in autumn, the thrust and fury of spring growth, the adjustment of trees and rocks and human beings to the fierceness of winter . . . as well as the supreme perception of man, woman and child of this expanding universe."[33] The very act of creating the sculpture *Madonna and Child* demonstrated how Hepworth understood war, life, and death and, despite the death of her son, communicated her deep hope, as she stated in 1959:

> Sculpture communicates an immediate sense of life—you can feel the pulse of it. It is perceived, above all, by the sense of touch which is our earliest sensation; and touch gives us a sense of living contact and security . . . That has nothing to do with the question of perfection, or harmony, or purity, or escapism. It lies far deeper; it is the primitive instinct which allows man to live fully with all his perceptions active and alert, and in the calm acceptance of the balance of life and death. In its insistence on elementary values, sculpture is perhaps more important today than before because life's continuity is threatened and this has given us a sense of unbalance.[34]

Overall, Hepworth intended her sculpture to be regenerative: "It's something you experience through your senses, but it's also a life-giving, purposeful force."[35]

Hepworth's sculpture *Madonna and Child* is cathartic, and by placing her war memorial in the Parish Church of St. Ives, Hepworth invited her community to share in her grief and hope. Indeed, *Madonna and Child* communicates the importance of community during a time of war and suffering. By giving her sculpture to St. Ives Parish Church, Hepworth demonstrated the importance she placed on the sacred, on the need for beautiful public sculpture, and on the need for grieving as a community after great sacrifice. Almost every British village has at least one war memorial, perhaps two, dedicated to those who fought and died in World War I and II. By placing the memorial to her son in a church, Hepworth made a private memorial public. Notably, she included in her memorial the grieving Mother, thus inviting all the mothers who had lost sons and daughters as a result of war to grieve with her, and made the memorial broadly relatable by portraying the Madonna and Child, rather than an individual image of her own son Paul. Hepworth's memorial brings hope to the viewer and focuses on the individual and the incarnational, as well as the public and the community.

Hepworth desired to explore the themes of motherhood and sacrifice in art as a means of expressing her deepest feelings, exploring the mysteries of the physical and spiritual realms, responding passionately to life's experiences, and endeavoring to make sense out of the fragmented pieces of earthly existence after the war. She rethought the concepts of motherhood and sacrifice not merely as sentimental or simply visually pretty or pleasing but instead as postwar catalysts for restoration and rebuilding, community and wholeness, and inspiration and imagination, signifying a spiritual reality. Hepworth's noteworthy sculpture *Madonna and Child* reveals an attempt to draw near and experience the holy, the presence of God. Overall, Hepworth's works of art demonstrate how the themes of motherhood and sacrifice form a particularly important topic in postwar British art and culture. Hepworth's complex artistic meditations on birth, motherhood, separation, and sacrifice grew into powerful symbols of postwar hope and renewal in Great Britain.

## Notes

1. An image of this sculpture can be found at the website organized by the Hepworth Estate: http://barbarahepworth.org.uk/sculptures/1954/madonna-and-child.
2. Barbara Hepworth, *Drawings from a Sculptor's Landscape* (New York: Frederick A. Praeger, 1967), 11.

3. Barbara Hepworth, *A Pictorial Autobiography* (New York: Frederick A. Praeger, 1970), 37.
4. Barbara Hepworth, *Carvings and Drawings* (London: Lund Humphries, 1952), Facing Plate 36.
5. Ibid., Facing Plate 60.
6. Matthew Gale and Chris Stephens, *Barbara Hepworth: Works in the Tate Gallery Collection and the Barbara Hepworth Museum St. Ives* (London: Tate Gallery, 1999), 17.
7. Ibid., 137.
8. Hepworth, *Carvings and Drawings*, vii.
9. Gale and Stephens, *Barbara Hepworth*, 179.
10. Quoted in Penelope Curtis, *Barbara Hepworth* (London: Tate Gallery, 1998), 16.
11. Hepworth, *Drawings from a Sculptor's Landscape*, 19.
12. John Skeaping, *Drawn from Life: An Autobiography* (London: Collins, 1977), 207.
13. Curtis, *Barbara Hepworth*, 36.
14. Margaret Gardiner, *Barbara Hepworth: A Memoir* (Edinburgh: Salamander, 1982), 18.
15. Edwin B. Mullins et al., *Barbara Hepworth Exhibition 1970* (Hakone, Japan: Hakone Open-Air Museum, 1970).
16. Curtis, *Barbara Hepworth*, 7.
17. Hepworth, *Carvings and Drawings*, Facing Plate 1.
18. Chris Stephens, ed., *Barbara Hepworth, Centenary* (London: Tate Gallery, 2003), 51.
19. Ibid., 11–12.
20. J. P. Hodin, *Barbara Hepworth* (New York: David McKay, 1961), 23.
21. Hepworth, *A Pictorial Autobiography*, 81.
22. Gale and Stephens, *Barbara Hepworth*, 134–37.
23. Ibid., 137.
24. Hepworth, *Carvings and Drawings*, Facing Plate 36.
25. Gale and Stephens, *Barbara Hepworth*, 137.
26. Barbara Hepworth, Letter to Herbert Read, December 30, 1946, Sir Herbert Read Archive, University of Victoria, British Columbia.
27. Ann Wagner, "Miss Hepworth's Stone Is a Mother," in *Barbara Hepworth Reconsidered*, ed. David Thistlewood (Liverpool: Liverpool University Press and Tate Gallery Liverpool, 1996), 54.
28. Hepworth, *Carvings and Drawings*, Facing Plates 134 and 135.
29. Edouard Roditi, *Dialogues on Art* (London: Seeker and Warburg, 1960), 100.
30. Hepworth, *A Pictorial Autobiography*, 20.
31. Stephens, *Barbara Hepworth, Centenary*, 51.
32. Hepworth, *Drawings from a Sculptor's Landscape*, 10.
33. Ibid., 12.

34. J. P. Hodin, *Barbara Hepworth* (New York: David McKay, 1961), 23–24.
35. Alan Bowness, ed., *The Complete Sculpture of Barbara Hepworth 1960–69* (London: Lund Humphries, 1971), 14.

## Selected Bibliography

Bowness, Alan, ed. *The Complete Sculpture of Barbara Hepworth 1960–69.* London: Lund Humphries, 1971.
Curtis, Penelope. *Barbara Hepworth.* London: Tate Gallery, 1998.
Gale, Matthew, and Chris Stephens. *Barbara Hepworth: Works in the Tate Gallery Collection and the Barbara Hepworth Museum St. Ives.* London: Tate Gallery, 1999.
Gardiner, Margaret. *Barbara Hepworth: A Memoir.* Edinburgh: Salamander, 1982.
Hepworth, Barbara. *Carvings and Drawings.* London: Lund Humphries, 1952.
———. *Drawings from a Sculptor's Landscape.* New York: Frederick A. Praeger, 1967.
———. *A Pictorial Autobiography.* New York: Frederick A. Praeger, 1970.
Hodin, J. P. *Barbara Hepworth.* New York: David McKay, 1961.
Mullins, Edwin. "Barbara Hepworth." In *Barbara Hepworth Exhibition 1970.* Hakone, Japan: Hakone Open-Air Museum, 1970.
Roditi, Edouard. *Dialogues on Art.* London: Seeker and Warburg, 1960.
Skeaping, John. *Drawn from Life: An Autobiography.* London: Collins, 1977.
Stephens, Chris, ed. *Barbara Hepworth, Centenary.* London: Tate Gallery, 2003.
Thistlewood, David, ed. *Barbara Hepworth Reconsidered.* Liverpool: Liverpool University Press and Tate Gallery Liverpool, 1996.

# Chapter 10

## War Opponents and Proponents
### Israeli Military Mothers from Rivka Guber to "Four Mothers"

*Udi Lebel*[1]

### Introduction

Due to public pressure, primarily by the protest movement led by reserve troops and bereaved parents, a committee was established to examine the failure of the IDF (Israel Defense Forces) in the Second Lebanon War in 2006. Surprisingly, members of the committee noted a number of times in their summarizing report that Israel's failure in the war stemmed from the fact that "the IDF was managed during the war as one for whom the concern for casualties was an essential component of planning and part of the considerations of the campaigns." Thus they complained that "for all the sensitivity that one must feel for the lives of the soldiers, and the necessity to include this factor among all the guiding considerations, it is still difficult to accept the exceptional influence that this consideration had on the decisions made by the senior officers and the political decision makers."[2]

Between 1982 and 2000, during which the IDF maintained a presence in Lebanon, bereaved Israeli mothers of fallen sons and of soldiers serving there organized social protest movements, which succeeded in undermining the legitimacy of remaining in Lebanon as well as fighting there. Under the influence of "The Four Mothers," military theory and warfare doctrines were changed in a number of aspects and policy decisions were even undertaken, such as the withdrawal from Lebanon in 2000. This movement presented a maternal-feminist discourse and attempted to draft mothers of soldiers in order to join together in collective activities against the Israeli presence in Lebanon. They created a link between "Lebanon" and "Death," clarifying to each mother of a soldier in Lebanon that she is a potential bereaved mother. The bereaved mothers who led the "The Four Mothers" openly expressed their pain over their loss, deviating from the hegemonic discourse that glorified military bereavement. They explained that there was no meaning to death in Lebanon and encouraged mothers of soldiers as well as other bereaved mothers to join them in order to make clear to policymakers that they would not grant legitimization to defense policies as long as that would obligate their sons to serve in Lebanon. For example, in 1999, an active mother for the withdrawal of the IDF from Lebanon expressed, "When my son was in Lebanon, I felt as if the death penalty had been decreed upon an innocent person . . . My sense of loss was very strong . . . as if this loss had indeed taken place . . . but he did not die . . . I must fight for his life." The possibility of loss in military service became an inseparable part of various fears of Israeli mothers, who repeatedly saw on television bereaved mothers leaving funerals of soldiers who had fallen in Lebanon, holding up signs at the military cemetery entrances that read, "We do not have children for unnecessary wars." This development caused the establishment to have "Casualty Panic" and to be concerned that each loss of a soldier in Lebanon would diminish the legitimacy given by the mothers, family, and civilian society to serve there.[3]

The phenomenon of "The Four Mothers" was the continuation of events that had already taken place with the IDF's entrance into Lebanon and the First Lebanese War in 1982. Then under the umbrella organization of "Mothers against Silence," mothers of soldiers and casualties had worked to emphasize the price of bereavement for what was presented by them as a "War by Choice." The mothers daily tallied the death toll of fallen soldiers on signs held in continual protests taking place under Prime Minister Menachem Begin, thereby transforming themselves into a significant mass communications network as well as a cultural presence. They were interviewed by radio and television and made speeches at rallies on behalf of ending the war—often days after their sons had fallen. "Lebanonization of military motherhood" was a process that formed a new community of the bereaved, refashioning the role of bereaved mothers in addition to their public and self-images. They became the victims of the Israeli establishment, while the establishment leaders were considered perpetrators of their sons' deaths. Mothers accepted "new" expectations concerning proper behavior—to protect their living sons from the establishment's aggressiveness by protesting the Israeli presence in Lebanon or to grant meaning to their sons' deaths by joining the antiestablishment protest movement that would save the lives of others serving in Lebanon.

The influence of the mothers on the establishment was dramatic, especially in light of the fact that the main personalities of the bereaved mothers' movement belonged to the upper middle class, to the elite—the social strata identified with most middle and senior officers of the army, such as fighters in the elite forces. If indeed they had been able to influence their colleagues to convince their sons to refuse military service in Lebanon, it would have been a strategic influence, since the army was embedded in these social networks.[4]

The bereaved mother's discourse greatly influence military doctrine, which began to become more "Post-Heroic," essentially employing artillery and the air force, even becoming addicted to technological warfare, while refraining as much as possible from sending ground forces into battle. One of the "The Four Mothers" movement's leaders even expressed her views on this subject:

> Our questions weakened the IDF . . . Israeli society cannot absorb fallen soldiers because of all these years that soldiers were sent to their deaths for an unjustifiable cause. Because of this, in the first week [of the Second Lebanon War] the IDF attempted to fight a war of jets since it knew that we are unable to take casualties. In a certain sense, we, "The Four Mothers," have a part in this . . . we are all scorched by Lebanon. We are all scarred by Lebanon. The army also, the soldiers too . . . being exposed to crying soldiers and as soldier of mothers, has weakened our endurance.[5]

After what was considered a defeat in the Second Lebanese War in 2006, and especially on the tenth anniversary of the withdrawal from Lebanon, there began a social and mass communications debate in which one side designated the mothers of soldiers and casualties as accountable for various constraints that prevented the IDF from defeating Hamas and Hezbollah. The issue arose because the defeat in the war negated the meaning of the withdrawal from Lebanon, which was supposed to ensure quiet on the northern border as well as saving the lives of soldiers. This peace was broken by the war, which forced the Israelis to return to fight Hezbollah in Lebanon—this time from inferior positions, while enemy missiles rained down on Israel from the very position abandoned by Israel in 2000. Thus former Deputy Minister of Defense Reserve General Ephraim Sneh wrote, "The opinion of the general public, whose feelings for mutual responsibility had weakened, formed the 'The Four Mothers' movement, which placed the worry for the lives of the sons, the most deepest, basic of human feelings, above all consideration of national security, which in turn, almost became a contemptible concept." Ron Ben-Yisahi, a senior military commentator who wrote on the most popular Israeli Internet site, joined him in this critique: "To this very day, I cringe with shame when I remember that night in May 2000. I cannot forget the soldier in the tank brigade, who shouted from the turret of his tank into his cell phone: 'Mom, I'm out!'" When Reserve General Elazar Stern was asked at that time concerning the kidnapped soldier Gilead Schalit, then held captive by the Hamas, he replied, "If in past years we wouldn't have acted hysterically due to the pressure of the mothers, and I don't want to say anything more severe, then Gilead Schalit would be with us today, and he would have been liberated already." Similarly, after the First Lebanese War, there were those who blamed the defeat of the war on the activities of mothers who did not heed the call made by the prime minister "not to undermine morale." Parliament member Aryeh Nechamkin clarified that at the end of the war, the government responded to "mothers whose feelings are understood, but policy decisions cannot be made accordingly." How were mothers transformed into policy makers, into people considered influential on the chief of staff as well as the ministers in charge of defense? How did an official government investigative committee relate to the cultural shift led by the mothers concerning loss sensitivity influencing the fate of the campaign? This article presents an original study of the realm of cultural and political history, which will illuminate the link between political culture and the effectiveness of cultural agents, as well as the psychocultural and psychohistorical issues, whose long-term influences connect the culture and defense policies of the state of Israel.[6]

## The Objectives and Claims of This Study

1. During the first years of the state of Israel, a "deal" was presented to the mothers of soldiers, in order to motivate women to cleave to the model of the *Yiddeshe Mama* (Jewish Mother), who was expected to defend her son in private and to prevent him from endangering himself in public. From the viewpoint of this mother, the death of her son in battle means failure on her part and would

cause her to remain within the private domain with the perpetual image of one who failed to defend her son. Thus it was implicitly promised to her that should her son fall, she would then move from the private to the public sphere, and there she would not present the image of failure but one of a cultural hero, whose education of her son was appropriate according to patriotic expectations.
2. Laurence Mordekhai Thomas taught how certain sacrifices achieve preferred moral status, what he called "moral beacons," and thus are suitable for additional recompense.[7] This occurs when the hegemony locates those sacrifices that can fulfill political functions and by means of them can disseminate and reproduce the national episteme. The state of Israel located the mothers of soldiers, especially those of fallen soldiers, as characters that could be transformed into symbolic figures, morally strong. For that purpose a political culture was formed in which the bereaved mothers were merited by the deaths of their sons an entry ticket into the public arena. In this arena, one must be scrupulous about the Grief Regime, which elucidates what behavior and discourse is expected of them. If the bereaved mother adhered to the rules, she would enjoy a prestigious cultural status, entitled to the esteem of the nation and its leaders.[8]
3. Because of all this, when the bereaved mothers eventually adopted an antiestablishment political stance, employing their status in order to force the army to change its policies, the establishment should not have been surprised at the immense cultural importance they were given, since they used the very cultural status granted to them by the Establishment for its own interests in the early years of the state. The "Lebanonization of the military mothers" is a good illustration of the moral status granted to the bereaved mother becoming a two-edged sword, working from the beginning of the 1980s against the establishment.
4. This study also reveals that when the bereaved mothers protested against the army, demanding an IDF withdrawal from Lebanon and changed defense policies, it was not a case of demilitarizing culture, but at the most it represented "victimological militarism, which is a discourse that is facilitated by the militaristic culture resulting from the fact that status of these mothers is a consequence of the military culture in which the bereaved mother" or "mother of a soldier" has an abundance of moral capital. Therefore those mothers are not a counterculture; rather, they are a subculture within the Israeli culture of bereavement. Furthermore,

within the whole process of cooptation, there is a concealed element of subversiveness.[9]

## Reframing the "Jewish Mother": The "Heroic Bereaved Mother" and the Model of Hegemonic Bereavement

After Israel's War of Independence in 1948 and during the nation-building period, Israeli society organized around collective-republican values. This allowed the establishment to penetrate numerous intimate areas for the sake of emotional management and to nationalize them for its objectives. Thus the culture of military bereavement was built in order to serve the goals of the establishment. Within the framework of the "model of hegemonic bereavement," it was made clear to the parents of fallen soldiers, and especially to their mothers, that they have role demands even after the death of their sons, for the processing of loss is not just a private experience but a public one, and the parents were required to become "symbolic typecasts" that would adopt the prohegemonic discourse and behavior.

The image of the bereaved mother, her statements, and citations from her letters became part of Israeli culture. Bereaved mothers were quoted extensively in memorial volumes published by the establishment; stories in which the heroines are bereaved mothers became part of the texts taught in literature and civic classes in the schools. Plays, poems, songs, and films included them as characters. Bereaved mothers became regular speakers at public establishment events, becoming part of the environment close to the leading ministers of the state. For good reason, the Israeli mother was marked as the "weak link" that required a great deal of investment to mold her behavior and conduct in the public sphere, for the Jewish Mother (*Yiddeshe Mama*)—the same mother of the Jew from the years before the Zionist national revolution—would not have collaborated with the hegemonic Grief Regime in the national period. Likewise, she could not be counted on to fulfill civic expectations to act as one who encourages her son to join the army and endanger his life. On the contrary, the very thought that a Jewish Mother could become a bereaved mother would have killed her, as found in Rashi's exegesis to the binding of Isaac, where he commented that Sarah was totally unaware of this event, and when she heard of her husband's attempt to sacrifice her son, she simply dropped dead.[10]

In cultural depictions of motherhood, the Jewish Mother is viewed as an epistemic authority for her children, and especially for her sons.

In a chapter titled "The Mother," an Israeli psychiatrist wrote at the beginning of the 1960s that one is dealing with a person "who worries over and guards her children-sons, standing by this watch during her entire lifetime, and she knows how to stand heroically and courageously, with boundless devotion and unlimited self-sacrifice . . . The Jewish Mother views her children as the blessing of God, the source of all true happiness in her life . . . the ultimate reward, the greatest gratification possible." Literary and cultural texts, as well as scholarly studies, have taught that the Jewish Mother is totally identified with her motherhood. She maintains a motherhood that is embracing, strangling, and anxious concerning her son's health. She is especially identified as one who is anxious about his nutrition and health, his proper amount of sleep and his physical welfare, and being overprotective, which was considered by some to lead to the son's emasculation. Protection that does permit separation does not leave others to have epistemic authority over the son, which leads, according to Wincott, to preserving the primary maternal preoccupation, since the Jewish Mother refused to allow her son development space as a separate entity from. She works to preserve the total integration between herself and her son, nullifying any duality between them. The Jewish Mother refuses to allow her son to establish an individual identity and works to wholly integrate her life within her son's life. Hence it is no accident that some claim that Jewish identity is determined by the mother.[11]

Zionist ideology attempted to foster a psychopolitical revolution in the image of the Diaspora Jew from a vulnerable Jew who cannot defend his honor to a soldier and fighter—from someone whose mother directed him to an intellectual career (in the rabbinical academy) or in trade to one who desires sports, violence, and the military. In order to facilitate transforming the Jew into a fighter, a masculine and not a "feminized Jew,"[12] the designers of Zionist culture believed that a transformation in the image of the mother was required, for she was the personality that could motivate her boy to change "from zero to hero."[13]

David Ben-Gurion, minister of defense and prime minister from 1948 to 1954, argued "that the army needs maternal emotions more than any other public body or organization" and maintained that a mother should not feel betrayed by her son when she sends him off to be drafted into the army, for that very maternal emotion would be provided by his commanders. Ben-Gurion went on to say, "Every Hebrew mother who handed over the fate of her son to suitable officers should know that." This statement became a trademark, a social-family contract, engraved on the hearts of the Israeli people. This newfound dogma appeared in brass letters decorating the office of the minister of defense and in induction centers and boot camps throughout the country. In order to continue the mothers' willingness to educate their sons regarding the obligation of serving in the army, Ben-Gurion made it clear to his officers, "It's not enough that an officer knows his task, he must all love mankind . . . and especially arouse trust in the soldier and the soldier's mother."[14]

From the viewpoint of the state, the Israeli "child" was created to be a soldier, and his mother to be the mother of a soldier. Thus she was also the mother of a casualty, and this became normative, which found legitimacy within popular discourse and culture. When a midwife in an Israeli hospital was asked in an interview to report how many babies were born the previous night, she replied, "Five soldiers and three girls were born." National discourse, both on the right and on the left, supported this customary encouragement of mother to her son in joining the army. For this reason, a link was established between the Israeli mother and the imaginary "Jewish Mother." Prime Minister Yitzchak Rabin, in his speech celebrating the International Year of the Woman, clarified that the task of a "true woman" in the Land of Israel is to grant the "ultimate sacrifice": not her death, but the death of her husband or son.[15]

Many cultural illustrations clarified what was considered proper behavior for the new Israeli mother—the heroic mother who sends her son off to the army. An example of such a transformation from "Jewish Mother" to "Heroic Mother" can be seen in a segment that appeared in a Memorial Day pamphlet issued by the Defense Ministry. A column titled "Deborah or Eulogy" recounted the period of riots (the prestate era) when the blood of a Jew was worthless. In the story of Deborah, a mother named after the Biblical heroine, the mother is the heroine of the story and not her son who died in the narrative. The story describes how this mother, against a Diaspora Jewish Mother's instinct, turned to her son, not to spur him to find a hiding place, but just the opposite: "She called to her son and ordered him—Go there, to your people, and assist them. With her own hands, she helped him clean his rifle, took out his leather knapsack with lead bullets, preparing everything for his journey." Her response to her son's willingness to go and endanger himself does not overflow with her apprehension for his welfare. On the contrary, Deborah's face was "illuminated with joy when after a half hour she saw her son, properly dressed and armed." The story continues to report that her son fought courageously, "with all his strength he fell upon his enemy, aiding his colleagues from the Haganah who were tired . . . he destroyed many enemies, saving the lives of many. For three complete hours he fought savagely and heroically." However, in the end, in an alternative reading of the David and Goliath story, "a small non-Jew came, raised a heavy, sharp stone, slung it at Beryl, struck and crushed his head." The story does not skip the transformation of the "Jewish Mother" at the time when she was confronted with the experience of loss, teaching that there is still heroic behavior: "Silently, dressed in a black dress, head covered in a dark scarf, Deborah went to the funeral. She walking erectly not stooped . . . 'I am the mother of the killed boy . . . I sent him to them. I will not cry because God took my son from me. No man took him, I myself gave him. My heart said to me that he would not return alive, but I sent him in order that he should be with you and that he should die for you . . .'"[16]

## The Hegemonic-Heroic Motherhood Grief Regime

In order to clarify to bereaved mothers what was appropriate conduct and what the national establishment expected of them, what proper discourse should be employed in the public sphere, there developed a semiformal Grief Regime that elucidated to each bereaved mother that she was part of the epistemic community, called "The Family of Bereavement," as Israeli culture dictates that all Israeli people whose family members died in war and terror are bereaved. Thus the entire community is entrusted with providing meaning for loss, working toward memorializing their dear ones, and paving social networks for "appropriate conduct," while preserving the bereaved mother in her position in the higher echelons of civilian government.[17]

Consequently, bereaved mothers follow three core structures:

### The Bereaved Mother Is Reserved

It was made clear to bereaved mothers that they should not publically display any emotion, being self-controlled upon entering public memorial areas as well as military cemeteries, as these are public and not private. Likewise, it was made clear that the heroic mother was one who adopted a Western-masculine ethos, in which one refrained from displaying anger or pain in times of shock and trauma, for the loss of one's senses or a tempest of emotions is regarded as primitive, feminine conduct, and most important, as conduct that may instill anxiety in other mothers.

It was not easy for many mothers to refrain from crying in public, and those who succeeded included others in this effort, and it was reported as a real accomplishment. For example, one bereaved mother whose son fell in the Independence War recorded in the newsletter of the national memorialization organization, "For twenty years this feeling has been with me—we have inserted our pain into our hearts, and walk about with stone faces." Her friend, also a bereaved mother, noted that throughout all the years she "puts on a face before the entire world like a strong, heroic mother."[18]

In a newspaper issued the year of the establishment of the state of Israel, an essay by a bereaved mother was published. The article has been repeatedly printed in Israeli memorial literature and in various memorial perpetuation pamphlets throughout the years. It concerns the apology of a mother for weeping at her son's funeral. "Forgive me, my son, that I shed tears, given that for the death of heroes like you one does not weep. However, it is hard to remember you and not weep." In a volume published by the rehabilitation department of the Ministry of Defense and sent to all bereaved families whose sons died in battle, an essay appeared by a bereaved mother who declared that when in public she succeeds in fulfilling the national goal of retaining her self-control: "Proudly I will bear my pain . . . in silence I carry my grief, I will halt my crying in my throat, strangling the wailing before it bursts out . . . don't cry . . . proudly I will bear my pain."[19]

Many bereaved mothers explained that displaying sorrow in public is not legitimate, for parents must invigorate and strengthen the youth who would soon follow the paths of their sons. Should they see a mother's sorrow and distress caused by the death of her son, he would develop an ambivalent attitude before ever volunteering for any dangerous mission. Thus in the aforementioned article sent to bereaved families, a bereaved mother clarifies why she refrained from crying in the military cemetery: "This is not a time to weep or lament . . . No one knows who's next . . . This is not a time to be depressed . . . Self-control and cold thinking even in hours of bereavement . . . Tears, be silent in your hiding places." Following this piece, a poem was composed titled "Tears, Be Silent in Your Hiding Places," which was published in every memorial pamphlet published by the Ministry of Defense. Another mother described how she restrained herself from crying in public, even in front of a group of soldiers who carried her son to his grave. Even in this tragic situation she identified her task as guarding morale and as someone uninterested in sowing sorrow among young soldiers: "I overcame my sorrow in order not to distress them, so as not to crush their spirit . . . I felt that I must be strong for them . . . I don't wail, and look upon the broken mothers . . . who withhold the cry of their tragedy, for fortitude is required of us."[20]

## The Bereaved Mother Justifies Her Fate

The mother of an IDF casualty was meant to be just the opposite of Sarah, the mother of Isaac, who was annoyed with her husband who would have sacrificed her son if God had not prevented it. This was made clear to mothers of casualties, for example, in the letters by fallen soldiers written to their mothers, which were distributed by the state in various publications. In these letters, the sons identified themselves with the mission, as one soldier wrote to his mother in a letter that was made public after he fell in battle: "A man is examined by his love of the Land and his devotion to the Zionist idea—only if he knows how to sacrifice his fat and blood on its altar without withdrawing from the battle—only thus will a loyal Zionist will be tested." The letter by Shlomo ben Yosef, an underground fighter who was executed by the British, clarified to his mother that if he should die, she should know that he is totally at peace with his fate. As he explained, "Jewish sons ended their lives in far worse humiliating and tragic circumstances . . . I am quite happy with my fate."[21]

The heroic bereaved mother was required to adopt such a position. One mother wrote what became a well-known text that was taught in schools: "We observe our sons and do not recognize them . . . we have yearned for them for 2000 years . . . our sons and daughters who go out today with orders from the nation to give their lives . . . their share is not in the camp of the sacrificed. This is the generation . . . that heralds the bells of the Redeemer in the mountains. And we, their parents and teachers . . . today we have been raised and educated by them. They have comforted and encouraged us by their departure from us."[22]

The words of the mothers who embraced these antivictimological messages, absent of any anger and filled with acceptance and meaning, became public and widespread. Such messages offer information about the fallen and shed light on the patriotism of their mothers. Such nationalism is expressed, for example, in the memorial pamphlet issued by the Defense Ministry in 1978, where a bereaved mother is cited as asking, "Actually, what do I want? Why do I complain? Why do I cry? Finally, how did we educate Nimrod? . . . We educated our son to ascend the altar of sacrifice . . . Yes, we educated him to be ready for moment of trial. This is the moment, and we knew that we must pay for it . . . This is the generation that we hope for, and it carries out our enterprise to immortality." This is a discourse of antitraumatic grief that teaches that one can find meaning in loss, achieving depoliticization and detraumatizing of sorrow, which was reflected by one mother when she wrote, "I will not complain about my fate—the fate of thousands in present-day Israel. I know that this fate is unpreventable in the cruel bloody wars that the evil powers of the world have forced upon us."[23]

## The Heroic Mother Glorifies Military Death

The epistemic community as managed by bereaved mothers was entrusted with generating a national consensus that the death of sons took place in extraordinary heroic situations, even if this was not the case. Miriam Shapira, a bereaved woman, founded an organization for national memorialization, now known as *Yad leBanim* (Memorial for the Sons). Originally, she wanted to call it the Memorial for Israeli Heroes in order to stress the fact that the organization "sanctifies the memorialization of our heroes who by their ultimate heroism brought us our freedom." Consequently, all the dead soldiers, though only a minority of them actually fell in battle, achieved the status of heroes; thus their mothers were framed as persons who consciously molded their sons to achieve extraordinary bravery. Consequently, these mothers, no less than the sons themselves, deserved singular appreciation on the part of society, as expressed by Miriam Shapira, who said of her son's generation, "[We] took care of it, guided it in this direction, *and we finally sacrificed it on the altar of the future of our nation.*" For this reason, on many occasions David Ben-Gurion referred to the fallen soldiers as the "young lions of Israel" and their bereaved mothers as "lionesses."[24]

## RIVAK GUBER: THE HEROIC MILITARY BEREAVED MOTHER TYPECAST

Every epistemic community interested in forming a collective behavior within its members "requires a character that would foster moral leadership and be viewed as the ideal type to emulate." David Ben-Gurion found the person who was considered the ultimate heroic and bereaved mother; with his assistance, she became, formally and symbolically, the leader of the community of "Family of Bereavement," to serve as the guide and model for all bereaved mothers. This person was Rivka Guber, who was called by Ben-Gurion "the Mother of the Sons."[25]

Rivka Guber (1902–81) was remarkably suitable to serve as the symbol for both the "Family of Bereavement" and the Labor Movement led by Ben-Gurion. She was a member of a *Moshav*, a cooperative Israeli settlement, and was active in the Women's Organization of the *Histadrut* Labor Federation. She became famous in 1942 when, upon her husband's disqualification from serving in the British army for health reasons, she decided to serve in his stead and was appointed with the first group of volunteers of Auxiliary Territorial Services (ATS) in the British army. With this act, she shattered the stereotypical behavior of the protective Jewish Mother as she left three children at home, which garnered criticism and censure. After two years of military service, when her son Ephraim turned 16 she assisted him in falsifying his age in his identity card so that he could serve in the army in her place. He volunteered to the Jewish Brigade and was sent to the front in Europe. Rivka Guber wrote to him, "When I received your letter after the battle, I cried with happiness, not only because you survived, but because I was granted the privilege to raise a son like I dreamed of. In my heart, there is no cowardice, just as in yours."[26]

Sadly, Ephraim was killed on March 26, 1948, shortly after his younger brother Zvi joined the Palmach, also known as the "Crushing Company," which served as the military arm of the Hagana and was the precursor of the Israel Defense Forces. Zvi was killed months later on July 8, 1948. Rivka Guber became active in projects considered nationally significant and at all times emphasized that she was fulfilling her sons' testament. After the Independence War, she worked with her husband in the assimilation of new immigrants. In 1955, she decided to move to a different part of the country in order to assist new immigrants who settled there. She sold her house and donated the money to the Defense Fund in order to buy weapons for the army. In the new *Moshav*, the family lived without electricity and water, in conditions so primitive that even younger members found them difficult. But in response to this situation, she wrote, "Our special situation obligates us to grasp the meaning of life as a mission."[27]

A dramatic change in her public status took place when David Ben-Gurion read her book about her sons titled *The Brothers* (*Sefer haAchim*), a book without any grievances or anger at her loss, its entirety filled with meaning and significance for their deaths. Ben-Gurion quickly went to meet her and declared, "I don't know if in Israel there is—nowadays or at any time—anyone like the Mother of the Sons. Her words form a chapter unlike any in world literature." Ben-Gurion transformed the book into a mass-circulated pedagogical text, and the Ministry of Defense financed numerous publications of it. As Ben-Gurion reflected in a speech, "The unique thing of this book is the character of the mother shining above us from its pages. The mother's word will forever stand as symbol of heroism and loyalty of the Hebrew mother; she has succeeded in speaking for many mothers in Israel."[28]

Following her meeting with Ben-Gurion, not only did the book undergo a transformation, but Rivka Guber herself became a symbolic image in Israeli society. Ben-Gurion later wrote to Rivka Guber, "A great mother of Israel has arisen for us . . . I am sure that in future generations the light of your heroism will shine on . . . Your great and eternal words are for all of the Children of Israel wherever they are, and perhaps not just for them. If there are mothers like you in Israel—we can meet our future with a quiet heart." On another occasion he surmised, "In this book there is something exalted and dear . . . Fortunate is the generation in which women like these live in. Perhaps this is the true and deep secret of the great 'miracle' that happened to our people in this generation." Ben-Gurion suggested that "it would have also been fitting [for the book] to be called *The Mother*."[29]

Rivka Guber was appointed head of the organization for national memorialization, *Yad leBanim*. On Memorial Day, radio broadcasts included her remarks. She visited public forums and was part of official memorial ceremonies. Among the prizes she was awarded was Mother of the Year and the Israel Prize, a national prize granted each Israeli Independence Day to a few persons for their extraordinary contribution to the betterment of the state. In newspapers and public reports, she was described as "the symbol of the bereaved mother in Israel." Political leaders seeking legitimacy sought her for her blessing. Upon his election as president of the state of Israel, Yitzchak Navon chose to hold his first public meeting with Rivka Guber. Prime Minister Menachem Begin added Rivka Guber to national delegations and functions, declaring her the symbol of "all bereaved families in our land." He even took her along to the signing ceremonies of the peace treaty between Israel and Egypt. Even her funeral took on national significance, with many of the nation's leading personalities participating.[30]

## Celebritism in Bereavement: The Army and Mothers

Rivka Guber is an extraordinary example of the esteemed status granted by Israeli society to bereaved mothers. With the death of their sons, such mothers earned a ticket into the public conscious and mass communications of the nation. As an example, in a newspaper report about a mother of five sons that were all drafted into the army, her sons stated that "never did she express . . . any regrets that we were leaving her . . . even in the difficult days when two of her sons did not return from the front." The report ended by declaring her "the exemplary Hebrew mother." When Ben-Gurion granted the "Birth Prize" to mothers that gave birth to more than ten children, he gave first prize to a mother with five sons who had served in the IDF, saying, "[A] Hebrew mother like you (will become) the symbol of maternal heroism," while also giving a check for one hundred Israeli pounds. These mothers even became the dominant persons interviewed concerning current events and were invited to public communications forums during warfare in order to serve as framers and legitimizers of the defense policy that demanded the service and potential sacrifice of sons in battle.[31]

## Boomerang: The Two-Edged Sword in the Status of the Heroic Bereaved Mother

Among all the epistemic authorities who influence the soldier's spirit, the voice of the "soldier's mother" has the most dominant cultural and communicative aura in Israel. When the IDF was in Lebanon, for example, it was found that mothers of soldiers serving in the army as well as mothers of fallen soldiers went on the air and were interviewed by newspapers five times more than fathers. However, in order to provide legitimacy and a proestablishment discourse, the bereaved mothers were transformed by the establishment into a public category of their own with hefty moral weight, which significantly shaped public opinion.

Only in the 1980s did a number of phenomena come together for change. First, among the elite, who were the first to be exposed to globalization and new liberalism, a postnationalism chasm developed that began to distance the once interchangeably civilian and military identities of Israelis. Mothers stopped viewing themselves as persons whose mission was to instill national values into their children but rather began limiting the influence of the state on their children.

Values such as the comfort and welfare of the child became more important than any other objective of the State. Similarly, the age that children were still considered "children" was extended; thus an Israeli mother's duty to protect her child and not hand him over to the state was lengthened.[32]

Additionally, this era witnessed the development of victimological liberalism, in which the heroes of mass communication are the victims and not the traditional "heroes." Someone who was hurt as a result of an erroneous public policy on the part of the state would merit the greatest amount of coverage by mass communications, which views suffering as a type of merchandise that can be covered in colorful reports that fuel the anger toward the victimizer leadership.[33]

Finally, warfare necessary in this era has been dubbed the "new wars," in which extensive wars occur against terror and guerillas and often take place in urban spaces. This type of warfare has great potential for moral failure without the possibility for a decisive victory or a swift end to the war. Such warfare quickly fosters opposition, delegitimization, and public weariness from casualties in addition to constant doubts as to its justifiability.[34]

All these features have transformed what the state designed as a resource into a burden—a boomerang effect. The very mothers who underwent cooptation by the establishment in order to grant legitimacy to the defense policies have, in the era of neoliberalism, rejected the legitimacy of national defense policies. As far as the establishment is concerned, the concept of bereaved motherhood has blown up in its face. The hegemony does not employ the bereaved mother; rather, the bereaved mother employs the status granted to her by the hegemony in order to limit that very hegemony. Thus the use of the bereaved mother is dual: cooptation on one side of the coin is subversion on the other. The power of the bereaved mother seeks to encourage but also to dismantle the military hegemony.

## From Heroic Militarism to Victimological Militarism

Bereaved mothers from the period when the IDF occupied Lebanon did not establish a counter epistemic militaristic community. Instead, victimological militarism is a community that is counterestablishment, protesting against the state's policies but not against the cultural militarism. Only as a result of this cultural militarism did the mothers of soldiers and casualties achieve their symbolic status and cultural and communicative privileges, even while working against army policy.

Victimological discourse that is pushed forward by mothers is not a civilian discourse. Rather, it is a militaristic one, which preserves the singular status of one whose son serves in the army, hence the suggestion that this is a change from "heroic militarism" to "victimological militarism."

## Competitive Bereavement Communities

It should be emphasized that this essay describes processes relevant to mothers belonging to Israeli elites. In the last few years, as the IDF has come to be made up of many more soldiers not belonging to these elite groups but to "marginal" groups such as religious families, West Bank settlers, and new immigrants, there has arisen a "cultural nostalgia" that attempts to rejuvenate the model of hegemonic bereavement. Religious bereaved mothers, living in West Bank settlements, are loyal to the model of the heroic, military, bereaved mother. The present study does not deal with this group, but one can certainly surmise that the cultural models and the patterns of response to military loss are not disappearing—just "changing address." Certain mothers would prefer adapting what Neimeyer called grief staging due to the influences of the epistemic bereavement community they belong to. This testifies that loss, bereavement, and grief are not private but social processes adopted by individuals as part of the communities of feeling to which they belong. The Israeli bereaved mother will choose the path of grief that is suitable to her social and psychopolitical environment. Her social clique will mark those achievements that could be called posttraumatic growth. However, what is considered as conferring meaning to military loss in one group may not be considered as such in another group; thus these mothers may feel that they have to set out to enforce meaning to their sons' deaths by means of extensive public activities. The responses of bereaved mothers to the deaths of their sons in war are dependent on what community they belong to. As long as the national Israeli arena is characterized by a cultural maternal militarism, the mothers will continue to be central cultural agents framing the wars by granting or denying them military legitimacy.[35]

## Notes

1. I would like to thank Ayala Shaulson for assisting in locating archival sources and for the productive exchange of ideas. Many thanks to Prof. Claire Phelan and Prof. Dana Cooper for the exciting invitation to take

part in this pioneering and significant anthology and for Jay Knarr for professional editing assistance. I wish to dedicate the article to Neomi Lebel, my beloved, brave Jewish mother.
2. Winograd Commission, *The Commission of Inquiry into the Events of Military Engagement in Lebanon, 2006*, Final Report, 252. The commission was established as a response to public protest against heads of military and state after poor performance in the Second Lebanon War (2006). After the report's publication, the minister of defense and the commander in chief of the Israel Defense Forces resigned.
3. N. Livne, "Mothers Crying," *Haaretz*, March 13, 2002; Udi Lebel, "'Casualty Panic:' Military Recruitment Models, Civil–Military Gap and Their Implications for the Legitimacy of Military Loss," *Democracy and Security* 6, no. 2 (2010): 183–206.
4. Udi Lebel, "Militarism versus Security? The Double-Bind of Israel's Culture of Bereavement and Hierarchy of Sensitivity to Loss," *Mediterranean Politics* 16, no. 3 (2011): 365–84.
5. Ibid.; A. Shavit, "This Time We Have No Choice," *Haaretz*, July 28, 2007.
6. E. Sneh, "The Withdrawal which Empowers Hezbollah," *Haaretz*, May 21, 2010; R. Ben-Yishay, "The Disgrace which Costs Us," *Ynet*, May 25, 2010; H. Ezra, "Elazar Stern vs. Shalit Affair," *Channel 7*, October 4, 2010; Lebel, "Militarism versus Security," 371.
7. L. M. Thomas, "Suffering as a Moral Beacon: Blacks and Jews," in *The Americanization of the Holocaust*, ed. Hilene Flanzbaum (Baltimore: Johns Hopkins University Press, 1999).
8. Marie Breen-Smyth, "Hierarchies of Pain and Responsibility: Victims and War by Other Means in Northern Ireland," *Tripodos* 25 (2009): 27–40; Udi Lebel, "The 'Grief Regime' Gatekeepers: 'Victimological Militarism' and the Symbolic Bargaining over National Bereavement Identity," in *Culture and Rites/Rights of Grief*, ed. Zbigniew Bialas, Pawel Jedrzejko, and Julia Szoltysek (Cambridge: Scholars, 2013).
9. Lebel, "The 'Grief Regime' Gatekeepers."
10. Rashi [Rabbi Solomon ben Isaac], commentary to Gen. 23:3.
11. Amiram Raviv, Daniel Bar-Tal, Alona Raviv, and Daniela Peleg, "Perception of Epistemic Authorities by Children and Adolescents," *Journal of Youth and Adolescence* 19, no. 5 (October 1990): 495–510; M. Giladi, *Actual Issues in the Eyes of the Psychiatry* (Tel Aviv: author, 1963), 45; R. Kulka, "Between Tragedy to Compassion," in *How Does Analysis Cure?*, ed. Heinz Kohut, Arnold Goldberg, and Paul E. Stepansky (Tel Aviv: Am-Oved, 2005).
12. M. Berger, "The Mouse That Never Roars: Jewish Masculinity on American Television," in *Too Jewish? Challenging Traditional Identities*, ed. Norman Kleeblat (New Brunswick, NJ: Rutgers University Press, 1996).

13. T. Mayer, "From Zero to Hero: Masculinity in Jewish Nationalism," in *Israeli Women's Studies: A Reader*, ed. Esther Fuchs (New Brunswick, NJ: Rutgers University Press, 2005).
14. David Ben-Gurion, *Davar*, October, 31, 1971, 5.
15. B Channel, *Morning News*, January 1, 2002; Yitzhak Rabin, Knesset Protocols (February 12, 1975), Knesset Archives, Jerusalem, Israel.
16. Y. Bardichevsky, "Debora or Eulogy," in *Memorial Day's Book* (Jerusalem: Ministry of Defense, 1978), 34–37.
17. Hugh T. Miller and Charles J. Fox, "The Epistemic Community," *Administration & Society* 32, no. 6 (January 2001): 668–85; Stephen Castles, "Nation and Empire: Hierarchies of Citizenship in the New Global Order," *International Politics* 42, no. 2 (2005): 203–35.
18. M. Burstein, "For Remembrances," *Yad Labanim Journal* (September–October 1974): 75.
19. Udi Lebel and Yona Rochlin, "Soldiers and Families of MIAs and POWs," *Social Movements Studies: Journal of Social, Cultural and Political Protest* 8, no. 4 (2009): 365, 369.
20. Rubin Avinoam, ed., *Mumble Hurts* (Tel Aviv: Maarachot, 1954), 28–29, 38.
21. M. Burstein, "For Remembrances," *Yad Labanim Journal* (September–October 1974): 75; I. Oron, *Death, Mortality and Ideology* (Tel Aviv: Ministry of Defense, 2002), 113.
22. Avinoam, *Mumble Hurts*, 10–11.
23. Israeli Ministry of Defense, *Memorial Day's Book* (Tel Aviv: Ministry of Defense, 1978), 42, 57.
24. M. Shapira, "We Call All Mothers," *Devar Hapoolet*, November 23, 1948, 4. Emphasis in original. Udi Lebel, "'Blackmailing the Military'—'Military Strategic Refusal' as Policy and Doctrine Enforcement: Israeli Warfare at Lebanon, Samaria and Gaza," *Small Wars and Insurgencies* 24 (forthcoming).
25. William D. Greenfield, "Moral Leadership in Schools," *Journal of Educational Administration* 42, no. 2 (2004): 174–96.
26. Rivka Guber, *Hadoar*, June, 30, 1972, 4.
27. Rivka Guber, "Being Worthy," Speech at Bialik Haiuse, Tel Aviv, 1967, Speeches File, Rivka Guber Archive, Gnazim (the Israeli Authors Central Archive), Tel Aviv.
28. David Ben-Gurion, "Some Things about Rivka Guber" (1957), File 10c1, Ben-Gurion Archives, Sde Boker; David Ben Gurion, *Davar*, March 26, 1951, 4.
29. David Ben-Gurion to Rivka Guber, August 24, 1950, File 10c1, Ben-Gurion Archives, Sde Boker; David Ben-Gurion to Rivka Guber, December 13, 1953, File 10c1, Ben-Gurion Archives, Sde Boker.
30. Menachem Begin, *Maariv*, September, 11, 1978, 15.
31. David Ben-Gurion, *Davar*, March 26, 1951, 4; David Ben-Gurion, *Davar*, September, 23, 1949, 28.

32. Gabrielle M. Maxwell and Allison Morris, *Family, Victims and Culture: Youth Justice in New Zealand* (Victoria: University of Wellington, Institute of Criminology, 1993).
33. Lebel, "Blackmailing the Military."
34. Mary Kaldor, *New and Old Wars: Organized Violence in a Global Era* (Cambridge: Polity, 2012).
35. Lebel, "Blackmailing the Military"; R. A. Neimeyer, "The Staging of Grief," in *Studies of Grief and Bereavement*, ed. Shulamith Kreitler and Henya Shanun-Klein (New York: Nova, 2013); Natti Ronel and Udi Lebel, "When Parents Lay Their Children to Rest," *Journal of Social and Personal Relationships* 23, no. 4 (August 2006): 507–22.

## Selected Bibliography

Avinoam, Rubin, ed. *Mumble Hurts.* Tel Aviv: Maarachot, 1954.

Bialas, Zbigniew, Pawel Jedrzejko, and Julia Szoltysek, eds. *Culture and Rites/Rights of Grief.* Cambridge: Scholars, 2013.

Breen-Smyth, Marie. "Hierarchies of Pain and Responsibility: Victims and War by Other Means in Northern Ireland." *Tripodos* 25 (2009): 27–40.

Castles, Stephen. "Nation and Empire: Hierarchies of Citizenship in the New Global Order." *International Politics* 42, no. 2 (2005): 203–35.

Flanzbaum, Hilene, ed. *The Americanization of the Holocaust.* Baltimore: Johns Hopkins University Press, 1999.

Fuchs, Esther, ed. *Israeli Women's Studies: A Reader.* New Brunswick, NJ: Rutgers University Press, 2005.

Greenfield, William D. "Moral Leadership in Schools." *Journal of Educational Administration* 42, no. 2 (2004): 174–196.

Kaldor, Mary. *New and Old Wars: Organized Violence in a Global Era.* Cambridge: Polity, 2012.

Kleeblat, Norman, ed. *Too Jewish? Challenging Traditional Identities.* New Brunswick, NJ: Rutgers University Press, 1996.

Kohut, Heinz, Arnold Goldberg, and Paul E. Stepansky. *How Does Analysis Cure?* Tel Aviv: Am-Oved, 2005.

Kreitler, Shulamith, and Henya Shanun-Klein, eds. *Studies of Grief and Bereavement.* New York: Nova, 2013.

Lebel, Udi. "'Blackmailing the Military'—'Military Strategic Refusal' as Policy and Doctrine Enforcement: Israeli Warfare at Lebanon, Samaria and Gaza." *Small Wars and Insurgencies* 24 (forthcoming).

———. "'Casualty Panic': Military Recruitment Models, Civil–Military Gap and Their Implications for the Legitimacy of Military Loss." *Democracy and Security* 6, no. 2 (2010): 183–206.

———. "Militarism versus Security? The Double-Bind of Israel's Culture of Bereavement and Hierarchy of Sensitivity to Loss." *Mediterranean Politics* 16, no. 3 (2011): 365–84.

———. "'Second Class Loss': Political Culture as a Recovery Barrier?—Israeli Families of Terrorist Casualties and Their Struggle for National Honors, Recognition and Belonging." *Death Studies* 38, no. 1 (2014): 9–19.

Lebel, Udi, and Yona Rochlin. "Soldiers and Families of MIAs and POWs." *Social Movements Studies: Journal of Social, Cultural and Political Protest* 8, no. 4 (2009): 359–74.

Lev-Ami, Ayelet. "Public Discourse and Parental Involvement in the Army." Master's Thesis, Tel Aviv University, 2001.

Maxwell, Gabrielle M., and Allison Morris. *Family, Victims and Culture: Youth Justice in New Zealand.* Victoria: University of Wellington, Institute of Criminology, 1993.

Miller, Hugh T., and Charles J. Fox. "The Epistemic Community." *Administration and Society* 32, no. 6 (January 2001): 668–85.

Mosinzon, Yigal. *Chasamba and the Stranger in the Black Mask.* Tel Aviv: Shahaf Pub, 1954.

Raviv, Amiram, Daniel Bar-Tal, Alona Raviv, and Daniela Peleg. "Perception of Epistemic Authorities by Children and Adolescents." *Journal of Youth and Adolescence* 19, no. 5 (October 1990): 495–510.

Ronel, Natti, and Udi Lebel. "When Parents Lay Their Children to Rest." *Journal of Social and Personal Relationships* 23, no. 4 (August 2006): 507–22.

# Chapter 11

## Reproducing a Culture of Martyrdom
### The Role of the Palestinian Mother in Discourse Construction, Transmission, and Legitimization

*Michael Loadenthal*

### Introduction

Nestled between the Gaza Strip and the West Bank is the state of Israel, which since 1967 has occupied the Palestinian territories. After decades of failed negotiations, the Jewish state now competes with Palestinian militants and paramilitaries in an ongoing cycle of retaliatory violence. The West Bank, the larger of the Palestinian territories, is currently segmented into ever-shrinking enclaves of land, separated by military installations, Israeli settlements, and the vast infrastructure designed to control the Palestinian populace and guarantee the safety of Israeli citizens. As a result of the conflict, Palestine is host to a variety of Palestinian paramilitary, militant, and terrorist groups. These groups have large-scale social service, political, religious, media, and military wings—and while some are Islamist, others are secular nationalists or have their roots in anticolonialist leftist movements. Groups like Islamic Jihad—an Islamist paramilitary group—and Fatah—the ruling secular nationalist party—compete for popularity by waging a bloody war with the state of Israel fought through both military strikes and the rhetoric of propaganda.

The Gaza Strip is far smaller than the West Bank and shares a border with Egypt. In the summer of 2005, the Israel Defense Forces withdrew its military forces from the Strip, and the government of Ariel Sharon organized the evacuation of all Israeli settlers. The Gaza Strip, like the West Bank, is made up of small towns, rural villages, tightly packed cities, and large refugee camps. There is mass unemployment and poverty as the population attempts to build a viable state after more than four decades of harsh occupation. The Gaza Strip is regarded as more religious and destitute than the West Bank, exuding the graphic images of martyrs' parades and helicopter missile strikes. In lock step with the conflict, both the Gaza Strip and West Bank have witnessed religious reinvigorations as the conflict has dragged on.[1] Within Gaza, the Islamic Resistance Movement, known popularly as Hamas, garners a great deal of support and for many surpasses the Fatah-aligned Palestinian Authority in legitimacy. Hamas has grown to be the most popular militant group in the Palestinian territories and operates a wide network of social and religious institutions as well as an armed wing, known as the Ezzedeen al-Qassam Brigades. The Brigades has regularly engaged in paramilitary and terrorist attacks against the Israeli military and citizenry and organizes frequent military parades and political rallies. Hamas has a formidable presence in both Gaza and the West Bank, and it has elected members to all levels of local government. Hamas is strongest in the Gaza Strip, while Fatah along with its main armed wing, the al-Aqsa Martyrs Brigade, is strongest in the West Bank. Since the first Palestinian *intifada* (uprising or shaking off), Fatah and Hamas have competed for the people's support. Throughout Palestinian society, great diversity in class, religious background, and education exist, making the intifada one of the most constant socializing forces.

The most recent uprising, known as the al-Aqsa Intifada, began in September 2000 and has been more dominated by religion than prior uprisings. While some military organizations such as Hamas's armed wing state in public communications that the al-Aqsa uprising is continuing,[2] many conclude that the period of the second intifada ended around 2005. The end of this period can be marked by the death of Yasser Arafat in 2004, Israeli withdrawal from the Gaza Strip,[3] and the Sharm el-Sheikh peace talks[4] in 2005, or the armed clashes between Hamas and Fatah security forces[5] in 2006. Despite the difficulty with marking its end, the al-Aqsa Intifada is noted for the influx of religious overtones attributed to the rise of Islamists movements such as Hamas and Islamic Jihad. As such, the culture of the intifada has increasingly centered on jihadi martyrdom, as the influence and popularity of

Islamist movements increased in times of heightened violence. Since the 1970s, leftist and secular nationalist groups have continually lost ground, while the Islamists, advocating Islamicly derived martyrdom, have gained significant support and popularity. In the Palestinian context, jihadi martyrdom teaches that God rewards those who fight and die in pursuit of nationhood, and that achieving death through resistance is a victory in itself. To die for God is an aspiration held in high regard. This understanding does not discriminate between the deeply religious and the average secular nationalist. Regardless of group affiliation or religiosity, the martyrdom narrative is accepted and advanced by militants of all stripes.

During periods of high activity, the intifada directs the lives of many Palestinians. While the current period can be understood as existing in a temporal space *after* the second intifada yet *before* the third, the cultural reality of nationalist violence continues to pervade the social, political, and religious spheres of life. The militant factions that maintain the movement garner competing support with the quasigovernment of the Palestinian Authority by providing social services the government is unable to provide because of mismanagement and corruption. These groupings present themselves as the only active participants in an attempt to gain Palestinian statehood and the return of the Palestinian diasporic community. Through consistent polling, Palestinian support for an *armed* campaign for statehood remains between 51 and 88 percent according to two studies conducted in 2012.[6] The groups that fight for the Palestinians integrate entire communities and families into their operation. Fathers are told to bear weapons and plot attacks on soldiers while sons throw rocks at Israeli military vehicles and personnel. Daughters also confront soldiers and aid the militant groups in a variety of necessary supporting roles. Mothers are taught to raise children to become fighters and eventually sacrifice them to the war. The entire family attends rallies and prayer services—often along lines of familial affiliation—in spaces owned and operated by Hamas, Islamic Jihad, Fatah, and others. This is obviously a simplistic representation of the social order, and while it is well established in the literature[7] that women occupy a variety of roles in the armed segments of the movement, their most visibly prominent role is that of a mother.

This chapter examines how the mothers of these families have rhetorically integrated themselves into the conflict, reproducing a culture that justifies and promotes death for nationhood. The mothers in question lovingly praise their children's actions, even when they discover that their loved ones have died in combat. How has the reality of the intifada shaped the realities of these mothers, and how has it created a publicly preformed script that aids the cycle of violence by continuing the culture of martyrdom? We will seek to answer these questions and to trace what the dominant narrative is, as well as the factors that combine to create and sustain it.

There are sizeable segments of Palestinian society that disagree with and remove themselves from the methods of the armed intifada. Despite the diversity that exists in Palestinian society, an undeniable culture that praises death permeates throughout and serves to socially insulate the conflict. This cultural reality is emboldened by a protracted armed conflict that in only 8 years has killed more than 4,900 Palestinians and more than 1,030 Israelis.[8] This chapter argues that Palestine is socially molded by a culture that justifies and feeds the intifada through a discourse of self-sacrifice that provides a never-ending supply of fighters. To be considered a martyr in this conflict, one need not explode on a bus or attack a settlement. Militants who are assassinated, boys shot while throwing stones, and noncombatants hit in the crossfire are also deemed martyrs. The sacrifice of all is praised, as their death is seen to advance the intifada toward an eventual victory. Membership and involvement in the groups of the intifada is common across class, age, and religious lines. Though the exoticized, Orientalist portrayal of those creating this martyrs' culture often presents a poor and deeply religious young male, this image lacks the nuance that constitutes the ranks of the various paramilitaries. The martyrs who narrate the struggle are young and old, secular and Islamist, rich and poor. The arguments herein do not, therefore, reflect *the whole* of Palestinian society, though they do reflect the norms established by the intifada. I have attempted to paint an accurate picture of this culture, bearing in mind its placement within the whole of Palestinian society and among the combined societies that create the Israeli-Palestinian conflict.

## A "Culture of Martyrdom"

In order to frame the mother narrative within the larger discourse of the Palestinian antioccupation and nationalist movements, Anne Marie Oliver and Paul F. Steinberg's "culture of martyrdom" framework has been adopted.[9] Though other scholars have spoken of a socializing force within Palestinian society that promotes self-sacrifice as a means of nationalist struggle, Oliver and Steinberg's bounded model lends itself well to this analysis. The authors develop the concept throughout their book, and while discussing the martyrdom tape of Abu-Surur, a Palestinian fighter, they define the culture: "The idea that you had to prepare for self-sacrifice, rehearse your own death lovingly as many times as possible—indeed, think of it in terms of happiness—was commonplace during the uprising. Media often seemed to serve precisely this function, vivifying death with the notion of happiness. The 'natural' or 'accidental' death was something to be avoided at all cost—an idea aptly expressed in the PFLP [Popular Front for the Liberation of Palestine] imperative, 'Beware of natural death. Don't die except in a shower of bullets.'"[10]

The concept of a "culture of martyrdom," is this: the society has taught its children to expect and welcome a fate of either dying in combat with the Israeli army or as a result of Israeli defensive and/or retaliatory violence. This culture is infused with religious overtones that reinterpret death as a reward. The cultural artifacts of the intifada exemplify this through portraying death as a welcoming Paradise, a goal to be sought.

This reinterpretation of death can also be seen in the propaganda created by militant groups. One example is the "Slogan of the Hamas," crafted by the organization in their 1987 manifesto. Within this document, termed the "The Charter of Allah: The Platform of the Islamic Resistance Movement," Hamas states,

> Allah is its goal,
> The Prophet its model,
> The Qur'an its Constitution,
> Jihad its path,
> and death for the cause of Allah its most sublime belief.[11]

In both the Popular Front for the Liberation of Palestine and the Hamas slogans, the acceptability and aspiration for martyrdom is apparent. Slogans such as these are regularly included in movement publications, political statements, military communiqués, graffiti, and other forms of community-level messaging. In their discussion of a movement artifact, a poster in this case, Oliver and Steinberg provide the following description: "Human skulls are piled atop one another to form the word *Hamas* . . . Torches are fueled by human blood rather than oil. Kalashnikovs stack up to form the name of a particular faction. The blood of martyrs is transformed into stones in the hands of street fighters. Blood streams from the back of a boy-martyr to form the byword, 'The intifada continues.' The word 'freedom' is formed from miniature bombs ready to explode in the face of the reader."[12]

This description exemplifies the militarized society that Palestinian children are raised in; a society that honors martyrdom through guerilla warfare and resistance. Young boys, unable to attend school during times of conflict, spend their days imitating militants, brandishing toy rifles and throwing rocks at Israeli forces. The constant presence of violent, hypermilitant imagery normalizes the bloodshed of the struggle and helps frame suicide attacks and other martyrdom operations as simply another acceptable and praised tactic of war. Children march in funeral processions and paramilitary parades, chanting with thousands of others, promising their lives as future martyrs for the Palestinian struggle for statehood. These are scattered examples of the socializing forces that help create and reproduce the "culture of martyrdom" in children, as well as adults.

Some critics of the armed intifada have argued that the perpetrators of the conflict manipulate their ideology to create an overly broad definition of what constitutes a martyr. These critics accuse militant leaders of exploiting the deaths of some Palestinians by claiming their lives as sacrifices for nationalism when they are actually killed "accidentally"—for example, in a situation in which the victim was counted as collateral damage and not the intended target. This critique is not specific to the Palestinian arena, just as justifiable martyrdom is not confined to Islamic/jihadi movements. In his book, Robert Pape argues that religious conceptions of what constitutes a martyr are standardized and uniform across religions: "Although both secular and religious groups honor 'martyrs,' the idea of martyrdom is religious in origin and remains primarily a religious concept even today. 'Martyrdom' means death for the sake of faith, and it or closely related terms are common to all the world's major religions as the sole exception to the prohibition on voluntary death (suicide) . . . All the world's primary religions hold that the main indicator that one had died for faith is that one has been killed by someone from outside the faith, who is part of a community hostile to the faith."[13]

The flexible usage of the martyr label allows the community to envision its collectivity in a shared opposition to the opponent collectivity—in this case, the state of Israel. When militants claim bystander deaths as *martyrdom*, the losses are used as a rallying cry for collective retaliation and resistance. In this sense, every Palestinian killed in the conflict aids the "culture of martyrdom" by building an ever-larger case for retaliation. By operating within this framework of a "culture of martyrdom," we can begin to locate the mothers' discourse as one portion of this larger cultural reality. It can be argued that the discourse offered by the mothers is in many ways scripted by the larger promartyr culture. The mother discourse serves to validate the "culture of martyrdom" while simultaneously supporting it. Those who constitute the intifada script the "culture of martyrdom," and as Islamist militant groups gain more influence, the culture has become increasingly reliant on the imagery and ideology of martyrdom as a driving force.

## The Mother Narrative

We must first establish what constitutes the mother narrative prior to discussing possible explanations as to why such a unified set of arguments are presented to the public. Before doing this, it is important to state that this analysis focuses on the *public statements* made by mothers, while presenting little insight as to the emotional trauma felt by grieving parents. Mothers who lose their children through acts of martyrdom privately mourn their loss, though their public face is much different.[14] The culture surrounding the intifada has scripted the public response, but this narrative must not be confused with the maternal grief experienced by all mothers who have lost a child. A mother's praise for her dead child's actions is more akin to a form of coping, a method of grieving that supports the nationalist initiative.

When reading the interviews and testimonies of the mothers, their proclamations of pride emerge clearly as an overriding theme. The mothers praise the "heroic" actions of their children and legitimize the attacks with congratulatory admiration. Within this realm, one mother's name repeats throughout as a model for the sacrificial Palestinian mother: Maryam Mohammad Yousif Farhat, popularly known as Um Nidal. Um Nidal was the epitome of what militant groups like Hamas hope for in a mother.[15] Um Nidal had six sons. Of these six sons, three were killed carrying out armed attacks against Israel. Another son has been imprisoned for intifada activities, and the other two are said to reside in the Gaza Strip, serving high-ranking positions with Hamas's military. Um Nidal's son-in-law was also a very popular and well-known Hamas military commander before being killed by Israeli forces. Um Nidal's popularity allowed her to be elected into the Palestinian Legislative Council in 2006 on Hamas's ticket. She also served as the Gaza regional deputy for Hamas's Change and Reform political party formation. She served there until her death in March 2013.

Um Nidal is known throughout Palestine not only because she publicly supported attacks initiated by her sons—including those that led to their deaths—but also because she provided material support to her son Mohammed Farahat in an attack that killed five *yeshiva* (religious school) students. Before leaving for the 2002 attack, Mohammed and his mother appeared in a video together where Um Nidal is shown wishing her son off. In a later interview she stated, "I wish I had 100 boys like Mohammad . . . I'd sacrifice them for the sake of God."[16] Between September 24 and December 10, 2005, Hamas's English-language website, the Palestine Information Center, carried at least six articles in praise of Um Nidal. In one titled "Moments with Um Nedhal [sic] Farahat while embracing sand mixed with her son's blood," Um Nidal is quoted as saying, "This is a great dream; I never expected the day when I enter [the site of the attack] and see, with my own eyes, the sand mixed with my son's blood to come true . . . I feel proud and exalted that I have my share in defeating the IOF [Israeli Occupying Force] in Gaza Strip and forcing them out of it."[17]

In another Hamas-authored article, Um Nidal maintains her support for martyrdom operations and says, "I am proud of my sons, who selected the best way to die; martyrs . . . Palestinian mothers must tolerate the pains of losing their sons falling while defending the Palestinian honor."[18] Not only is Um Nidal held up as a model within the mother narrative; she has also been promoted by Hamas as a political candidate. In December 2005, Hamas announced that it would field Um Nidal as an electoral candidate in the January 2005 legislative elections. Um Nidal was described as "a sure vote-winner" and an "icon of the Palestinian uprising."[19] In an article produced by the pro-Hamas Palestine Information Center, Um Nidal is described as "a Palestinian intifada symbol."[20] She is termed the "Khansa of Palestine," a reference to a figure from the time of the Prophet Muhammad who sacrificed all her sons fighting non-Muslim "unbelievers." It should be noted that the model of al-Khansa (b. 575 AD) is not confined to the Palestinian arena. In 2004, the transnational terrorist network of al-Qaeda created a jihadi publication for women named *al-Khansa*.[21] This Internet magazine encouraged Muslim women to integrate themselves into the global jihad and instructed mothers to raise children who embrace jihadi martyrdom. In very similar ways, both Hamas and al-Qaeda have signaled to Muslim women that al-Khansa is a model to be imitated in the modern fight for a revived Islamic empire.

Um Nidal's words represent a major theme in the mother narrative—namely, the supporting role mothers play in both the culture of martyrdom and the legitimacy of self-sacrifice. The words of Um Nidal are repeated throughout the mother discourse. While Um Nidal is a single example of a socially promoted version of motherhood, her public comments are common among mothers who have lost children in martyrdom attacks. In another example, the mother of the first female Palestinian suicide bomber, Wafa Idris, praised her daughter's actions as well. Wafa's mother is described as "tearful . . . [yet] proud of her daughter [hoping] more women will follow her example."[22] The words of Wasfiyeh Idris reflect the themes in the testimony of Um Nidal. Both mothers praise the actions of their children, and both encourage the continuation of martyrdom attacks as a tactic of war with Israel.

Though Um Nidal is presented as a model for other mothers to imitate, not all mothers react with the same praise. In her book, Joyce Davis analyzes conversations with three mothers who express three diverse points of view regarding the martyrdom of their children. The first mother, Munabrahim Daoud (mother of Mohammed al-Daoud), supports the narrative offered by Um Nidal in her praise of her son's actions. The mother advocates for armed struggle to resist occupation, offers herself as a potential martyr for Palestine, and argues that her son has the right to sacrifice himself for the sake of the nation.[23] She openly laments that the youths of Palestine are dying in pursuit of nationhood but appears to accept these as necessary losses in the continuation of nationalist resistance. Her story serves to legitimize the accounts offered throughout the discourse, exemplified by Um Nidal, and is surely representative of a *portion* of society.

The public discourse of the mothers of martyrs, at first glance, appears quite homogenous. It has been argued by some within the security apparatus that the whole of Palestinian society embraces Um Nidal's version of struggle, and thus the whole of Palestinian society is suicidal and opposed to any peaceful resolution. This statement is obviously untrue, as are all statements that attempt to describe an entire society through single declarative statements. Examining the example of Amal Zaki Ahmad (mother of Mohammed al-Durrah), we can see divergence in the mother narrative. In her testimony, Ahmad argues that the Palestinian intifada is needlessly killing the country's youth and says that if she was able, she would have stopped her son from attacking Israel and killing himself in the process.[24] It is likely that many mothers identify with this critique of martyrdom and armed struggle, though their testimonies are absent from the public discourse. This lack of diversity within the public mother discourse suggests that the media's presentation serves to filter out those whose words would be damaging to the promotion of a culture of martyrdom. Many of the mothers' testimonies are broadcasted via media networks with clearly stated, pro-armed-struggle policies. In at least two of the interviews surveyed, the segments were aired on Lebanon's al-Manar TV network, which is operated by the Iranian-backed paramilitary group Hezbollah.[25] In other instances, the television networks of the Palestinian Authority have hosted martyrs' mothers. As the Palestinian Authority acts as a quasigovernment for the Palestinian people, it maintains a vested interest in maintaining the armed nationalist movement. Examples like the mothers on al-Manar TV show an element of selection in the mothers' testimonies. If a mother is interviewed prior to the broadcast time and she appears hesitant or opposed to speaking positively about her child's attack, she would likely be passed over for another interviewee. It is difficult to determine how often this type of filtering occurs, but the testimony of Amal Zaki Ahmad shows that throughout Palestinian society a vibrant discourse is being played out, one that exhibits great diversity internally and little diversity when presented to the outside world.

These examples display numerous possible reactions to the martyrdom of a child. Davis's examples demonstrate that some mothers break from the normative praise narrative and outwardly express sorrow, regret, and sadness. Though we can determine that a portion of mothers would condemn martyrdom as a method of struggle, these testimonies are absent from the public discourse promoted in the public media sphere. While diverse reactions are seen in portions of the narrative, none of the mothers surveyed question the cause of their hardship; all blame the Israeli occupation. Though the mothers agree on the cause of their suffering, they do not agree as how to best confront it. Time and again mothers are interviewed on television, asked to speak at militant rallies, and are given prominence at religious services. In these settings, the mothers that advance socially are those that enforce the narrative. Those wishing to express grief and sadness are told to channel that into a sense of anger and resistance. When the discourse of the mother is packaged and transmitted throughout the society, it is stamped with the promartyrdom ideology of the militants, and when it is not, it is silent and kept within the arena of the home and family.

## Supporting Children— Encouraging Martyrs

The discourse of the mothers of martyrs is filled with recurring, overriding themes. In the generalized narrative, mothers present themselves as proud of their children's actions. They speak of their children's ascendance to Paradise and of the status the living gain from the sacrifices of the deceased. For jihadi Islamists, martyrdom promises entrance into Paradise, the equivalent of the Judeo-Christian concept of Heaven. This concept is developed by the Islamist jihadis, but it is found throughout the intifada in both secular and religious groups. While it is incorrect to assert that martyrs attack *solely* to gain entrance into Paradise, the promise of a Heavenly afterlife is commonly cited as a comforting factor. Through Davis's descriptive interview accounts, she implies that in the realm of martyrdom, mothers are expected to accept the decisions made by their children. If the child believes that Paradise awaits them following their death as martyrs, the mother must desire the best for their child and thus encourage martyrdom.[26] In an interview with Um Nidal, published in the London-based Arabic-language daily newspaper *Al-Sarq al-Awsat*, the "mother of martyrs" makes this point clearly: "I am a compassionate mother to my children, and they are compassionate towards me and take care of me. Because I love my son, I encouraged him to die a martyr's death for the sake of Allah . . . Jihad is a religious obligation incumbent upon us, and we must carry it out. I sacrificed Muhammad as part of my obligation."[27] Here, Um Nidal argues that love for her son *requires* her to encourage his martyrdom. In many cultures mothers are expected to make sacrifices for their children's well-being; in the Palestinian martyrdom narrative, this means offering children as martyrs, hoping that they will be successful in reaching Paradise.

Scholarship on the topic of martyrdom appears to agree on this point. Mothers are expected to support the choices their children make, and if their child desires martyrdom, the mothers are expected to support them and be joyful.[28] According to Oliver and Steinberg, as well as Davis, Islamist social forces have promoted the idea that mourning for a martyr is a sin. This belief is recurrent within intifada culture, and children are taught that after they die as martyrs, they are immediately transported to Paradise as heroes forgiven for their sins. With this belief in mind, mothers who argue against their children's planned self-sacrifice could be deemed un-Islamic in their attempt to prevent their children from reaching Paradise in the service of Allah. This tendency to support the will of the child shapes the mothers' discourse in powerful ways. It forces the words of mothers to mimic the words of their children, which in many cases is a reproduction of the messaging provided by militant groups. If the mother repeats the child, and the child repeats the militants, then who is shaping the mothers' discourse? The tendency to tacitly accept the will of the child is one element that allows this narrative transfer, traveling from the agenda-setters in militant groups to the mothers and martyrs.

## Rewarding Martyrs—Influencing Mothers

In attempting to determine the place of the mother within the discourse they present, it is necessary to examine the effects martyrdom has on the family, specifically on the mother. Throughout the stories of the intifada, accounts of incentives provided to those killed in combat have sparked a great deal of controversy. In some cases these rewards are monetary, but more often they take the form of social capital—namely, fame and prestige. The mother of a successful martyr gains a great deal of community status after her child is announced to have died in pursuit of the nationalist agenda. The neighborhood hosts parties for the family, the mother is framed as selfless, and the dead child is memorialized as a nationalist hero. Within the refugee camps, villages, towns, and cities that make up Palestinian society, the mothers of martyrs are made into stars overnight. In Davis's account of the aforementioned mothers, they all speak of some level of community celebration. Of these three women, one received financial gifts from sympathetic parties, one received gifts she donated to the needy, and one received no offers of charity at all. Once again the varied financial rewards and the varied celebratory practices show a great deal of diversity within the experience of losing a child.

Prior to deciding to participate in an attack on Israel, Palestinian martyrs-to-be likely consider the impact their actions will have on their families. The families of martyrs are collectively penalized by the Israeli state, and in the past, the family homes of suicide bombers have been demolished via bulldozer soon after the attack. The financial rewards attempt to serve as compensation for these retaliatory measures. Potential martyrs can predict the rewards and hardships their family may experience and may see their attack as a way to aid their family after they are dead.[29] If the child sees their actions as helping to liberate their homeland, the added bonus of personally elevating one's family would likely influence their decision. During childhood, Palestinians learn from local examples that martyrs' families are rewarded with notoriety, praise, social status, and gifts. The title given to the mothers of martyrs, *Um Shahid* (literally the mother of the martyr), is a sign of honor and respect. Throughout interviews with mothers, as well as with the martyrs themselves, themes of nationalism, religious duty, and revenge are dominant. It is far too simplistic and incorrect to argue that potential rewards are a motivational force for martyrs, though one cannot deny the effect their promise has on the unknown children who become well known, celebrated, nationalist icons.

Beyond financial gifts, the issue of community status appears to dominate the mothers' discussions. When a child becomes a martyr, the experience is felt by the family through both personal loss and community reactions. While the martyr experienced the attack, the family only experiences the aftermath—including such community support structures as visits from prominent movement leaders.[30] After a martyrdom attack, leaders within the armed movements will often visit the homes of the martyrs to speak with the family, paying special attention to the mother. Julie Peteet argues that this style of visiting carries unique connotations in Arab culture. She explains that the visitor's social positioning carries important social connotations, and that the fame of the visitor is a "crucial index of status and social hierarchy."[31] When movement leaders visit a martyr's home to spend time with the mother, she becomes the subject of praise and is recognized as garnishing the necessary importance to grant such a special visit. The visit acts as an additional social reward and a central element of gained community status.

These elements of reward, as experienced by the mothers of martyrs, have a definite effect on the narrative these women offer to the public. If no cultural support for martyrdom existed, and no community support for the families existed, it is unlikely that a sense of pride would dominate the mother narrative. The rewards, both financial and social, aid the militant groups by positively framing martyrdom through the perception of widespread community and social support. This sense that the entire community supports the actions of the martyr influences the reaction of the mother as she attempts to align her public reaction with accepted community norms.

## Spheres of Gendered Involvement

In attempting to place the experience of the mothers of martyrs within the larger context of the Palestinian intifada, we can conceptualize their actions as filling a traditionally female sphere of activity. Since the start of the al-Aqsa Intifada, women have increased and diversified their roles within militant groups; however, the roles of paramilitary fighter and suicide bomber are still relegated to the young, and thus mothers are not ideal candidates for these positions. Since the start of the al-Aqsa Intifada, there have been at least ten attacks by female suicide bombers,[32] and the Israel Defense Forces claim to have arrested more than fifty in the process of organizing attacks. In 2004, Hamas, with the assistance of Fatah's al-Aqsa Martyrs Brigade, dispatched Reem al-Riyashi, a female suicide bomber who was also a mother of two. In her martyrdom tape, al-Riyaski spoke of sacrificial motherhood: "God has given me two children. I love them [with] a kind of love that only God knows, but my love to meet God is stronger still."[33] In 2006, Fatimah al-Najar, a 57-year-old mother of 9 (grandmother to 41), killed herself in a suicide bombing targeting Israeli troops conducing military operations in the Gaza Strip. In her martyrdom tape, al-Najar stated, "I ask Allah to join us with martyrs and to get my sons and daughter into [al-Aqsa] mosque. I wish that my family will give sweets when hearing of my martyrdom."[34]

Though evidence has shown Palestinian women to operate in a variety of armed roles, the numbers of *visible* male fighters vastly overshadows that of females. Therefore nationalist-minded women are forced to find other ways to support the resistance. In practice, many women are prevented from participating as fighters in the public sphere, and as such, mothers' actions as propagandists can be deemed the fulfillment of a proscribed nationalist role. In this role as propagandist, the power of the narrative is its ability to transform the private experience of grieving into a public performance in support of the nationalist movement. Feminist scholar and conflict analyst Simona Sharoni argues that throughout the world women are excluded from the politics of nationalist struggle and are therefore encouraged to serve the cause by operating in the private sphere of the home.[35] Both within the world at large and within the Palestinian context, women are encouraged to serve the nation by birthing male fighters, maintaining the home, and otherwise remaining within a traditionally female, private sphere of influence.

When mothers praise the actions of their martyred children, they are not confronting these gendered assumptions, as their praise still emulates and is associated with the space of the home. The actions of the praising mothers do not challenge gendered norms and are therefore accepted by the larger male-led nationalist movement. Cynthia Cockburn, a feminist scholar focused on the intersection of gender and conflict, shares this view and discusses "acceptable private spheres," noting women's lack of autonomy in nationalist movements.[36] She explains that women's roles in nationalist movements inextricably link them to the home and family. In areas with ongoing nationalist movements, women often find themselves as the teachers of children, the supporters of male fighters, and the key players in an ongoing demographic war. Women in the Gaza Strip have one of the highest fertility rates in the world, as the Palestinian population attempts to shift demographics in their favor. In essence, the females are charged with reproducing the nation, both physically and socially.

Within the model of gendered spheres of involvement, we can question the consistent representation of mothers as linked to their sons. It is exceedingly rare in the discourse of martyrdom to find publicized reactions from fathers, brothers, sisters, or spouses. This discourse largely ignores fathers and focuses solely on female parents and their male or female children. This peculiarity begs the question, why does the Palestinian discourse focus so heavily on the connection between a mother and her son? This formulaic reliance reflects an essentialist view of motherhood as somehow embodying a unique connection, unable to be experienced by other members of the family. This view implies that women have occupied this linked role throughout time, and that their status as the repository of grief is static. Within the discourse of the intifada, the mother-of-martyrs narrative can be seen as a genre of propaganda, equivalent to graffiti, leaflets, or videotaped martyr testimonies. All these artifacts serve to form the culture of the intifada. In placing Palestinian mothers within a private sphere of gendered activity, her role is to represent the family's grief, to present a proud face for the fathers, siblings, spouses and extended family. That is her role, to represent the normative reaction, and to bear the grief privately while displaying the family's collective pride publicly.

When women are selected to represent the family, they are further inundated with an inherently reactionary role. While traditionally, males occupy the active battlefront and women the reactionary home front, the nature of the Israeli occupation and the resulting Palestinian uprising has created an unclear, deterritorialized line of battle.[37] This has led women into the realm of a defensive war. The Palestinian home, managed by the mother, is often a battleground due to the nature of the conflict, its lack of dually opposed state actors, and the use of community-based, guerilla warfare tactics. Since the protests, arrest raids, and militant organizing occur in neighborhoods and homes (and not military bases), the Israeli army is often fighting in the homes and yards of the populace. This has blurred the demarcation that traditionally excludes the home front from the battlefront. This muddled distinction means that the home front is often a scene of conflict and war.

## Celebration as Resistance

As women are kept absent from the public sphere of the nationalist movement, mothers have created a space for themselves as propagandists, crafting a discourse of resistance and perpetuating the culture of martyrdom. After a martyr is killed and the community swarms the home of the family, the sense of celebration is unmistakable. Community members distribute sweets to children, posters displaying the martyr's picture are plastered around, and mass funeral marches pass through the streets triumphantly exhibiting the martyr overhead. These elements of celebration are essential to the culture of martyrdom and thus essential in constructing the mothers' discourse. The addition of a sense of celebration in the face of death is itself a loud statement of defiance directed at Israel. By celebrating death, the Palestinians convey a message of uncompromising struggle—a sense that the parade of future martyrs will never cease. The mass funerals of martyrs celebrate this sense of collective resistance and serve to solidify the community in its support of the family. The community joins together to resist collectively, and thus the mothers' praise is simply another element of this self-promoting, celebratory cycle.

One theory explaining the displays of joy at martyrs' funerals links these celebrations to the missed opportunity to express similar joy during a child's wedding. While there have been numerous examples of married men and women becoming martyrs, in the majority of cases the fighters are unmarried. In Palestinian society, marriage is an important part of the life cycle. Men and women are often married young, and in the absence of a wedding, the family has missed one of the central ceremonies that frames the life of their child. Anthropologist Julie Peteet hypothesizes that mothers may compensate for missing their child's wedding by equally celebrating their martyrdom.[38] Though not an example from the Palestinian arena, this hypothesis may help to explain the testimony offered by the mother of Bassel Ala' al-Din, a martyred Hezbollah fighter, broadcast on Hezbollah-controlled television in 2005. In the interview the mother says, "Bassel had a wish . . . Whenever I told him I wanted to marry him off, he would say: 'Yes, mother, you'll marry me off like this in paradise.' And indeed, the martyr Bassel got married in paradise. I congratulate the black-eyed virgins who took Bassel from me, who took my entire life."[39]

In the absence of a wedding, the mother praises her child's ascendance to Paradise and his eventual "wedding" with *hur al-'ain*, the virgins of Paradise. The martyrdom discourse is spotted with wedding parallels. In another example, Palestinian Um Taysie (mother of Taysir al-'Ajrami) dreams about her martyred son. In her interview on Palestinian Authority TV, Um Taysie describes her dream encounter with her son, who was killed in a Hamas suicide bombing. Um Taysie draws a connection between martyrdom and weddings, stating, "That very night his brother Taysir came to me in a dream. I was standing at the entrance to the house and he appeared, wearing a groom's suit and his face was lit up like the moon. This is what Taysir's face looked like in the dream . . . I dreamt it the night he committed martyrdom. In the morning I said to his wife . . . Naji is going to be martyred today.'"[40] This statement shows that while Taysir was already married, he still appeared in the dream "wearing a groom's suit." This dress symbolizes his wedding to the *hur al-'ain*, and though his mother had the opportunity to celebrate her son's earthly marriage, the wedding in Paradise is also celebrated.

In order to further draw the connection between the celebratory nature of weddings and martyrdom, we can examine the Arab custom of vocal ululations. During weddings, funeral processions, as well as smaller community celebrations, women can often be located by tuning one's ear to the sound of ululation. Peteet argues that the mother who most bravely ululates in celebration of martyrdom is praised and considered a desired example of "militant motherhood."[41] This practice honors those who praise the loudest and thus acts as a type of social natural selection advancing the praising mothers and passing over those who resist the celebration. This form of social selection is the same process that fosters a seemingly homogenous discourse concerning mothers' reactions toward martyrdom. Those who speak in praise are promoted socially, and those who hesitate to enforce the narrative are penalized by invisibility, social isolation, and stigmatization. The funeral processions and interviews teach the lesson that regardless of the grief experienced in private, when in the public sphere one must serve the nationalist agenda and praise the martyr.

## Mothers' Sacrifices Are Expected

In surveying the active participants in the Palestinian intifada, one first highlights the roles played by suicide bombers, armed fighters, and stone-throwing children. When discussing the actions that constitute the resistance movement, the role of the mother as propagandist and martyrdom supporter is rarely identified. I have argued that the role played by the mothers' discourse is integral to the continuation of the culture of martyrdom—a culture that guarantees an unending supply of bodies willing to die for nationhood. In this role, the mother is expected to not only continuously birth children—fighting an ongoing demographic war with the Israeli populace—but eventually sacrifice those children for the nationalist agenda. Within this logic, mothers' contributions to the nationalist movement can be overlooked because of an assumption that such sacrifice is the fulfillment of a proscribed duty. Journalist and Middle East specialist Barbara Victor takes care to interview many mothers who have lost their children as martyrs. In one interview, Samira, the cousin of female suicide bomber Darine Abu Aisha, speaks to this proscribed duty: "It is the duty of every Palestinian mother to encourage her sons and daughters to become martyrs. I adore my children, but if I help them achieve martyrdom, it only means that Allah has chosen them because he loves them more than I do."[42] Samira's words show the pressure placed on mothers taught to encourage jihadi tendencies in their children. If the mothers were to prevent their children from becoming active in the movement, they could be seen as barriers to the nationalist agenda. This message is clear within the Palestinian nationalist movement, so much so that prominent mothers have publicly declared their children as potential martyrs.

In 2002, Suha al-Taweel Arafat, wife of former Palestinian leader Yasser Arafat, declared publicly that there was "no greater honor" than offering her son to the nationalist movement as a future martyr.[43] The wife of Hamas leader Abdel Aziz al-Rantissi was publicly scorned for failing to offer her son as a potential martyr after a phone call with her was broadcast globally by the Israeli government.[44] Abdel Rantissi later responded to the phone call, accusing the Israeli intelligence service of attempting to entrap his wife.[45] Rantissi accused Israel of attempting to weaken the Palestinian resistance by presenting their son Muhammad's mother as selfish, unwilling to support the martyrdom narrative. In Rantissi's accusation, he was clear to argue that his family would contribute their children, as all Palestinians are expected to do:

> The Mossad [Israeli intelligence] announced that it had a voice recording of my wife in which she voiced her rejection that her son Muhammad should carry out a martyrdom operation . . . A Zionist intelligence officer assumed the identity of Hamas military wing . . . and telephoned my home asking for my son . . . [Umm Muhammad] realized that the speaker was a member of the Zionist intelligence service so she spoke with great reservation . . . [Mossad] wished to undermine the Palestinian youths' psychological preparedness to seek martyrdom. The Zionist enemy realizes that Hamas's leaders have a great willingness to sacrifice themselves and their sons, for they are more eager than others to go to Paradise and wish their sons to do the same.[46]

Rantissi's defense was prompt, and he sought to assure the Palestinian people that his wife, like all nationalist wives, was willing to sacrifice for the larger goal of statehood. While it is impossible to know if Umm Muhammad's taped reaction is an accurate reflection of her personal views, Abdel Rantissi's reaction asserted Hamas's official position. Though Umm Muhammad may not personally want to lose her son, Rantissi's political concerns dominated publicly, and their son Muhammad was offered to the resistance as a future martyr.

It is assumed that an archetypal Palestinian mother would be willing yet not necessarily eager to sacrifice her child for nationhood. Peteet argues that throughout the Arab world the assumption that mothers are "sacrificial" is consistent and uncontested.[47] If one accepts Peteet's argument, then the actions of the martyrs' mothers are within expected gendered roles. The mother is expected to suffer throughout the struggle, her identity seen not only as the "giver of life" but also as the benevolent entity of sacrifice. These demands on the reproductive faculties of the Palestinian women are socially constructed, necessitated by the conflict, and presented as unchallenged expectations. If a mother defies these expectations—for example, by refusing to birth children or insulating her children from the intifada—she can be labeled as an Israeli collaborator or a traitor to the nationalist movement.

In their work, both Sharoni and Peteet agree that the nationalist movement often overlooks the contributions of mothers, as such sacrifices are seen as normal fulfillment of the motherly duties.[48] The mother is *expected* to praise the actions of her children, and she is *expected* to raise her children to desire martyrdom. If the mothers are expected to fill this role, then their contributions as praise-giving propagandists can be overlooked. This expectation robs mothers of their agency as nationalist actors and paints their actions as reactionary, solely responsive to the actions of their children. If the mothers are expected to simply raise the children and praise their actions, then their responses to the choices their children make will remain reactionary. With the men fighting Israel, they have become increasingly absent from the home, forcing women to adapt their roles to compensate. As supporters, women's contributions are accepted, as they show "loyalty to both the men in their families and the larger collectivity."[49] Within this social stalemate, the efforts of the mother are not afforded praise but rather assumed. This assumed role allows the culture of martyrdom, and specifically the discourse of the mothers of martyrs, to be transmitted from mother to child without interruption, failing to regard the mother as integral to the ideology crafting the intifada.

## Mothers as Icons and Repeaters

In arguing that mothers are confined to operate within the private sphere and their contributions are expected and not praised, we must avoid assuming that their role is not *important* in the nationalist movement. Within Palestinian society, mothers are seen as national icons, representatives of the larger society. They are seen as the "reproducers of the nation's culture,"[50] as they are the agents that teach the children and pass on tradition. The 1987 Hamas Charter explicitly names these female roles: "Muslim women have a role in the liberation struggle that is no less important than the role of men; woman is the maker of men, and her role in guiding and educating the generations is a major role."[51] The charter proceeds to state that the mother must educate the child in preparation for "their contribution to the jihad that awaits them." If mothers are instructed to teach the culture to the children, and the culture praises martyrdom, are we then surprised that many mothers teach and raise their children to embrace self-sacrifice? By having the national icon repeat the martyrdom narrative, it is granted great legitimizing power and influence. This further extends the reproductive pigeonholing of the mother, as she transmits cultural norms she did not herself create.

Within the society, the mother's words are seen as highly representative of the average mind-set within that culture, as women's voices are "highly valued in the nationalist discourse and often symbolize the spirit of the nation."[52] Thus if the spirit of the nation is martyrdom for nationhood, it is no surprise that the mothers transmit this understanding to their children. This is not to argue that the mothers are the sole enforcers of this culture, though their socializing effects on their children are extensive. The nature of a *culture* of martyrdom indicates that the influence is multifaceted and total. It is seen in graffiti scrawled on the walls, on children's Saturday morning cartoons, in posters lining shops and homes, and in the words and deeds of respected leaders. The culture of martyrdom is all around the youth of Palestine, yet when enforced by the word of the mother, it is given interfamily legitimacy and the power of a mother's voice.

Some have argued that mothers are not icons of tradition but icons of sacrifice.[53] The experiences of mothers under occupation have made these women into emblems for the suffering and loss of Palestinian society. This explanation exists not in contrast to the aforementioned argument but serves to complement it. Peteet argues that in making mothers into icons of sacrifice, the title of "mother of martyr" is adopted as a legitimized form of recognition.[54] By naming the explicit role of mothering successful attackers, the role is deemed legitimate. Palestinian politicians and movement leaders often include greetings to the mothers of martyrs in public statements, giving the title prominence and publicly recognizing the mothers' sacrifice. Combining the dual analyses offered, the mothers of Palestine can be considered emblems of tradition and emblems of suffering concurrently. In one regard, the mothers embody tradition, thus acting to transmit the culture to the youth, while in another sense, the mothers embody sacrifice and thus act to legitimize martyrdom. If we embrace these two tendencies simultaneously, the Palestinian mother, in reproducing the discourse of martyrdom, is acting as the embodiment of traditional sacrifice. By normalizing sacrifice as traditional, the mother helps shape the culture of martyrdom and continue the flow of recruits toward militants waiting to equip them with explosives and rifles.

## Conclusion

The sociocultural norms that constitute the Palestinian culture of martyrdom are lived by the populace, taught to the children by the mothers, and acted out in the daily activities of the intifada. The children learn about the society from their mothers, and thus the mothers' words are reflective of the dominant social norms, which in Palestinian society include the glorification of death for the cause of nationhood. Upon initial examination, the narrative offered by the mothers appears to be homogeneous, but when probed further, we can conclude that this public presentation of motherhood is selective and not fully representative. Complex systems of social and financial incentives allow mothers who enforce the dominant narrative to thrive, while those who stand opposed are kept absent from the public testimonies of the intifada. Through the statements presented in the media, it is impossible to determine the pervasiveness of the mother narrative in the larger Palestinian society. We know that the narrative discusses martyrdom in positive terms, but we are not able to determine how representative this narrative is among Palestinian women, and while the mothers' narrative remains dominant in the public sphere, it is not representative of the entirety of Palestinians. Furthermore it is difficult (if not impossible) to determine where sincere, self-sacrificial offering ends and nationalist performativity begins; in other words, how much of the mother narrative is for the purpose of media spectacle and how much is an accurate reflection of one's views? The answer remains unknown.

The mothers' discourse is a reflection of the culture of martyrdom as present in modern Palestinian society. The armed, nonstate actors that wage the continual war foster this culture. These groups actively infuse themes of martyrdom and religio-nationalist duty into the Palestinian reality. This prointifada-nationalism touches all aspects of Palestinian life and is embraced widely throughout the society. When the mothers relay this culture via representation in the media, and when it is taught to their children, they are acting within a traditionally female role as a repository and transmitter of culture. These communicative roles are both public and private, yet they remain within a feminine sphere of involvement, reactionary in nature, and inseparable from the actions of the children. Within the roles adopted by the mothers of Palestine, they are positioned to reproduce the nation in both sexual reproduction and discourse reproduction. In this role, the mother is positioned as a dual reproducer—birthing both future fighters and the dominant narrative that serves to continue the intifada until nationhood is achieved.

## Notes

1. Rema Hammami, "Women, the Hijab and the Intifada," *Middle East Report* 164/165 (August 1990): 24–28, 71, 78; Amal Jamal, "Engendering State-Building: The Women's Movement and Gender-Regime in Palestine," *The Middle East Journal* 55, no. 2 (Spring 2001): 256–76; Susan Muaddi Darraj, "Palestinian Women: Fighting Two Battles," *Monthly Review* 56, no. 1 (May 2004): 32–33; Beverley Milton-Edwards, *Islamic Politics in Palestine* (London: I. B. Tauris, 1999).
2. Ezzedeen Al-Qassam Brigades Information Office, "Military Communiqué: Al Qassam Brigades Mourns the Death of Saleh Al Basheti," Ezzedeen Al-Qassam Brigades Information Office, October 27, 2013, http://www.qassam.ps/statement-1493-Al_Qassam_Brigades _mourns_the_death_of_Saleh_Al_Basheti.html.
3. "Israel Completes Gaza Withdrawal," *BBC*, September 12, 2005, http://news.bbc.co.uk/2/hi/middle_east/4235768.stm.
4. Inigo Gilmore, "Palestinian Ceasefire Ends Four-year Intifada," *Telegraph*, February 4, 2005, http://www.telegraph.co.uk/news/ worldnews/middleeast/israel/1482803/Palestinian-ceasefire-ends -four-year-intifada.html.
5. "Over 600 Palestinians Killed in Internal Clashes Since 2006," *Ynetnews.com*, June 6, 2007, http://www.ynetnews.com/articles/0 ,7340,L-3409548,00.html.
6. "Poll No. 78, Dec. 2012—Gaza, Resistance and the UN Bid," Jerusalem Media and Communication Centre, December 22, 2012,

http://www.jmcc.org/documentsandmaps.aspx?id=858; Arab World for Research and Development, *Results of an Opinion Poll: The Public Mood, UN Vote, Gaza Confrontation, Elections, PA and Government, Evaluation of Leadership* (Ramallah, Palestine: author, 2012), 3, http://www.awrad.org/files/server/20121512014342.docx.

7. Sherna Berger Gluck, "Palestinian Women: Gender Politics and Nationalism," *Journal of Palestine Studies* 24, no. 3 (April 1995): 5–15, doi:10.2307/2537876; Karla J. Cunningham, "Cross-Regional Trends in Female Terrorism," *Studies in Conflict & Terrorism* 26, no. 3 (2003): 171–95, doi:10.1080/10576100390211419; Barbara Victor, *Army of Roses: Inside the World of Palestinian Women Suicide Bombers* (London: Constable, 2004); Debra D. Zedalis, *Female Suicide Bombers* (Honolulu: University Press of the Pacific, 2004); Cindy D. Ness, "In the Name of the Cause: Women's Work in Secular and Religious Terrorism," *Studies in Conflict and Terrorism* 28, no. 5 (2005): 353–73, doi:10.1080/10576100500180337; Rosemarie Skaine, *Female Suicide Bombers* (Jefferson, NC: McFarland, 2006); Israeli Security Agency, *2006 Summary—Palestinian Terror Data and Trends* (Jerusalem: Israeli Security Agency, 2006); Yoram Schweitzer, "Palestinian Istishhadia: A Developing Instrument," *Studies in Conflict and Terrorism* 30, no. 8 (2007): 667–89, doi:10.1080/10576100701435761; Anat Berko and Edna Erez, "Gender, Palestinian Women, and Terrorism: Women's Liberation or Oppression?" *Studies in Conflict & Terrorism* 30, no. 6 (2007): 493–519, doi:10.1080/10576100701329550; Anne Speckhard, "The Emergence of Female Suicide Terrorists," *Studies in Conflict and Terrorism* 31, no. 11 (2008): 995–1023, doi:10.1080/10576100802408121.

8. The casualty numbers were derived from data collected from the BBC, as well as data collected by B'Tselem. The data range for the BBC study is September 29, 2000—January 15, 2005. The date range for the B'Tselem study is September 29, 2000—December 26, 2008. "Intifada Toll Sept 2000—Sept 2005," *BBC*, September 30, 2005, http://news.bbc.co.uk/2/hi/middle_east/4294502.stm; "Fatalities before Operation 'Cast Lead,'" *B'Tselem*, 2008, http://www.btselem.org/statistics/fatalities/before-cast-lead/by-date-of-event.

9. Anne Marie Oliver and Paul F. Steinberg, *The Road to Martyrs' Square: A Journey into the World of the Suicide Bomber* (New York: Oxford University Press, 2006).

10. Ibid., 122.

11. Hamas, "The Charter of Allah: The Platform of the Islamic Resistance Movement (Hamas)," trans. Raphael Israeli, Harry Truman Research Institute, The Hebrew University, April 5, 1998.

12. Oliver and Steinberg, *The Road to Martyrs' Square*, 62.

13. Robert Anthony Pape, *Dying to Win: The Strategic Logic of Suicide Terrorism* (New York: Random House, 2005), 91.

14. The use of the term *child* and *children* throughout this chapter is not meant to reference the subject's age but rather to denote their relation to the mother. Men and women engaging in suicide bombings and other armed attacks are mainly between the ages of 18 and 30. Though some have carried out attacks at later points in their lives, the use of young children and teenagers is exceedingly rare. Young children are often engaged in stone throwing and may possibly provide material assistance to militant groups, but they do not carry out armed assaults endorsed by paramilitaries. Therefore when the "children of mothers" are discussed, the term is not meant to convey age but simply a relationship.
15. Nidal Al-Mughrabi, "Hamas 'Mother of Martyrs' Runs in Palestinian Poll," *Reuters*, December 8, 2005.
16. William Yardley, "Mariam Farhat, Palestinian 'Mother of Martyrs,' Dies at 64," *New York Times*, March 20, 2013, http://www.nytimes.com/2013/03/20/world/middleeast/mariam-farhat-palestinian-mother-of-martyrs-dies-at-64.html.
17. "Reports: Moments with Um Nidhal Farahat While Embracing Sand Mixed with Her Son's Blood," Palestine Information Center, October 6, 2005, http://www.palestine.co.uk/am/publish/printer_14775.shtml.
18. "Daily News: Palestinian Mother Remembers Her Martyred Sons, Proud of Their Heroism," Palestine Information Center, November 7, 2005, http://www.palestine.co.uk/am/publish/printer_15203.shtml.
19. Al-Mughrabi, "Hamas 'Mother of Martyrs' Runs in Palestinian Poll."
20. "Daily News: Hamas Nominates Khansa of Palestine for PLC Elections," Palestine Information Center, December 10, 2005, http://www.palestine-info.co.uk/am/publish/printer_15771.shtml.
21. "Militants Launch Internet Magazine Encouraging Women to Take up Arms," *Boston Herald*, August 27, 2004.
22. "Female Bomber's Mother Speaks Out," *BBC*, January 30, 2002, http://news.bbc.co.uk/2/hi/middle_east/1791800.stm.
23. Joyce Davis, *Martyrs: Innocence, Vengeance, and Despair in the Middle East* (New York: Palgrave Macmillan, 2004), 122–25.
24. Ibid., 124–25.
25. Al-Manar TV, *MEMRI: Mother of a Hizbullah "Martyr" Tells Her Story (#714)*, Video clip, vol. 714 (Lebanon: Al-Manar TV, 2005), http://www.memritv.org/clip/en/714.
26. Davis, *Martyrs*, 130–32.
27. Maryam Mohammad Yousif Farhat, "An Interview with the Mother of a Suicide Bomber (Special Dispatch No. 391)," trans. Middle East Media Research Institute, June 19, 2002, http://www.memri.org/report/en/print683.htm.
28. Oliver and Steinberg, *The Road to Martyrs' Square*, 126,159.
29. Ibid., 148.

30. Julie Peteet, "Icons and Militants: Mothering in the Danger Zone," *Signs* 23, no. 1 (October 1, 1997): 116–17.
31. Ibid., 117.
32. Victor, *Army of Roses*.
33. Chris McGreal, "Human-bomb Mother Kills Four Israelis at Gaza Checkpoint," *Guardian*, January 15, 2004, http://www.theguardian.com/world/2004/jan/15/israel.
34. "Fatimah Omar Mahmoud Al-Najar," *Ezzedeen Al-Qassam Brigades Information Office*, 2006, http://www.qassam.ps/martyr-80-Fatimah_Omar_Mahmoud_Al_Najar.html.
35. Simona Sharoni, "Rethinking Women's Struggles in Israel-Palestine and in the North of Ireland," in *Victims, Perpetrators or Actors?: Gender, Armed Conflict and Political Violence*, ed. Caroline N. O. Moser and Fiona Clark (New York: Zed, 2001), 86.
36. Cynthia Cockburn, *The Space between Us: Negotiating Gender and National Identities in Conflict* (New York: Zed/St Martin's, 1998), 43.
37. Peteet, "Icons and Militants," 108.
38. Ibid., 116.
39. Al-Manar TV, *MEMRI*.
40. Palestinian Authority TV, *MEMRI: Mother of Palestinian Suicide Bomber Interviewed on PA TV (#271)*, Video clip, vol. 271 (Palestine: Palestinian Authority TV, 2004), http://www.memritv.org/clip/en/271.htm.
41. Peteet, "Icons and Militants," 115–16.
42. Victor, *Army of Roses*, 102.
43. "Israel: Palestinian First Lady Speaks Out (Suha al-Taweel Arafat)," *Info-Prod Research (Middle East)*, April 14, 2002, http://www.highbeam.com/doc/1G1-84784327.html.
44. "Hamas Leader's Wife Forbids Son to Become Suicide Bomber," *Jerusalem Post*, August 2, 2002.
45. Abdel Aziz Rantissi, "My Wife Told the Truth and the Jews, the Corrupters, Lied," *BBC*, August 9, 2002.
46. Ibid.
47. Peteet, "Icons and Militants," 105.
48. Sharoni, "Rethinking Women's Struggles in Israel-Palestine and in the North of Ireland," 92.
49. Ibid.
50. Cockburn, *The Space between Us*, 43.
51. Khalid Hroub, *Hamas: Political Thought and Practice* (Washington, DC: Institute for Palestine Studies, 2000), 234.
52. Ibid.
53. Peteet, "Icons and Militants," 110.
54. Ibid., 112.

## Selected Bibliography

Berko, Anat, and Edna Erez. "Gender, Palestinian Women, and Terrorism: Women's Liberation or Oppression?" *Studies in Conflict and Terrorism* 30, no. 6 (2007): 493–519.

Cockburn, Cynthia. *The Space between Us: Negotiating Gender and National Identities in Conflict.* London: Zed, 1998.

Cunningham, Karla J. "Cross-Regional Trends in Female Terrorism." *Studies in Conflict and Terrorism* 26, no. 3 (2003): 171–95.

Darraj, Susan Muaddi. "Palestinian Women: Fighting Two Battles." *Monthly Review* 56, no. 1 (May 2004): 25–36.

Gluck, Sherna Berger. "Palestinian Women: Gender Politics and Nationalism." *Journal of Palestine Studies* 24, no. 3 (April 1995): 5–15.

Hammami, Rema. "Women, the Hijab and the Intifada." *Middle East Report* 164/165 (August 1990): 24–28, 71, 78.

Hroub, Khalid. *Hamas: Political Thought and Practice.* Washington, DC: Institute for Palestine Studies, 2000.

Jamal, Amal. "Engendering State-Building: The Women's Movement and Gender-Regime in Palestine." *The Middle East Journal* 55, no. 2 (Spring 2001): 256–76.

Milton-Edwards, Beverley. *Islamic Politics in Palestine.* London: I. B. Tauris, 1999.

Ness, Cindy D. "In the Name of the Cause: Women's Work in Secular and Religious Terrorism." *Studies in Conflict and Terrorism* 28, no. 5 (2005): 353–73.

Oliver, Anne Marie, and Paul F. Steinberg. *The Road to Martyrs' Square: A Journey into the World of the Suicide Bomber.* New York: Oxford University Press, 2006.

Schweitzer, Yoram. "Palestinian Istishhadia: A Developing Instrument." *Studies in Conflict and Terrorism* 30, no. 8 (2007): 667–89.

Sharoni, Simona. "Rethinking Women's Struggles in Israel-Palestine and in the North of Ireland." In *Victims, Perpetrators or Actors?: Gender, Armed Conflict and Political Violence,* edited by Caroline N. O. Moser and Fiona Clark, 85–98. New York: Zed, 2001.

Skaine, Rosemarie. *Female Suicide Bombers.* Jefferson, NC: McFarland, 2006.

Speckhard, Anne. "The Emergence of Female Suicide Terrorists." *Studies in Conflict and Terrorism* 31, no. 11 (2008): 995–1023.

Victor, Barbara. *Army of Roses: Inside the World of Palestinian Women Suicide Bombers.* London: Constable, 2004.

Zedalis, Debra D. *Female Suicide Bombers.* Honolulu: University Press of the Pacific, 2004.

# Chapter 12

## Motherhood as a Space of Political Activism

### Iraqi Mothers and the Religious Narrative of Karbala

*Fatin Shabbar*

### Introduction

During the Ba'ath regime, Iraq underwent one of the most brutal political periods of its history. Since the very beginning of its establishment, the regime used violence to maintain control over the country. The Ba'ath party was the only official and legal party in the country; its ideology was forced on citizens, and every Iraqi individual had to adhere to the official philosophy and worldview, as any conflicting ideas would lead to severe punishment. The education system, cultural narratives, and history were reoriented and Ba'athized.[1] Membership and full commitment to the party was compulsory among high school and university students as well as public servants, politicians, and journalists.[2] Saddam Hussein positioned himself as the leader of the Ba'ath party in Iraq and therefore held sole authority over Ba'ath philosophy.[3] In reality the party had no significance when compared to the person of Saddam Hussein, as the whole power and authority given to the Ba'ath party was only to facilitate and ensure "the President's absolute political control and psychological hold over people's lives."[4] During his time in power, Saddam Hussein established several loyal organizations that had full authority to investigate, detain, torture, and execute any Iraqi individual suspected of working against the regime.[5]

The presence of these organizations and the regime's use of force to dominate the nation created a culture of violence in Iraq. Rape, torture, displacement, forced divorce, and murder were common events within Iraqi society. The chairperson of the UK-based Organization of Human Rights in Iraq, Dr. Sahib Alhakim, reports that more than 4,000 incidents of rape, murder, and torture occurred under the Ba'ath regime.[6] However, alongside state political violence, Iraq has also gone through four destructive wars in the past three and a half decades. The first was the Iraq-Iran war that started in 1980 and continued for eight years, followed by the Iraq-Kuwait war in 1990, and then the Gulf War in 1991. The Gulf War was then directly followed by UN-imposed economic sanctions that continued for 13 years and was described as "genocide" by Denis Hallidery, the UN humanitarian coordinator in Iraq. The end of the regime in 2003 started a new era of violence in Iraq. After almost 11 years since the US invasion of Iraq, security and safety are still considered major issues for the Iraqi people along other issues such as poverty, corruption, and a lack of necessary resources, including clean drinking water and electricity.

This long history of political instability has left its imprint on the Iraqi identity, particularly in relation to violence and terror. When violence was used as a primary tool of communication and domination in Iraq, fear became a prominent emotional experience among Iraqi people. Saddam Hussein held a particular interest in producing a Ba'athized generation that held an eternal loyalty to their leader, therefore he focused on the children and the youth, emphasizing that "the Party and the State should be their family, their father and mother."[7] With this philosophy, children and youth were brainwashed not only through Ba'athized education but also through compulsory military trainings that taught children to safeguard the Ba'ath regime and their leader and "godfather" Saddam.[8] In an effort to diminish this influence, mothers worked to develop a counteridentity in their children.

Generally, the political instability in Iraq in the last three and a half decades has significantly reshaped roles and experiences of mothers. The contribution of mothers in war time and in militarized societies is not merely one of nurturing but rather one of indemnifying survival for their families, which may include carrying out domestic duties, providing a living, and engaging in direct and indirect conflict with the enemy.[9] It is important to emphasize that ensuring the survival of family extends beyond the physical domain to the psychological.

Psychological survival can include mothers developing "psychological resistance" in their children against violence and oppression.[10] However, when living in a state of violence and fear, developing and maintaining psychological survival mechanisms within children can become a very complex process for mothers and often requires innovative methods of child rearing. Mothering children in war zones and in militarized societies is inevitably a political act, because it most often involves the nurturing of *safe* resistance within children. In her research on Palestinian mothers, anthropologist Julie Peteet explains that her research participants considered their motherhood as a form of "*nidal*," which means political struggle.[11] Such a discursive portrayal of motherhood embraces the understanding that the political domain is an integral part of everyday mothering.

The analysis provided in this chapter focuses on the ways that mothers negotiate their religious and cultural environment to politicize their mothering. In other words, there is particular attention paid to mothers' transformational engagement with religious and cultural discourses and practices to perform political resistance. Some women in Iraq mobilize religious and cultural practices to create and claim a political space for their struggle as mothers. In this argument a nontraditional analysis of motherhood in Iraq is employed to shed light on the different ways that Shi'a women mobilize significant religious narratives and practices, such as the narrative of Karbala and the mourning rituals associated with it.[12] This religious narrative of Karbala is also examined in relation to the cultural practice of storytelling and the role it plays in advancing the cause of political motherhood. This chapter is part of a larger project that focuses on examining Iraqi women's experiences during war, sanctions, and occupation, in which 31 Iraqi women were interviewed.

## Motherhood and Mourning Ceremonies: Understanding the Narrative of Karbala

In the Shi'a sect of Islam, mourning is considered an important political project that builds the collective identity of the community. Shi'a Muslims hold structured mourning ceremonies in remembrance of the martyrdom of Imam Hussein (the grandson of Prophet Muhammad, peace be upon them)[13] in a battle known as the Battle of Karbala. Mourning ceremonies in the Shi'a sect of Islam are usually carried out throughout the year marking the anniversaries of the deaths of different members of the Prophet's family. However, they reach their climax in the two months of sadness of the lunar calendar, Muharram and Sufer, in which the Battle of Karbala was carried out on the tenth day of *Moharram* known as *Ashura*. The Battle of Karbala holds great political significance for Shi'a Muslims; it is used as a political symbol that exemplifies the fight against oppression and injustice.[14] Shi'a Muslims believe that the narrative of Karbala is retractable and can be used to explain, and respond to, contemporary political events. The ongoing oppression faced by the Shi'a community on the whole had further strengthened the political dimension of the Karbala narrative because the injustice faced by Imam Hussein is seen reflected in the contemporary political reality experienced by his followers.[15] One of the famous slogans used by Shi'a Muslims is "Every day is *Ashura* and every land is Karbala." This philosophy is clearly found in the work of the famous Iranian Islamic thinker Ali Shari'ati, who argues, "Every place should be turned into Karbala, every month into *Moharram*, and every day into *Ashura*."[16] In this philosophy, the narrative of Karbala is transformed from a historical event into a political paradigm that symbolizes an act of rebellion against oppression, injustice, and state corruption. Accordingly, many governments tried to ban any ceremonies associated with the narrative of Karbala, fearing the political motivation and the revolutionary potentials found in these rituals.[17] The success of the Islamic revolution of Iran in mobilizing the narrative of Karbala to overthrow the Shah had further amplified the anxiety about this narrative in many neighboring states, resulting in increased suppression of rituals associated with it.[18] For example, in Iraq the practices that commemorate the Battle of Karbala were banned and criminalized until the fall of the regime in 2003, and since then they are continuously targeted by terrorist attacks and aggressively criticized by some neighboring governments.

The observances of Karbala's commemoration vary from one culture to another; however, among the most popular traditions are mourning ceremonies that consist of different activities, including "recitation of the Karbala narrative [and] . . . recitation of rhythmic lamentation poetry" that inflame emotions of deep sadness, which often leads to communal weeping and chest beating.[19] Substantial research has been done regarding the significance and the gendered dynamic of these performances, though the aspect of motherhood is almost nonexistent in this body of literature in spite of its centrality to the mourning rituals, particularly in times of political violence. However, the concept of motherhood is not only central to these rituals but also fundamental to their politicization, particularly in war-torn and militarized societies like Iraq. In Iraq, some mothers adopt the narrative of Karbala to nurture the political dimension of their mothering in an act of resistance.

The significance of motherhood in mourning ceremonies is observed through the stories told and practices curried out in the first ten days of Muharram. Each of these ten days is designated for the remembrance of the death of one member of Imam Hussein's family. The first three days take an introductory form where the overall story of Karbala is recalled and interpreted in relation to contemporary political events. On the third day, however, there is more focus on the story of Imam Hussein's companions and his father's wife, Om Al Baneen, who is perceived as a symbol of the "sacrificial mother," having lost four of her biological sons in the battle. The fourth day of Muharram is then designated for Fatima Al Sughra, a young daughter of Imam Hussein who was left behind in Medina because she was ill. The fifth day is designated for Muslim Bin-Akheel, the cousin of Imam Hussein who was killed before the start of the battle. The sixth day is designated for the two sons of Muslim Bin-Akheel who became lost in Kufa and were eventually killed. The seventh day is designated for Al Abbas, who was the half-brother of Imam Hussein and the eldest son of Om Al Baneen. The eighth day is designated for Al Qasim, who was the nephew of Imam Hussein; he was not yet married and so he is known as the groom.[20] The ninth day is designated for Ali Al Akber, the eldest son of Imam Hussein; the night of that day is designated to baby Abdullah, who is also known as Ali Al Asghar, the youngest son of Imam Hussein who was also killed in the battle. The tenth day, *Ashura*, is designated for Imam Hussein and is in fact the day when the battle took place.

On each of these days, there is a particular mention of motherhood, especially from days six to nine, when the lamentations normally revolve around the tale of the mother who lost her child. There are five women who are central to the narrative of Karbala in their roles as mothers: Al Saydah Fatima't Al Zahra, Om Al Baneen, Laila, Ramleh, and Al Rabab.[21] Those women are symbolized as icons of motherhood, for although they would have undertaken other duties in the battle, their roles as mothers give them more prevalence in the rituals commemorating Karbala.

Generally, the most prominent motherhood icon is Al Saydah Fatima't Al Zahra, the daughter of the prophet and the mother of Imam Hussein. Despite her death long before the battle, her centrality to the narrative of Karbala centers on two main elements. First, she is recalled in lamentations as a gesture of condolence for the loss of her son. Second, her identity as a strong and resilient woman is recalled in the storytelling of the Karbala narrative to make a connection between her and her daughter Al Saydah Zaynab, who was present in the battle of the Karbala and who had a prominent role in keeping the family safe and speaking against Yazid, the caliph of the day. In this element, the Battle of Karbala is presented as a mother and daughter journey in which the daughter has learnt resilience and bravery from her mother's teaching.

Apart from Al Saydah Fatima't Al Zahra, other mothers are also made central to the narrative of Karbala and its rituals, but to a lesser extent. Among the highly regarded mothers is Om Al Baneen, who was the wife of Imam Hussein's father and who lost four of her sons in the Battle of Karbala. Om Al Baneen is presented as an icon of sacrifice who endured the death of her sons and faced her loss stoically. A day is often designated for her remembrance when her story of patience and endurance is told to invoke resilience among mothers who have lost their children as a result of political violence. She is also a central character in day seven, which is designated to her son, Al Abbas; she is remembered as a brave mother and true believer. Similar images of loss and patience is drawn from Laila (the mother of Ali Al Akber), Ramleh (the mother of Al Qasim) and Al Rabab (the mother of Abdullah). Those mothers are believed to be of a lower religious ranking than Al Saydah Fatima't Al Zahra; therefore they are seen as representative of the average mothers of today's society, and so their stories of loss are exemplified in contemporary stories of loss. In this sense, the Iraqi Shi'a mothers who lost their children in today's political violence present themselves as the new Laila, Ramleh, and Al Rabab and will also identify with Om Al Baneen if more than one child is lost.

## Mothers Reenacting Karbala through Mourning Ceremonies

Under Saddam Hussein, the Shi'a community was classified as "unfaithful" and therefore targeted by the Ba'ath regime. The failed uprising against Saddam Hussein by the Shi'a community in 1991 only worsened this situation, and many Shi'a men were killed, kidnapped, and tortured; the two holy cities for Shi'a Muslims were demolished, and almost two million people were displaced.[22] The situation devastated the Shi'a community, particularly the families of those killed, as they were denied funeral rights because their sons where considered traitors by the state.[23]

In these conditions, mourning ceremonies became an important outlet for expressing political anger. Lara Deep, an anthropologist and a prominent scholar on the gender dynamics of Karbala, argues that the "changing political and social realities influence the ways narratives are produced and rituals are practiced [in Ashura]. Thus the ritual provides comprehension of present-day events in Iraq, and the horrific impact it has on women's lives."[24] Although Karbala commemoration rituals and mourning processions were banned by Saddam Hussein, women continued to hold these ceremonies in the private setting of their homes.[25] In these mourning ceremonies, individual stories of loss were identified within religious holy narratives, which helped reinterpret the death of their loved ones from traitors to martyrs.

In the contemporary Middle East, every war/politically related death is identified with martyrdom[26] and therefore for Shi'a Muslims is identified with *Sayed al Shohada* (The Master of Martyrs), a title given to Imam Hussein. This project of identifying the death of ordinary people with a highly religious figure helps mobilize the community politically and build their resilient identity. Mourning ceremonies become a political voice where not only the death of Imam Hussein is mourned but also the generational death of his followers. Mothers take the lead in these mourning ceremonies as they become an embodied image of Om Al Baneen, Laila, Ramleh, and other mothers of Karbala. Mothers who lost their children under the Ba'ath regime or in the current sectarian violence in Iraq take mourning ceremonies as an opportunity to reenact Karbala and revolutionize these rituals by assuming the role of the mothers of the modern Karbala, where Yazid is signified by modern enemies such as Saddam Hussein and al-Qaeda. In this sense, the Shi'a community lives the story of Karbala through those mothers, and this evokes a sense of political resistance and social resilience in the community.

Interviewees confirmed that mourning ceremonies are ideal for connecting individual loss to *Ahlu-al-Bayt* loss (*Ahlu-al-Bayt* means "the people of the house" and it refers to the family of the Prophet). As Om Baqer, one of the participants, stresses, "This is not only useful in building emotional resilience so that mothers can cope with their loss, but it is also useful in building political resilience where injustice is fought and condemned." In this account, mourning ceremonies are presented as a site of political resistance where individual loss, although mourned, is also celebrated as an extension of the revolution of Imam Hussein. For Shi'a Muslims, this symbolic connection denotes that the injustice under which they lived is a continuation of the injustice as experienced by Imam Hussein and his family in Karbala. Therefore contemporary wars and militarization are symbolically presented as a "modern Karbala." In this sense, the role of motherhood that proved very powerful in Imam Hussein's Karbala becomes of particular importance in the "modern Karbala." This is because the resilience depicted by the mothers of martyrs in Imam Hussein's Karbala is encouraged to be reenacted. Shi'a women living through political conflict are "encouraged to find strength in and to emulate the female figures of Karbala";[27] however, they still have the space to mourn and grieve their loss through mourning ceremonies.

The rituals carried out by mothers and their symbolic embodiment of the mothers of Karbala is very powerful in continuously renewing the spirit of Karbala and reviving its revolutionary potential. For example, one of the common rituals held by mothers who lost their young sons in war was to prepare wedding trays (a wedding tradition in Iraq) on the eighth day of *Muharram,* known as *saineiet Al Qasim.*[28] Om Ali,[29] one of the research participants who lost her unmarried son during the US invasion, dignifies this specific ritual with Al Qasim's remembrance. Om Ali links the death of her son to Al Qasim's martyrdom because, as she says, neither "put the Henna on their hands" (an Iraqi tradition in weddings). Subsequently, Om Ali prepares wedding trays on the eighth day of *Muharram* and on the anniversary of her son's death. This symbolic ritual is powerful in transforming individual loss into a communal one that exemplifies the injustice suffered by the community. These rituals held by Om Ali and other mothers can indirectly present them in the community as the modern "Ramleh" of the "modern Karbala." Accordingly, mothers alongside martyrs become the transmitters of Karbala and the bearers of its revolutionary principles, which helps evokes the spirit of political resistance.

As Elizabeth Warnock Fernea argues, "The Ta'ziyeh [one form of mourning ceremony] is the literal voice of ordinary people attempting to deal symbolically (and pragmatically) with violence against their community, with what they perceive as age-old persecution and discrimination."[30] Therefore mourning ceremonies nurture a collective identity where the mourning of the traumatized self is linked to a communal cause. Mothers attend mourning ceremonies regularly and consider them an important part of their lives, because it can help them find purpose in their journey against the oppression of wars and militarization. Mourning ceremonies are useful not only to facilitate political resistance but also to heal the wounds of loss and be a motivational thrust for mothers to endure.[31]

Om Hadeel confirms that mothers who lost their children in political violence in Iraq find refuge in mourning ceremonies, because these ceremonies give them the space to "equate their loss to that of Ahlu-al-Bayt," and this in turn can be a path to redemption. This is an important point that communicates the significance of the Karbala narrative in developing community resilience in facing political violence and premature death. This concept of resilience is clearly seen in Om Khalid's narrative when she recalled her first reaction to her son's death as the result of injuries sustained in a bomb blast not far from her home: "When I heard the bomb, I said, 'my son has died.' I felt that my son has died, I had a mother's feeling. But when I went out [to check] I said, 'oh God give me patience,' I remembered the suffering of Al Saidah Zainab, peace be upon her, and her loss of her brothers and sons." In this narrative Om Khalid develops her resilience through the spiritual connection she makes with the loss of Al Saydah Zaynab. By taking the mothers of Karbala as role models, Om Khalid faces the death of her son with patience and strength, the qualities known of the mothers of Karbala. The lessons learned from Karbala become central to community development in times of political instability. Therefore the role of mothers in reenacting Karbala does not stop at the aspect of embodiment but is also practiced through storytelling, in which the narrative of Karbala becomes educational material used in "motherhood teaching" to resist the social impact of war on the identity of children.

## Motherhood Teaching and Storytelling

Teaching through storytelling is a very strong theme within some nonwestern cultures, particularly the Arab culture, in which teaching is an attribute that is mostly attached to the feminine identity—that is, mothers building generations through teaching.[32] *Inheriting Our Mothers' Gardens* is among the most informative books about storytelling that examines the "power of stories" for nonwestern women.[33] The book highlights the power of storytelling in building individual and collective identities, emphasizing that "there is nothing like a story to help fix one's self-image."[34] In fact, it is about not only one's self-image but also a collective one. Building the nation through motherly stories or "motherhood teaching" is an important concept, particularly for the Arab community, which values the sharing of experiences and the tradition of storytelling.[35] As indicated by several researchers, many nonwestern women consider their mothers' teaching and stories as the building blocks of their strength, resilience, and identity.[36]

A famous Arabic poem reads, "A mother is a school; if you invest in her, you invest in a well-raised generation." This eminent verse implies that mothers hold a strong power in constructing a collective national identity and could therefore shape the existence of a whole nation.[37] Motherhood teaching is particularly important in times of war and political violence because it can construct an oppositional voice within the community using unstructured, *safe* methods of political activism. In other words, mothers turn their conceived apolitical everyday mothering into a form of political activism that can be a practice of peaceful resistance. Research shows that "motherhood teaching" is a significant way in which some women practice culturally nonthreatening political activism, especially in Muslim societies.[38] The honorable position given to mothers in Islam contributes greatly to how Muslim mothers practice their motherhood teaching. Muslim women use their religious privilege within the practice of their motherhood teaching, in which their role as educators is culturally embraced and thus would not be considered threatening. The concept of motherhood teaching, when combined with religious authority, can transform into a politically powerful practice that embraces the centrality of motherhood to community and nation building, and this in turn can help endorse further political activism in mothers.[39]

Raising children in a country like Iraq where fear and violence dominates the relationship between the state and its citizens is never merely a domestic matter. Participant mothers discussed their mothering duties as political practice, highlighting the political challenge they faced in raising their children under the Ba'ath regime where the enemy was the state. Mothers emphasized that there was a need to nurture a political identity in children that was publically confirmative but privately oppositional to the Ba'athist state. In this regard, Om Imad states, "As a mother I had a difficult task of protecting my family, but at the same time I had to keep pace with the society . . . because the political society puts pressure on the families, they want children to be raised their way and be under their control." Om Noor calls it "Saddamist upbringing," where children are taught criminality and disloyalty to everyone but the leader. Therefore Iraqi women as nurturers considered themselves to be carrying a significant responsibility for developing a non-Ba'athist political identity in their children while at the same time keeping them safe. Om Hadeel confirms that this is a very difficult task: "We raised our children in a way that they love Saddam and even call him Uncle Saddam but at the same time they hate him because he is bad." As it can be seen in Om Hadeel's narrative, mothering was extremely complex under the Ba'ath regime; Om Hadeel, along other participants, used "motherhood teaching" to manage this challenging task.

For example, Om Hadi confirms that storytelling was an effective way of building a non-Ba'athist political identity in her son: "I tell him about his cousin's story, I say to him, 'See, he lost his father, his uncle and his other uncle, Saddam executed them.' I would teach him and he would listen." In this narrative, Om Hadi uses storytelling as an educational tool. Research shows that storytelling can be an effective way of motherhood teaching in which "mothers transmit their expectations, beliefs, and knowledge to their children."[40] In this sense, the political significance of motherhood teaching rests in the power it holds in transmitting specific worldviews, ideologies, and morality to children. Family stories are important in constructing "a sense of right and wrong, duty, understanding of family, and how to behave in the world"; therefore they are powerful means of building identity and self-conceptualization.[41]

Although storytelling has always played an important role in motherhood teaching for Iraqi women, the type of stories told to children have transformed with the rise of political violence. For example, Om Imad gives a critical summary of how Iraqi mothers adapted new ways of teaching to protect their children from the "Saddamist uprising" and to safeguard their maternal authority:

> Prior to Saddam and his brutal regime, our grandmothers would tell us stories about witches and fairy tales. However, when we became mothers, we realized that fiction was no longer useful in the raising of our children . . . we had to teach our children reality, because innocence was diminished. The regime had taken away children's innocence; they were getting them engaged in military training like Ashbal Saddam (Saddam's Cubs, an official military group for minors) . . . So, we said that's it, the stories of the witch are no longer useful, I have to bring my child down to reality. I would have to tell my child stories from my life, from my neighbor's life, from my friend's life, and from my ancestors' lives. I would have to take the story and tell it in a way that conveys the messages I want to present to my child. I tell him that this is the truth, and this story is useful for you, and that you should derive your life on the basis of this story, and it should be a lesson for you in life.

This is a very powerful narrative that pulls together several important points. It first focuses on the conceptual transformation in storytelling, in which imaginative and fictional stories were no longer an effective method in performing motherhood teaching. For storytelling to be an effective teaching method, Om Imad and many other women had to tell the stories of war with all its brutality and pain. This practice can be a form of "counterstorytelling" that helps develop an oppositional voice within children and "open new windows into reality" where practices of oppression are made visible.[42]

As in Om Imad's narrative, women are turning their female-based life experience into educational material and life-learning examples for new generations. Om Noor, who had to leave school at the age of 15 due to war conditions, returned to high school at the age of 24 after she had become a mother of two. She states, "I wanted to become an example for my children . . . I wanted to become an incentive for them; a powerful incentive." Although she has not mentioned the word story, Om Noor implies that her life experience has become important educational material that can teach her children persistence and a positive outlook for success. However, not only personal stories were identified as useful in developing children's identity; religious stories, like the story of Karbala, were also recognized as educational.

## Revolutionizing the Story of Karbala

The mobilization of the Karbala story is useful in fostering social and political resilience in children. Many of the participants in this research emphasized that the story of Karbala is a story of political salvation that can help build the political identity of their children and encourage them to resist the psychological effects of political oppression. Om Baqer confirms that "as a mother I see the Karbala story as a political approach to life and so for me it is important to embrace this in my children." Other participants affirmed that it is important for children to attend mourning ceremonies so that they can listen to the story of Karbala and learn from the lessons it offers. Om Zahra states, "I insist on taking my children to Hussayniya [a place where mourning ceremonies are held] so they can listen and learn, I know that maybe they don't understand everything said in there but it is important that they go because it helps build their identity." Other women argued that mourning ceremonies are useful in teaching children morality and principled behavior.

The different wars and political conflicts in Iraq resulted in changing the social morality and ethics, creating a moral crisis within the community.[43] Violence was gradually disseminated as an acceptable form of communication, and some people resorted to lying, cheating, spying, and fraudulency as means of survival. With such a decline in the moral environment, the raising of children and the attempt to uphold high moral standards becomes a very challenging task. Mothers indicated that they needed to always find innovative methods of educating their children and disciplining their morals, as the traditional methods of child rearing were no longer effective in the current political climate. Therefore many mothers adopt the narrative of Karbala as a disciplinary paradigm that not only cultivates the political identity of their children but also helps in developing their moral selves. The mothers in this research indicated that one of the valuable elements of the Karbala story is its flexibility and fluidity; it can be discursively reshaped to suit different ages and different contexts. For those with very young children, the story is told in a basic form to embrace the dichotomy between good and evil. However, as the child grows, the story can discursively evolve to include more complex concepts and meanings.

Mourning ceremonies are seen as spaces of "manufacturing identity," and so they are considered exceptionally important for the new generation.[44] It is important to reiterate that mourning ceremonies are not only places of mourning; they are also places of teaching where the story of Karbala is recited and analyzed in relation to modern political reality.[45] Accordingly, the narrative of Karbala has never been static; it has always been subjected to reinterpretation depending on the cultural and political context. Over time, the narrative transformed significantly from a story of grief to a concept of political activism that simulates the political reality experienced by the Shi'a community.[46] Om Manar confirms that "we hold mourning ceremonies to say that the revolution of Imam Hussein has not ended yet, we are its bearers and we encourage our children to continue that path." In this account, mourning ceremonies are presented as a political statement that people make against injustice,[47] with the intent that the ritual should be passed from one generation to the next to ensure the continuation of the message. Thus although mourning is usually seen as a sign of weakness, Shi'a mourning ceremonies, on the contrary, signify spiritual empowerment for individuals and political solidarity and activism for the community.[48] Given the centrality of the concept of motherhood to mourning ceremonies, many Shi'a mothers in Iraq consider themselves responsible for transmitting and revolutionizing the principles found in these rituals.

## Notes

1. Adeed Dawisha, *Iraq: A Political History from Independence to Occupation* (Princeton: Princeton University Press, 2009), 215.
2. Sahib Alhakim, *Untold Stories of More than 4000 Women Raped, Killed and Tortured in Iraq, the Country of Mass Graves* (London: Merowh, 2003), 8.
3. Efraim Karsh and Inari Rautsi, *Saddam Hussein: A Political Biography* (New York: Grove, 1991), 176.
4. Dawisha, *Iraq*, 215.
5. Alhakim, *Untold Stories*, 6–7.
6. Ibid.
7. Ibid., 176–77.
8. Ibid., 177.
9. Nadera Shalhoub-Kevorkian, "Liberating Voices: The Political Implications of Palestinian Mothers Narrating Their Loss," *Women's Studies International Forum* 26, no. 5 (2003): 391–407; Julie Peteet, "Icons and Militants: Mothering in the Danger Zone," *Signs* 23, no. 1 (1997): 114.
10. Victoria J. Ward, "Raising Resisters: The Role of Truth Telling in the Psychological Development of African American Girls," in *Urban Girls: Resisting Stereotypes, Creating Identities*, ed. Bonnie J. Ross Leadbeater and Niobe Way (New York: New York University Press, 1996), 85–99. Although psychological resistance is discussed in relation to racism in this reference, its theoretical application is relevant to the context of the chapter.
11. Peteet, "Icons and Militants," 114.
12. Shi'a is a term that refers to followers of Shi'ism, which is one of the two main sects of Islam. The narrative of Karbala and the mourning rituals associated with it are more significant for Shi'a Muslims, and therefore the analysis provided in this chapter is mostly, but not entirely, relevant to Iraqi Shi'a mothers. However, I have not made this distinction in the title, because other women can still identify with some of the analysis made in this chapter.
13. Feminist epistemology highlights the importance of the positioning of the researcher within the research, emphasizing the subjectivity of academic writing, where the identity of the researcher should be explicit within the research. The inclusion of "Peace Be Upon Them," although considered academically inappropriate under some western protocols of writing, is perceived appropriate within postcolonial feminism that stresses the importance of decolonizing knowledge production through the employment of nonwestern intellectual processes and academic styles, particularly in research that involves nonwestern subjects.
14. Dena Al-Adeeb, "From Sacred Ritual to Installation Art: A Personal Testimony," *Alif: Journal of Comparative Poetics* 28 (2008): 18.

15. Dan Murphy, "Islam's Sunni-Shiite Split," *Christian Science Monitor*, January 17, 2007, http://www.csmonitor.com/2007/0117/p25s01-wome.html, accessed October 29, 2008.
16. Scot K. Aghaie, *Martyrs of Karbala: Shi'a Symbols and Rituals in Modern Iran* (Seattle: University of Washington Press, 2011), 87.
17. Edith Szanto, "Beyond the Karbala Paradigm: Rethinking Revolution and Redemption in Twelver Shi'a Mourning Rituals," *Journal of Shi'a Islamic Studies* 6, no. 1 (2013): 88.
18. Aghaie, *Martyrs of Karbala*, 87.
19. Ali J. Hussain, "The Mourning of History and the History of Mourning: The Evolution of Ritual Commemoration of the Battle of Karbala," *Comparative Studies of South Asia, Africa and the Middle East* 25, no. 1 (2005): 79.
20. There is a legendary story about Al Qasim that is often told in mourning ceremonies. The story emphasizes that Al Qasim was engaged to Imam Hussein's daughter but did not end up marrying due to his martyrdom.
21. Wilferd Madelung, "Husayn B'Ali: Life and Significance in Shi 'ism." *The Institute of Ismaili Studies* 12 (2012): 2. *This is an edited version of an article originally published in the Encyclopedia Iranica on December 15, 2004, available at http://www.iranicaonline.org.*
22. Eric Goldstein, *Endless Torment: The 1991 Uprising in Iraq and Its Aftermath* (New York: Human Rights Watch, 1992), 26, 27, 32.
23. It is difficult to locate this data in academic scholarship, as in militarized societies there are a lot of experiences that are lived but not necessarily documented. However, McNeil writes briefly about this trend (paying for the bullets and denying the families' right to mourn their loss publicly) in the context of the Iraq-Kuwait war, which indicates that there is a legitimate grounding to the claims made by the women.
24. Lara Z. Deeb, "From Mourning to Activism: Sayyedeh Zaynab, Lebanese Shi 'i Women, and the Transformation of Ashura," in *The Women of Karbala: Ritual Performance and Symbolic Discourses in Modern Shi 'i Islam*, ed. Kamran Scot Aghaie (Austin: University of Texas Press, 2005), 15.
25. The argument for this can be found in Szanto, "Beyond the Karbala Paradigm," 88.
26. See Shalhoub-Kevorkian, "Liberating Voices."
27. Abir Hamdar, "Jihad of Words: Gender and Contemporary Karbala Narratives," *The Yearbook of English Studies* (2009): 98.
28. This tray is also prepared by other women, but the day has special significance for mothers who lost their young sons in to premature deaths.
29. *Om* means "mother," and in the Arab culture parents' names derive from their eldest child, because calling them by their first names is

considered impolite. This research follows this cultural tradition in the naming of participants.
30. Elizabeth Fernea, "Remembering Taziyeh in Iraq," *TDR/The Drama Review* 49, no. 4 (2005): 139.
31. This argument is also found in Liz Stanley, *Mourning Become... : Post/Memory and Commemoration of the Concentration Camps of the South African War 1899–1902* (Manchester: Manchester University Press, 2006). See also Shalhoub-Kevorkian, "Liberating Voices."
32. Shalhoub-Kevorkian, "Liberating Voices," 400. Shari Stone-Mediatore, *Reading across Borders: Storytelling and Knowledges of Resistance* (New York: Palgrave Macmillan, 2003), 1. Rosemary Sayigh, "Remembering Mothers, Forming Daughters: Palestinian Women's Narratives in Refugee Camps in Lebanon," in *Women and the Politics of Military Confrontation: Palestinian and Israeli Gendered Narratives of Dislocation*, ed. Nahla Abdo and Ronit Lentin (New York: Berghahn, 2002), 68.
33. See Letty Russell et al., eds., *Inheriting Our Mothers' Gardens: Feminist Theology in Third World Perspective* (Philadelphia: Westminster, 1988).
34. Mercy A. Oduyoye, "Be a Woman, and Africa Will Be Strong," in *Inheriting Our Mothers' Gardens*, 37.
35. Bouthaina Shaaban, *Both Right and Left Handed: Arab Women Talk about Their Lives* (Bloomington: Indiana University Press, 1988), 153.
36. See Russell et al., *Inheriting Our Mothers' Gardens*; Angelita Reyes, "From a Lineage of Southern Women: She Has Left Us Empty and Full of Her," in *Unrelated Kin: Race and Gender in Women's Personal Narratives*, ed. Gwendolyn Etter-Lewis and Michele Foster (New York: Routledge, 1996), 25; Nancy Greenman, "More than a Mother: Some Tewa Women Reflect on Gia," in *Unrelated Kin*, 58.
37. A similar argument can be found in Nancy A. Naples, "Activist Mothering: Cross-generational Continuity in the Community Work of Women from Low-Income Urban Neighborhoods," *Gender & Society* 6, no. 3 (1992): 443.
38. Ibid.
39. Angelita Reyes, *Mothering across Cultures: Postcolonial Representations* (Minneapolis: University of Minnesota Press, 2002), 13.
40. Nancy Weitzman, Beverly Birns, and Ronald Friend, "Traditional and Non-traditional Mothers' Communication with Their Daughters and Sons," *Child Development* 56, no. 4 (1985): 894–98.
41. Jody K. Kellas, "Narrating Family: Introduction to the Special Issue on Narratives and Storytelling in the Family," *Journal of Family Communication* 10, no. 1 (2010): 1.
42. For a complete account of the argument, see Richard Delgado, "Storytelling for Oppositionists and Others: A Plea for Narrative," *Michigan Law Review* 87, no. 2411 (1989).

MOTHERHOOD AS A SPACE OF POLITICAL ACTIVISM    223

43. Nadje S. Al-Ali, "Reconstructing Gender: Iraqi Women between Dictatorship, War, Sanctions and Occupation," *Third World Quarterly* 26, no. 4–5 (2005): 748.
44. Mottahedeh Negar, "Women of Karbala: Ritual Performance and Symbolic Discourses in Modern Shi'ism," in *The Martyrs of Karbala: Shi'i Symbols and Rituals in Modern Iran*, ed. K. Scot Aghaie (Seattle: University of Washington Press, 2004).
45. Al-Adeeb, "From Sacred Ritual to Installation Art," 15.
46. Zeynab B. Ali, "Contemporary Karbala Narratives and the Changing Gender Dynamics in Shi'i Communities," Academic Commons, Columbia University, 2011, http://hdl.handle.net/10022/AC:P:13597, accessed October 22, 2013.
47. Al-Adeeb, "From Sacred Ritual to Installation Art," 18.
48. Hussain, "The Mourning of History," 85.

SELECTED BIBLIOGRAPHY

Abdo, Nahla, and Ronit Lentin, eds. *Women and the Politics of Military Confrontation: Palestinian and Israeli Gendered Narratives of Dislocation*. New York: Berghahn, 2002.
Aghaie, Kamran Scot. *The Martyrs of Karbala: Shi'i Symbols and Rituals in Modern Iran*. Seattle: University of Washington Press, 2004.
———, ed. *The Women of Karbala: Ritual Performance and Symbolic Discourses in Modern Shi'i Islam*. Austin: University of Texas Press, 2005.
Al-Adeeb, Dena. "From Sacred Ritual to Installation Art: A Personal Testimony." *Alif: Journal of Comparative Poetics* 28 (2008): 7–40.
Al-Ali, Nadje. "Reconstructing Gender: Iraqi Women between Dictatorship, War, Sanctions and Occupation." *Third World Quarterly* 26, no. 4–5 (2005): 739–58.
Alhakim, Sahib. *Untold Stories of More Than 4000 Women Raped, Killed and Tortured in Iraq, the Country of Mass Graves*. London: Merowh, 2003.
Ali, B. Zeynab. "Contemporary Karbala Narratives and the Changing Gender Dynamics in Shi'i Communities." Academic Commons, Columbia University, 2011. http://hdl.handle.net/10022/AC:P:13597. Accessed October 22, 2013.
Dawisha, Adeed. *Iraq: A Political History from Independence to Occupation*. Princeton: Princeton University Press, 2009.
Etter-Lewis, Gwendolyn, and Michele Foster, eds. *Unrelated Kin: Race and Gender in Women's Personal Narratives*. New York: Routledge, 1996.
Fernea, Elizabeth. "Remembering Taziyeh in Iraq." *TDR/The Drama Review* 49, no. 4 (2005): 130–39.
Hamdar, Abir. "Jihad of Words: Gender and Contemporary Karbala Narratives." *The Yearbook of English Studies* (2009): 84–100.
Hussain, J. Ali. "The Mourning of History and the History of Mourning: The Evolution of Ritual Commemoration of the Battle of Karbala."

*Comparative Studies of South Asia, Africa and the Middle East* 25, no. 1 (2005): 78–88.

Karsh, Efraim, and Inari Rautsi. *Saddam Hussein: A Political Biography*. New York: Grove, 1991.

Kellas, Jody Koenig. "Narrating Family: Introduction to the Special Issue on Narratives and Storytelling in the Family." *Journal of Family Communication* 10, no. 1 (2010): 1–6.

Langellier, Kristin. *Storytelling in Daily Life: Performing Narrative*. Philadelphia: Temple University Press, 2004.

Makiya, Kanan. *The Republic of Fear: The Politics of Modern Iraq*. Berkeley: University of California Press, 1998.

Naples, Nancy A. "Activist Mothering: Cross-generational Continuity in the Community Work of Women from Low-Income Urban Neighborhoods." *Gender and Society* 6, no. 3 (1992): 441–63.

Peteet, Julie. "Icons and Militants: Mothering in the Danger Zone." *Signs* 23, no. 1 (1997): 103–29.

Reyes, Angelita. *Mothering across Cultures: Postcolonial Representations*. Minneapolis: University of Minnesota Press, 2002.

Ross Leadbeater, Bonnie J., and Niobe Way, eds. *Urban Girls: Resisting Stereotypes, Creating Identities*. New York: New York University Press, 1996.

Russell, Letty, Kwok Pui-lan, Ada Maria Isasi-Diaz, and Katie Geneva Cannon, eds. *Inheriting Our Mothers' Gardens: Feminist Theology in Third World Perspective*. Philadelphia: Westminster, 1988.

Shaaban, Bouthaina. *Both Right and Left Handed: Arab Women Talk about Their Lives*. Bloomington: Indiana University Press, 1988.

Shalhoub-Kevorkian, Nadera. "Liberating Voices: The Political Implications of Palestinian Mothers Narrating Their Loss." *Women's Studies International Forum* 26, no. 5 (September–October 2003): 391–407.

Stanley, Liz. *Mourning Become . . . : Post/Memory and Commemoration of the Concentration Camps of the South African War 1899–1902*. Manchester: Manchester University Press, 2006.

Stone-Mediatore, Shari. *Reading across Borders: Storytelling and Knowledges of Resistance*. New York: Palgrave Macmillan, 2003.

Szanto, Edith. "Beyond the Karbala Paradigm: Rethinking Revolution and Redemption in Twelver Shi'a Mourning Rituals." *Journal of Shi'a Islamic Studies* 6, no. 1 (2013): 75–91.

Weitzman, Nancy, Beverly Birns, and Ronald Friend. "Traditional and Nontraditional Mothers' Communication with their Daughters and Dons." *Child Development* 56, no. 4 (1985): 894–98.

CHAPTER 13

## MOTHERS AND MEMORY
### SUFFERING, SURVIVAL, AND SUSTAINABILITY IN SOMALI CLAN WARS

*Mohamed Haji Ingiriis*

Many mothers around the world face violent attacks, both physically and mentally, every day in diverse conflict-ridden settings. Countries that suffer from international and domestic conflicts are almost all located in the Global South, exacerbating the lack of sustainable development compared to the Global North, and nearly all clan (and tribal) conflicts occur in Africa. Contemporary Somalia is a quintessential case of clan warfare and has come to embody one of the worst countries in which to be a mother. The nation has been embroiled in armed conflict since the 1970s, when resistance groups took advantage of the deteriorating circumstances of a brutal regime to resist a clan-military dictatorship.

Three decades of war impacted Somalis in unexpected ways, and compartmentalizing rival clans into warring subclans resulted in unprecedented catastrophe. The conflict and conflagration reached a climax in 1977 when fratricidal killings plagued many areas of the country following the defeat of the Somali military regime in its attempts to "liberate" Somali territories in Ethiopia and incorporate them into Somalia.[1] Even though the war started as a war of liberation against dictatorial military rule (1969–91), it soon developed into a free-for-all—the phenomenon of a "murderous pattern of internecine aggression and reprisals and later into a seemingly purposeless war between clan-based feuding militia groups, punctured only by asymmetrical and unconvincing claims to clan supremacy by one leader or another."[2] For mothers and children, the consequence of such conflict is everlasting trauma inflicted on them ever since.

This chapter focuses on the methods used by Somali women in enduring and overcoming the violence that occurred following the fall of the military dictatorship. It examines the ways in which mothers coped with armed conflict and how they articulated survival, suffering, and sustainability while employing their maternal agency. Apart from the devastation of such warfare over three decades, mothers have emerged as crucial peace builders during the era of anarchy since 1991, when Somalia's image has been characterized by the collapsed-state category.[3] While the country still continues to head the list of the world's failed states, many women remain resilient and work to promote communal peace. This has provided them with the opportunity not only to organize collectively in participating in community development initiatives, such as peace building through poetry and economic reconstruction through remittance, but also to undertake the responsibility for being the heads of their households as they replace husbands who might be either dead or displaced.

Recent studies on gender and conflict have portrayed mothers in Africa as passive and have overlooked women's agency in surviving, suffering, and sustaining conflicts. The existing literature is limited to the suffering of women during the war and tends to neglect or ignore women's contributions—both positive and negative—to the war. Over the past two decades, several scholars have carried out studies that examine how war has affected the lives of mothers. Most of these studies have devoted a great deal of effort to analyzing a woman's position in terms of war and deprivation, and as the victim of violence, without considering how the war enabled mothers to become more active economically and socially.[4] In the course of employing a paradigm of war theory, these analyses concentrated on the process of conflict rather than the outcome of the conflict, even though they noted that the war has caused women to pay a highly gender-specific price. Matt Bryden and Martina Steiner observe, "The direct impact of war upon Somali women has been dramatic. Tens of thousands of men have been killed, leaving widows and orphans behind. Bereavement and separation have forced thousands of women to live displaced within Somalia or as refugees in foreign countries. Thousands more women face a similar fate simply because the pressures of war-displacement, poverty, and despair—have destroyed their marriages. Today, many women live alone or without relatives to support them, and a significant number of the women in Somalia are the only breadwinners in the family."[5] Observers have emphasized the social effects of war and how these have shaped mothers' lives. Some have continued to record the atrocities committed against women, emphasizing their place as victims of vicious fighting.[6] In Judith Gardner and Judy El Bushra's edited volume, several Somali women evaluated the social impact that armed conflict had on them, described their experiences, and considered the difficult choices they had to make daily and how they managed to survive.[7] Unfortunately, political instability and safety concerns make it difficult for more of these interviews to occur in the field, leading to a lack of nuanced, contextual studies, particularly in South-Central Somalia, the most conflict-ridden area in Somalia.

## The Collision of Conflict

The fall of the military regime on January 26, 1991, and the subsequent outbreak of the Hobbesian clan wars heralded the most dramatic change in the position of women in Somali society. As the military dictatorship was ousted, the scene was filled by chaos and anarchy. The lack of central government became a "blessing" for mothers, as they employed idiosyncratic efforts and methods in order to survive, which contributed to improving their social status and position in the society. The absence of their husbands, who either were killed or fled, has provided mothers with an opportunity to take on a more active and leading role in their households and their communities in various ways, including the practice of *buraanbur* (the Somali genre poetry exclusive for women) as a tool to promote peace *or* ignite warfare. The lack of any formal government also ushered in a new era that allowed them to take a more prominent role in their communities at large, not only in private businesses, but also in peace-building, leadership, and state-reinstating processes.[8]

Upon seizing power in October 1969, the military regime banned the democratic structures in which the previous civilian government had operated. Besides political parties, women's associations were banned, press freedom was forbidden, and censorship was employed liberally. In 1975, the regime sought to adopt a controversial military legislation, which advocated equality between men and women. This garnered a strong reaction from Islamic scholars who denounced such legislation as contradictory to religious values. As Abdirahman Abdullahi Baadiyow pointed out, Somali women had already "enjoyed enormous freedom in comparison with many Muslim societies in the world."[9] The military regime responded to the religious outcry by executing ten sheikhs. This event marked the first active rebellion against the military regime.

Armed confrontation began as a result of an attempted coup in 1978.[10] Mothers were confronted by such an extreme level of insecurity that killing, looting, and rape became a part of everyday life in Somalia.[11] In 1988, the regime launched airstrikes on specific major towns in the northwest Somalia (present-day Somaliland).[12] Mothers and children bore the brunt of those state-structured attacks and began to flee en masse from Hargeysa, Berbera, Bur'o, and other towns.

As the fighting erupted in the capital of Mogadishu in January 1991, the violence shifted from state structured to clan structured. In her eyewitness account, Asha-Kaha, a Somali midwife and mother, recounted seeing a woman lying on the street after having been killed in the clan wars between the regime and the resistance groups. Even as she died, her baby continued to feed at her mother's breast.[13] As she fled with her two sons, Kaha called on other escapees to help her retrieve the baby. Many also reported witnessing similar cases on their way to the Somali border with Ethiopia and Kenya. The consequence was "a combination of intense physical and psychological stress for rape victims, provoking reactions that range from general aggression towards men to mental sickness."[14]

In the course of the conflict, arising from what Asha Haji Elmi describes as a "politicised clan identity," Somali mothers experienced the horrors of ferocious confrontations between hostile political entrepreneurs vying for power and economic resources by seizing state power.[15] Today, nearly every Somali family has had at least one member or relative who was killed in the war. The result of three decades of continual conflict has been the loss of almost a million lives.[16] Many more suffered physical and psychological wounds, while nearly 3.5 million have sought safety as refugees in neighboring countries such as Djibouti, Ethiopia, and Kenya, while others have fled as far as Europe, North America, or Australia.

## Rape Survival and Suffering

When the conflict reached a point of no return in Mogadishu, women were taken as war booty by both sides of the conflict—the regime and the resistance groups. As an example of such violence, Kaha was close to being raped twice. In the Gedo region, she recounted meeting two women being taken as sex slaves by the local clan militia.[17] Likewise, another interviewee, Mrs. A, was married to Mr. J by compulsion following the downfall of the regime, and she bore him two daughters. After several years with him, Mrs. A received a message from her family asking her to join them in Kenya. There she obtained permission to travel to the United States. After several years of difficulties, she sponsored her husband, who was able to join her in the United States, even though their marriage was coercive. It was very difficult to record and document her experiences due to cultural restrictions.[18] In Somali culture, women hide personal traumas such as these to circumvent "reputation injury" from their communities.

As the war shifted from state structured to clan orchestrated, rape occurred frequently throughout Somalia, and many mothers endured the physical horrors of rape. *Beijing Report* pointed out, "Although sexual assault was not unknown in traditional, pastoralist Somali society, mechanisms existed that served to deter and redress sexual assault. Within traditional Somali society it is the duty of a woman's family to protect and honour her status within the community. Thus in cases of sexual assault or abuse it is her family or clansmen who are charged with seeking redress of the situation and by the same token receive compensation from the offending parties."[19]

As the clan violence escalated on an unprecedented scale, rape was employed as a tool used to humiliate women belonging to rival warring clans. Human rights groups interviewed a Somali mother who was targeted by the regime forces by virtue of her clan identity. Hailing from a particular clan that the regime viewed as an enemy, the mother was among many other mothers who had been abused in front of her children.[20] The consequences of such cases had no less devastating effects on children than their mothers. Children who witnessed their mothers killed or molested were traumatized more than children who witnessed the same act inflicted on their fathers.[21] It is likely that many of the affected children emerged as militiamen in order to avenge their loved ones.

More often than not, mothers were not even spared by the clansmen that were supposed to protect and shield them in the context of clan wars. One shocking and ghastly incident was relayed by a group of Somali women concerning a young mother captured by a militia belonging to her subclan in central Somalia during the height of the clan wars in the 1990s.[22] When asked to provide her clan identity, the woman, showing a sign of confidence, proudly informed her captors that she belonged to "clan so and so." Only after being told to prepare herself for rape did she genuinely exclaim again, "I'm subclan so and so." She was blatantly informed by the militia, who was the same subclan as her, that they did not care about her clan or subclan. They explicitly stated that what they cared about was her body as sexual comfort from the conflict in which they were involved. Another mother was caught up in the midst of two warring clans. She identified one of the militiamen's subclans. When asked her clan identity, she identified herself with the man who stopped her. She was spared.[23] Another woman was captured in another clan war. Two militiamen from clan X stopped her while escaping from the crossfire, shouting at her and asking, "Aren't you from clan Y?" When she replied that she was from clan Z, they sarcastically laughed at her, reiterating and insisting that she was from clan Y. She was told to prepare herself for rape. While crying, she insisted, "Rape me as a clan Z woman, but you can't change my clan." With all the horror of the story, the woman refused to allow the militiamen to justify her rape case by cementing her to a clan to which she did not belong.[24] These incidents indicate that the opportunities for survival and suffering varied with the women's ordeals.

Many married women who survived rape could never return to their husbands due to the social stigma associated by members of their communities with the culture of abandonment. When unreported rape cases perpetuate during warfare, the rape experience in many Global South conflicts supersede a socially constructed consequence, depending on the reaction of communities operating under specific conditions:[25] "[T]he incidence of rape has overwhelmed traditional forms of protection and redress—a problem compounded by the disproportionate targeting of militarily weak minority groups."[26]

## Agents of Warfare

When state institutions cease to exist, there is a lack of conceptual framework to analyze women's experiences, especially in countries like Somalia where the state collapsed completely. Despite the evolving trends of the conflict-ridden conditions in Somalia, scholars have largely ignored women's contributions to Somali society and post-conflict reconstruction, partly because mothers remained peripheral to the traditional base of state power.[27]

Drawing on fieldwork in the mid-1990s, Virginia Luling challenged the assumption that women were merely "a force for peace." She observed that mothers were no less partisan than their husbands, arguing that "women have egged their menfolk on (their traditional role in Somali warfare)."[28] Women participated physically and materially in the war against the military regime. Faiza Jama observed that the war against the regime in the 1980s was seen as a "just cause" by many women who actively part took in the struggle to end the dictatorship.[29] Thus some women became leading members in mobilizing the militias in overthrowing the regime.

The methods of women in Kismaayo, for instance, were unique in some ways, as they were driven by clan superiority rather than the welfare of their children. When Siad Barre's forces, under the banner of a particular clan, retreated to Kismaayo, wishing to recapture the capital city of Mogadishu, they found support from several elder mothers who sang and chanted for them. Advertently or inadvertently, their direct involvement in the conflict aggravated not just mothers and children on the enemy side but also themselves and their children.[30] A relief officer who worked in Somalia during the height of such wars described the horror he had seen:

> My business is epidemiology (births, deaths, and health statistics of all kinds), and yet I can hardly believe the numbers from Afgoi. In this small farming town, only 30km northwest of the capital, my colleagues found by survey that nearly 3 of every 10 children under 5 who were alive in January of 1992 were dead by mid-November . . . a number that my mind struggles to accept as realistic, even now. Moreover, it is a number that my heart simply will not translate from the abstract into the beautiful happy faces that should be in Afgoi but which are not and will not be there. Although I have tried to dismiss the numbers on one ground or another, data from other surveys and anecdotes from my own experience, such as one-child families and the virtual absence of pregnant women in many settings, confirm that the substance of the terrible numbers are correct if not the specific percentage.[31]

## "Peace Is a Collective Responsibility"

During the battle for power and state resources, some of the women who initially aligned themselves with their clans reversed their actions and became promoters of peace. Inspired by the support they solicited from womenfolk, a considerable number of women have worked tirelessly to transform their communities politically, economically, and socially.[32] As one outcome of the perpetual warfare, many mothers led their households and became successfully productive in labor market.

Traditional Somali wisdom that excluded women from the center of political power has been reversed when women's genuine peace-building skills have been sought and seen as a crucial for solution to community crisis.[33] Here, at the community level, "conflict may create space to make a redefinition of social relations possible, but in so doing it rather rearranges, readapts or reinforces patriarchal ideologies, rather than fundamentally changing them."[34] The gender positions in building peace were so different that women faced distinct experiences and relationships. When the war was at its zenith, women were able to play "the role of peace envoy or messenger between her husband's clan and her father's clan," as rival clans engaged in fierce warfare throughout the 1990s.[35] This difference of relationship engagement provides women with the opportunity to find considerable agency in conflicts initiated by men. As one mother stated, it was a moral obligation for them to seek and foster peace.[36]

The Somali term for "peace building" is *nabad-dhalin*, referring to policies and programs for restoring stability and "effective social, political and economic institutions after a war or serious upheaval."[37] As such, Somali women, as mothers and leaders, developed strategies for peace builders to broaden the ethos of peace in their houses and within the wider community. During periods of fierce fighting, women organized and held demonstrations for peace, chanted slogans against hostilities, and proclaimed that "Somali women need peace, not war." Mothers as peace promoters have employed distinct strategies and approaches to end fighting between warring factions. Standing for a communal well-being, some women carried out peacebuilding initiatives by negotiating agreements between warring clans. Through these mediations, many mothers appeared to be "the most able peacemakers and developers of their country."[38]

## The Rise of Civil Society Organizations

During the civil war, Somali mothers have reframed the way they approach community development issues, in spite of limited capacity-building projects.[39] One significant method they employed in advocating their rights was the establishment of nongovernmental organizations (NGOs) within the framework of civil society movements. Perhaps one of the most influential among those NGOs seeking to provide a voice to women's concerns was Save Somali Women and Children (SSWC). Founded in 1992 by Asha Haji Elmi, a women's rights activist in Somalia, and other like-minded women, SSWC was one of the first cross-clan women's movements to be established during the civil war.[40]

In some areas, when women had passed child-bearing age, they might be "accepted as elders to help settle disputes, though they cannot participate in all the activities of elders." In an address given at Dialogue with Arab Women on Economic and Political Issues,

Pan-African Centre for Gender, Peace and Development, held in Dakar, Senegal, on May 1, 2005, Elmi recounted her attempts to extricate Somali mothers from clan rivalry. To make this an issue for men required practical action:

> The Sixth Clan was born out of frustration. Within our society, although [we are] victims of conflict we had no voice for the national solution. In a patriarchal society such as ours, women have no right to represent their clan, nor any responsibility for protecting the clan. A group of us had the idea to form our own clan, in addition to the five pre-existing clans. The Sixth Clan gave us the first political entry point for women as equal partners in decision making. The women elected me to be their leader. We went to the negotiation table with the five clan leaders. We put women's interests into the peace process . . . we engendered the language. Instead of merely referring to men, the language [in government documents] now says "he or she."[41]

## THE STRUGGLE FOR POLITICAL CIRCLES

The armed conflict and chaos led from the "practical disappearance of all state structures to a major disruption of economic, social and political life and to an unforeseen humanitarian catastrophe."[42] Many men lost their positions as family breadwinners and became economically unproductive in their households owing to the conflict's repercussions. In this context, mothers filled such a gap and became economically active by taking on the traditional positions of men as chief breadwinners. The influence of women in the public varied considerably from region to region with regard to their position. Aid agencies, such as those affiliated with the United Nations, acknowledged that women who were "economically independent, culturally aware and highly educated command more respect in the society."[43] In other words, educated women had a better chance of offering "alternative solutions to long-standing problems of Somalia."[44]

Women's positions as mothers, breadwinners, and household leaders presented a new conundrum in the transformation of gender in Somalia. Many men became reluctant to assume their wives' traditional role of looking after children. As a result, women were encumbered with two colossal tasks as both the breadwinner and prime caregiver for the family. As their husbands were engrossed in warfare, many mothers cultivated self-employment schemes to work for their families as *khat*-sellers, housemaids, butchery managers, transporters, and animal brokers.[45] Perhaps due to the pressure of finding food for their families, a considerable number of women "have been forced into other, less remunerative forms of petty trade, such as firewood and charcoal sales."[46] Even in the countryside where nomadic pastoralism still remained a way of life, the "most arduous work of loading and unloading pack animals is done by women."[47] By contrast, it is commonly acknowledged that "the economy has in some ways favoured women and has obliged them to replace men as the principal wage-earners in their families and has also empowered them in important ways."[48]

## Healing Mothers and Children

Excluding children from the analyses of women in war has obfuscated the wider picture of their share of the suffering. Understanding the dimensions and dynamics of war cannot neglect a likeminded focus on children. In her excellent essay, "Revisiting Women and Social Change: Where are the Children?" sociologist Barne Thorne has challenged traditional feminist discourse that excluded children.[49] This is relevant in most of the Global South, and nowhere is this truer than in the Somali case, where there is no single study that focuses on mothers and children. Many children who experienced violence in Somalia suffer from mental health disorders. Unfortunately, what is expected from their society is little, as Somali culture isolates all mental health patients—men, women, and children. Given the lack of assistance for victims of mass atrocities, many mothers suffer from posttraumatic stress disorder that stems from their experiences. Comprehensive psychotherapy has yet to be provided for grief-stricken mothers and their children who fled during the peak of the war and endured years of drought and starvation.

Somali mothers have paid a high price in intra- and interclan conflicts, and it remains an arduous task to obtain statistics to assess the widespread scale of violence against them.[50] Mothers have endured the agonies of separation and loss during the war. For those mothers who were unable to escape, many have lost their lives, along with the lives of their children, a condition experienced by others in conflict zones in Africa in the 1990s.[51] This conflict has intensified what Bryden and Steiner termed "the feminization of poverty." Because "many women live alone or without relatives to support them and a significant number of the women in Somalia are the only breadwinners in the family . . . the feminisation of poverty is thus on the increase."[52] The poverty of single mothers who resorted to refugee life and widows whose husbands were either killed or displaced by the war further alienated and marginalized them. Terrified and overwhelmed, many mothers cannot escape the mental depression if they indeed survived physically.

## NOTES

1. Mark Bradbury, "The Somali Conflict: Prospects for Peace," Oxfam Research Paper no. 9, 10.
2. Matt Bryden and Martina Steiner, *Somalia between Peace and War: Somali Women on the Eve of the 21st Century* (Nairobi: UNIFEM, 1998), 2. For studies on the causes of Somalia's descent into interclan "fractionalisation" and protracted "civil" war, see Mohamed Haji Ingiriis, "The Making of the 1990 Manifesto: Somalia's Last Chance for State Survival," *Journal of Northeast African Studies* 12, no. 2 (2012): 63–94; Samuel M. Makinda, "Politics and Clan Rivalry in Somalia," *Australian Journal of Political Science* 26, no. 1 (1991): 111–26.
3. Mary Harper defines the phenomenon of the failed state as when "everything has collapsed [and] where violence and hunger dominate." Mary Harper, *Getting Somalia Wrong? Faith, War and Hope in a Shattered State* (London: Zed, 2012), 105. For an insightful critique of the notion of the failed state mostly applied to Somalia, see Branwen Gruffydd Jones, "The Global Political Economy of Social Crisis: Towards a Critique of the 'Failed State' Ideology," *Review of International Political Economy* 15, no. 2 (2008): 180–205.
4. Bryden and Steiner, *Somalia between Peace and War*; Judith Gardner and Judy El Bushra, eds., *Somalia: The Untold Story: The War through the Eyes of Somali Women* (London: Pluto, 2004).
5. Bryden and Steiner, *Somalia between Peace and War*, 49.
6. Fatuma Ahmed Ali, "Women and Conflict Transformation in Africa," *Feminismo/s* 9 (2007): 67–78; Bryden and Steiner, *Somalia between Peace and War*; Asha Haji Elmi et al., "Women's Roles in Peacemaking in Somali Society," in *Rethinking Pastoralism in Africa: Gender, Culture and the Myth of the Patriarchal Pastoralist*, ed. Dorothy L. Hodgson (Oxford: James Currey, 2000), 121–41; Gardner and El Bushra, *Somalia: The Untold Story*.
7. See Gardner and El Bushra, *Somalia: The Untold Story*.
8. UN-INSTRAW, *Women, Peace and Security in Somalia: Implementation of UN Security Council Resolution 1325* (New York: United Nations International Research and Training Institute for the Advancement of Women, 2008), 22. See also Rima Berns McGrown, "Redefining Social Roles: The Extraordinary Strength of Somali Women," *Women and Environments* 58–59 (2003): 13–14.
9. Abdurahman M. Abdullahi (Baadiyow), "Women, Islamists and the Military Regime in Somalia: The New Family Law and Its Implications,"

in *Milk and Peace, Drought and War: Somali Culture, Society, and Politics, Essays in Honour of I. M. Lewis*, ed. Markus Hoehne and Virginia Luling (London: Hurst, 2010), 144.
10. Maria H. Brons, *Society, Security, Sovereignty and the State: Somalia, From Statelessness to Statelessness?* (Utrecht: International, 2001); Alice Bettis Hashim, *The Fallen State: Dissonance, Dictatorship and Death in Somalia* (Lanham, MD: University Press of America, 1997); and Anna Simons, *Networks of Dissolution: Somalia Undone* (Boulder, CO: Westview, 1995).
11. Cynthia Cockburn, *The Space between Us: Negotiating Gender and National Identities in Conflict* (London: Zed, 1998); David Turton, *War and Ethnicity: Global Connections and Local Violence* (Rochester, NY: Boydell, 1994). See also UN-INSTRAW, *Women, Peace and Security in Somalia*, 21.
12. See Mark Bradbury, *Becoming Somaliland* (Bloomington: Indiana University Press, 2008).
13. Asha-Kaha, *Gumaadkii Muqdisho iyo Hargeysa* (London: Lower Shabelle, 2000).
14. Bryden and Steiner, *Somalia between Peace and War*, 50.
15. Elmi et al., "Women's Roles in Peacemaking in Somali Society," in *Rethinking Pastoralism in Africa: Gender, Culture and the Myth of the Patriarchal Pastoralist*, ed. Dorothy L. Hodgson (Oxford: James Currey, 2000), 16.
16. For excellent analyses of the Somali conflict, see Bradbury, *Becoming Somaliland* (Bloomington: Indiana University Press, 2008); Afyare Abdi Elmi, *Understanding the Somalia Conflagration: Identity, Political Islam and Peacebuilding* (London: Pluto, 2010).
17. See Asha-Kaha, *Gumaadkii Muqdisho iyo Hargeysa*.
18. This family lived in Minneapolis, when I stayed that city from mid-May until mid-August 2008 (except brief visits to Atlanta, Nashville, and Washington, DC).
19. Quoted in Bryden and Steiner, *Somalia between Peace and War*, 50.
20. Africa Watch, *Somalia: A Government at War with Its Own People: Testimonies about the Killings and the Conflict in the North* (New York: Africa Watch Committee, 1990), 131.
21. Helene Berman, "The Relevance of Narrative Research with Children Who Witness War and Children Who Witness Woman Abuse," *Journal of Aggression, Maltreatment & Trauma* 3, no. 1 (2000): 107–25.
22. Conversation with anonymous women, Copenhagen, Denmark, June 2012. For how women's bodies are exploited during the conflicts, see H. Patricia Hynes, "On the Battlefield of Women's Bodies: An Overview of the Harm of War to Women," *Women's Studies International Forum* 27, no. 5–6 (2004): 413–45.
23. Anonymous, interview, August 10, 2013.

## Mothers and Memory 237

24. Anonymous, interview, August 10, 2013. For how women suffered (and at times acted as an agency) in the clan wars, see Mohamed H. Ingiriis and Markus H. Hoehne, "The Impact of Civil War and State Collapse on the Roles of Somali Women: A Blessing in Disguise," *Journal of Eastern African Studies* 7, no. 2 (2013): 314–33.
25. It was reported that Rwanda has roughly 5,000 children born out of rape. These children are known as little *interahamwe* (devil's children). See Meredeth Turshen and Clotilde Twagiramariya, eds., *What Women Do in Wartime: Gender and Conflict in Africa* (London: Zed, 1998).
26. Bryden and Steiner, *Somalia between Peace and War*, 50.
27. Ali, "Women and Conflict," 78.
28. Virginia Luling, "Come Back Somalia? Questioning a Collapsed State," *Third World Quarterly* 18, no. 2 (1997): 297.
29. Faiza Jama, "Somali Women and Peace-Building," *Conciliation Resources*, http://www.c-r.org/our-work/accord/somalia/somali-women-peacebuilding.php, accessed September 19, 2012; See also Bryden and Steiner, *Somalia between Peace and War*.
30. There is a clip recorded in this era on YouTube showing women being interrogated by warlords: https://www.youtube.com/watch?v=F1Yxck1Zy6M, accessed on December 29, 2013. The Somali novelist Nuruddin Farah reports that women of (his clan) in Kismaayo provoked their men to take action: "[D]efying the conviction that enjoins female sartorial modesty, [they] bared their breasts in public in front of a crowd of men. Fists raised, voices harsh, they shouted 'Rise, Rise!' challenging the men to action." The type of action followed the event was not clear. See Nuruddin Farah, "The Women of Kismayo: Power and Protest in Somalia," *Times Literary Supplement* 15 (1996): 18.
31. John Prendergast, "The Gun Talks Louder than the Voice: Somalia's Continuing Cycles of Violence," report prepared for the Center of Concern, Washington, DC, 1994, 15.
32. Faduma Ahmed Alim "Ureeji," telephone interview, May 6, 2011.
33. For a fictionalized account of women's peace-building potential in times of war, see Abdibashir Ali, *Dumar Talo Ma Laga Dayey* (Stockholm: Scansom, 2003).
34. Ali, "Women and Conflict," 70.
35. Gardner and El Bushra, *Somalia: The Untold Story*, 9–10.
36. Asha Haji Elmi, personal communication, February 11, 2011, and May 17, 2013.
37. Mary E. King, "What Difference Does It Make? Gender as a Tool in Building Peace," in *Gender and Peace Building in Africa*, ed. Dina Rodríguez and Edith Natukunda-Togboa (Costa Rica: University for Peace, 2005), 37.
38. UNHCR, "Women in Somalia," *Refugee Survey Quarterly* 13 no. 2–3 (1994): 114. For firsthand accounts, see Gardner and El Bushra, eds., "Women and Peace-Making in Somaliland," in *Somalia: The Untold*

*Story*, 142–52, from a paper by Zeynab Mohammed Hassan, with additional information collected through interviews with Noreen Michael Mariano, Shukri Hariir Ismail, and Amina Yusuf.
39. Asha Haji Elmi, personal communication, London, November 2009, and May 17, 2013.
40. However desirable the cross-clan concept may be, it seems to have constructed its base on the account of only the so-called big clans, since cross-clan has always meant putting all assumed majority clans on board without mulling over the minority groups among society, such as the Bravenese, Banadiri, and Bantu.
41. King, "What Difference Does It Make?" 38–39.
42. Riika Koskenmaki, "Legal Implications Resulting from State Failure in Light of the Case of Somalia," *Nordic Journal of International Law* 73 (2004): 2.
43. UNDP, *Somalia Human Development Report* (Nairobi: UNDP, 2012), 59.
44. Bryden and Steiner, *Somalia between Peace and War*, 59.
45. *Khat* is a stimulant drug used in eastern African countries, as well as Yemen in the Arab peninsula.
46. Peter D. Little, *Somalia: Economy without State* (Indiana: Indiana University Press, 2003), 61.
47. Ibid., 71.
48. Bryden and Steiner, *Somalia between Peace and War*, 40. For a comparative analysis on Somali women's economic power, see Christine Choi Ahmed, "Finely Etched Chattel: The Invention of Somali Women," in *The Invention of Somalia*, ed. Ali Jimale Ahmed (Lawrenceville: Red Sea, 1995), 154–65.
49. Barne Thorne, "Revisiting Women and Social Change: Where Are the Children?" *Gender and Society* 1, no. 1 (1987): 85–107.
50. The unprecedented atrocities that women have experienced during the fratricidal war was briefly chronicled in Inger Skjelsbaek and Dan Smith, eds., *Gender, Peace and Conflict* (London: Sage, 2001), 4.
51. See Teckla Shikola, "We Left Our Shoes Behind," in *What Women Do in Wartime*, 150–62.
52. Bryden and Steiner, *Somalia between Peace and War*, 49.

## Selected Bibliography

Ahmed, Ali Jimale. *Daybreak Is Near: Literature, Clans, and the Nation-State in Somalia*. Lawrenceville: Red Sea, 1996.

Ahmed, Christine Choi. "Finely Etched Chattel: The Invention of Somali Women." In *The Invention of Somalia*, edited by Ali Jimale Ahmed, 157–89. Lawrenceville: Red Sea, 1995.

Ali, Fatuma Ahmed. "Women and Conflict Transformation in Africa." *Feminismo/s* 9 (2007): 67–78.

Alim, Faduma Ahmed. *And Then She Said: The Poetry and Times of Hawa Jibril.* Toronto: Jumblies, 2008.
Andrzejewski, B. W., and I. M. Lewis. *Somali Poetry.* Oxford: Clarendon, 1964.
Bradbury, Mark. *Becoming Somaliland.* Bloomington: Indiana University Press, 2008.
Bryden, Matt, and Martina Steiner. *Somalia between Peace and War: Somali Women on the Eve of the 21st Century.* Nairobi: UNIFEM, 1998.
Cockburn, Cynthia. *The Space between Us: Negotiating Gender and National Identities in Conflict.* London: Zed, 1998.
Elmi, Afyare Abdi. *Understanding the Somalia Conflagration: Identity, Political Islam and Peacebuilding.* London: Pluto, 2010.
Elmi, Asha Haji, et al. "Women's Roles in Peacemaking in Somali Society." In *Rethinking Pastoralism in Africa: Gender, Culture and the Myth of the Patriarchal Pastoralist,* edited by Dorothy L. Hodgson, 121–41. Oxford: James Currey, 2000.
Gardner, Judith, and Judy El Bushra, eds. *Somalia: The Untold Story: The War through the Eyes of Somali Women.* London: Pluto, 2004.
Goetze, Catherine, and Dejan Guzina. "Peacebuilding, Statebuilding, Nationbuilding—Turtles All the Way Down?" *Civil Wars* 10, no. 4 (2008): 319–47.
Gruffydd Jones, Branwen. "The Global Political Economy of Social Crisis: Towards a Critique of the 'Failed State' Ideology." *Review of International Political Economy* 15, no. 2 (2008): 180–205.
Hansen, Stig J. "Warlords and Peace Strategies: The Case of Somalia." *Journal of Conflict Studies* 23, no. 2 (2003): 57–78.
Harper, Mary. *Getting Somalia Wrong? Faith, War and Hope in a Shattered State.* London: Zed, 2012.
Ingiriis, Mohamed Haji. "The Making of the 1990 Manifesto: Somalia's Last Chance to the State Survival." *Journal of Northeast African Studies* 12, no. 2 (2012): 63–94.
Johnson, John W. "Orality, Literacy and Somali Oral Poetry." *Journal of African Cultural Studies* 18, no. 1 (2006): 119–36.
Kapteijns, Lidwien. "Discourse on Moral Womanhood in Somali Popular Songs, 1960–90." *Journal of African History* 50, no. 1 (2009): 101–22.
King, Mary E. "What Difference Does It Make? Gender as a Tool in Building Peace." In *Gender and Peace Building in Africa,* edited by Dina Rodríguez and Edith Natukunda-Togboa, 27–50. Costa Rica: University for Peace, 2005.
Koskenmaki, Riika. "Editorial Note: Legal Implications Resulting from State Failure in Light of the Case of Somalia." *Nordic Journal of International Law* 73, no. 1 (2004): 1–36.
Lewis, I. M. *Blood and Bone: The Call of Kinship in Somali Society.* Lawrenceville: Red Sea, 1994.
Little, Peter. *Somalia: Economy without State.* Oxford: James Currey, 2003.

Littlewood, Roland. "Military Rape." *Anthropology Today* 13, no. 2 (1997): 7–16.
Luling, Virginia. "Come Back Somalia? Questioning a Collapsed State." *Third World Quarterly* 18, no. 2 (June 1997): 287–302.
Makinda, Samuel M. "Politics and Clan Rivalry in Somalia." *Australian Journal of Political Science* 26, no. 1 (1991): 111–26.
McCrone, Paul, et al. "Mental Health Needs, Service Use and Costs among Somali Refugees in the UK." *Acta Psychiatrica Scandinavica* 111, no. 5 (2005): 351–57.
Molyneux, Maxime, and Shahra Razawi, eds. *Gender Justice, Development and Rights*. New York: Oxford University Press, 2000.
Nakaya, Sumie. "Women and Gender Equality in Peace-building: Somalia and Mozambique." In *Building Sustainable Peace*, edited by Tom Keating and W. Andy Knight. Edmonton: University of Alberta Press, 2004.
Raeymaekers, Timothy, et al. "State and Non-State Regulation in African Protracted Crises: Governance without Government?" *Afrika Focus* 21, no. 2 (2008): 7–22.
Reese, Scott. *Renewers of the Age: Holy Men and Social Discourse in Colonial Benaadir*. Leiden: Brill, 2008.
Renders, Marleen. *Consider Somaliland: State-Building with Traditional Elders and Institutions*. Leiden: Brill, 2012.
Skjelsbaek, Inger, and Dan Smith, eds. *Gender, Peace and Conflict*. London: Sage, 2001.
Sørensen, Birgitte R. *Women and Post-Conflict Reconstruction: Issues and Sources*. Geneva: UNRSID, 1998.
Turshen, Meredeth, and Clotilde Twagiramariya, eds. *What Women Do in Wartime: Gender and Conflict in Africa*. London: Zed, 1998.
Turton, David. *War and Ethnicity: Global Connections and Local Violence*. Rochester: Boydell, 1994.
Walls, Michael. "The Emergence of a Somali State: Building Peace from Civil War in Somaliland." *African Affairs* 108, no. 432 (July 2009): 371–89.

# Chapter 14

## Grieving US Mothers and the Political Representations of Protest during the Iraq War and Beyond

### Francis Shor

The figure of the grieving mother has been intrinsic to the long history of war. That history has been particularly gendered inflected, deriving from what some feminist analysts see as the divisions between masculinity, militarism, and motherhood. According to Sara Ruddick, "Mothering begins in birth and promises life; military thinking justifies organized deliberate deaths. A mother preserves the bodies, nurtures the psychic growth, and disciplines the conscience of children she cares for; the military deliberately endangers the same body, mind, and conscience in the name of victory and abstract causes. Mothers protect children who are at risk; the military risks the children mothers protect."[1] While the somewhat essentialist constructions of motherhood expressed by Ruddick suggest a natural opposition to militarism, in fact mothers have often been enablers of patriotic and patriarchal militarism. Even in suffering the loss of a child during war, that grief has been buried in private rituals of implied consent.

On the other hand, recent wars, from Vietnam to Iraq, have been subjected to media exposure and political protest that have created the social space for grieving mothers to challenge publicly the legitimacy of those wars. In the case of the Iraq War, two grieving mothers, Lila Lipscomb and Cindy Sheehan, became both iconic media figures and political representatives of forms of antiwar protest. This essay will highlight how and why Lipscomb and Sheehan were thrust into the media spotlight and the particular ways in which they articulated their critique of the Iraq War. Although each became representative of different forms of political protest that marked the mobilization of antiwar sentiments and activism, their positions also demarcated the constraints and contradictions of sustained radical opposition to the Iraq War and the imperialist policies undergirding that war.

Lila Lipscomb gained national attention as the grieving mother at the emotional core of Michael Moore's 2004 polemical documentary, *Fahrenheit 9/11*. As noted by Cynthia Weber, "Lipscomb represents not just a mourning mother but the moral center of a betrayed America."[2] Indeed, Moore's presentation of Lipscomb as a flag-waving patriotic mother who encouraged her children to join the military is essential to her political legitimacy as a grief-stricken opponent of the Bush administration's promotion of the Iraq War. Both in the film and in a later interview, Lipscomb attests to the fact that she comes from "a long line of service and duty to the United States of America. I believe in this country. I do wave my flag every single day."[3]

Yet Lipscomb's faith in the country—or, more precisely, in the particular political leadership of the United States—was shattered by the death of her son, Michael Pederson, in the early days of the Iraq War when his helicopter gunship crashed, killing all the crew members aboard. Almost at the same time as receiving news of her son's death, she received his last posted letter that contained a clear indictment of Bush's rush to war. Reading tearfully from the letter in the film, Lipscomb quotes the following sentences (sentences that concisely summarize the outrage and message of Moore's film): "What in the world is wrong with George. He got us out here for nothing. I really hope they don't re-elect that fool." In turn, Lipscomb makes clear that her "son got sent into harm's way by a decision made by the president of the United States that was based on a lie."[4]

Lipscomb is thus situated in Moore's film as a grieving mother whose loss is directly attributable to the Iraq War policies of the Bush Administration. Yet she is also a figure whose opposition is clearly rooted in populist sentiments that circumscribe Moore's politics. As constructed by Moore, Lipscomb is "someone who can offer her testimony to the families of state policy while keeping her patriotism intact."[5] Outside the film, Lipscomb's antiwar opposition found an outlet in Military Families Speak Out, the organization for those with relatives in the military who oppose the war in Iraq. While Lipscomb's role as a grieving mother and opponent of Bush policies helped to legitimatize opposition to the Iraq War, its populist political perspectives also circumscribed that role.

Another grieving mother started from that sense of betrayal and populist outrage but continued on a more radical journey to seek the larger, if less popular, meaning of US imperial war. In the process, Cindy Sheehan confronted a more complicated range of issues around motherhood and militarism than Lila Lipscomb. Cindy Sheehan's life was profoundly altered when her son, Casey, was killed in combat on April 4, 2004, in Sadr City, Baghdad. Within a short period of time, she transformed her private grief into a series of public protests against the war policies of President George W. Bush. From an open letter to Bush on the seven-month anniversary of Casey's death that excoriated his "reckless and wanton foreign policies," to appearing as part of a political advertisement against Bush in fall 2004, to her prominent August 2005 vigil in Crawford, Texas, the site of Bush's vacation ranch, Sheehan became a visible symbol and lightning rod for opposition to the Iraq War.[6]

Reflecting on her grief at the loss of her son in the 2004 political commercial, Sheehan uses the pain and anger of the aggrieved mother to indict Bush's warmongering: "I imagined it would hurt if one of my kids was killed, but I never imagined it would hurt this bad, especially someone so honest and brave as Casey, my son, when you haven't been honest with us, when you and your advisers rushed us into this war. How do you think we felt when we heard the Senate report that said there was no link between Iraq and 9/11?"[7]

Yet, in using her position as grieving mother to attack Bush and his war policies, Sheehan entered an arena fraught with ideological overtones. As noted by Laura Knudson, the "identity of Sheehan-as-mother enabled her activism and stance on the war to be framed by rhetorics of motherhood on the part of both the political left and right. The rhetoric of the left used Sheehan's motherhood to elevate and validate her activism, while on the right her mothering was questioned and problematized."[8] Responding to attacks on her as a bad mother for inserting herself in such a public way in a national debate about the war and, in the process, "neglecting" her other children, Sheehan opines, "I have received dozens of emails with this heading: Go Home and Take Care of Your Kids . . . I think of all the name calling and unnecessary and untrue trashing of my character, this one offends me the most . . . First . . . because it is so blatantly sexist . . . second . . . is that I believe that what I am doing is for my children, and the world's children . . . I think that the strategy of eternal baseless war for corporate profit and greed is bad for all of our children: born and unborn . . . Constant war is not a family value."[9]

While Sheehan's embrace of the "Peace Mom" as a family value did attract national support, especially in the aftermath of the media attention to her Crawford Ranch vigil, she could garner that sympathy as a consequence not only of her gender but also of her race. As argued by Tina Managhan, Sheehan's whiteness "enabled this particular grieving mother to occupy the space of and symbolically become the *grieving mother in all of 'us'* (a symbolic mother to the nation)—constituting a particular 'us' and nation in turn."[10] Given what other critics have commented on concerning the remoteness of this "new American way of war" from the average US citizen, Sheehan's aggrieved public status provided many with the kind of emotional connection absent for most (white) Americans.[11]

Yet even as the invisible appeal of the whiteness in her grief bestowed legitimacy on Sheehan, the partisan nature of her attacks on Bush (and later the Democrats) would transfigure her role as a "counterpublic catalyst" for the antiwar opposition. Counterpublic catalysts provide "alternative styles of political behavior and alternative norms of public speech."[12] Certainly, as noted by cognitive linguist George Lakoff, Sheehan was able to reframe the debate on the war by embodying the metaphor of a nurturing parent versus Bush's embodiment of the strict disciplinary father. Beyond that metaphorical reframing, Sheehan was able to "re-energize the antiwar movement and enlarge the legitimate arena of public debate by articulating doubt."[13] However, to the degree that Sheehan raised public doubt and dissent, she opened herself up to vitriolic denunciations from those hyperpatriots who supported Bush and his wars. One sign among those counterdemonstrators who showed up at Camp Casey, as the vigil in Crawford came to be known, read, "Bin Laden says keep up the good work Cindy."[14]

To focus her growing dissent from hyper and militaristic patriotism and to expand her role as a counterpublic catalyst, Sheehan embraced the concept of "matriotism." In her book, *Peace Mom*, she notes how "matriotism" is an attempt "to balance out the destructive militarism of patriotism."[15] Elsewhere she writes that a "true Matriot would never drop an atomic bomb or bombs filled with white phosphorous, carpet bomb cities, and villages, or control drones from thousands of miles away to kill innocent men, women and children." Beyond this critique of war making, Sheehan urged those among her readers who would join other matriots "to stand up and say: 'No, I am not giving my child to the fake patriotism of the war machine which chews up my flesh and blood to spit out obscene profits.'"[16]

By articulating a more generalized critique of war with specific references to the Iraq War, Sheehan provided the antiwar movement with a counter to what emerged as the flag-waving hyper patriotism promoted by the Washington war machine. Such patriotism was deployed as ideological cover for the mendacity of the ruling elites. However, it also became a kind of compensatory status for the powerless. Indeed, the desperate need to display the flag, from the phalanxes of those that accompany the public appearances of US presidents to the periodic fluttering outside the homes of average citizens (including someone like Lila Lipscomb), operates as a symbolic ritual for imperial legitimacy. In effect, the "more uncritical the kind of patriotism that rules popular imagination and public discourse, the more alone, insulated, special and different the American ethos makes people feel, the more incomprehensible the rest of the world becomes, full of inarticulate, hostile elements."[17]

That distorting mirror is not only part of the imperial narrative that represents the United States as the repository of good in the world, but it is also a function of the role of the corporate media's presentation of the world. Through the use of framing and filtering devices, US corporate media, especially television, manage to narrow and exclude critical perspectives, leading to significant misperceptions. Added to media distortions, misrepresentations, and complicity, the Bush administration's deliberate policy of disinformation in the lead-up to the Iraq War in 2003 further eroded the public's critical understanding of the situation in the Middle East and Iraq. Erroneously insisting on ties between Saddam Hussein and al-Qaeda and the presence of weapons of mass destruction in Iraq, the Bush administration and complicit corporate media helped to frame the invasion and occupation of Iraq. Such misperceptions persisted into 2006 when a Harris Poll found that 64 percent still believed that Hussein had strong links to al-Qaeda and 50 percent were convinced that Iraq had weapons of mass destruction when the United States invaded.[18]

In calling out the Bush administration for its mendacious manipulation of information and images, both Sheehan and Lipscomb became critical voices raising doubt about Washington's policies in Iraq. Certainly, even more than Lipscomb, Sheehan turned her criticism of the Bush administration into a more thorough going political opposition. Although the mainstream media picked up on Sheehan's opposition to Bush, the framing of that antagonism was reduced to an apolitical anger that circumscribed the larger critique of the Bush administration and Pentagon policies.

In turning her antiwar activism into a more inclusive, albeit counterpublic, critique, Sheehan became the kind of political activist whose dissent moved beyond just Bush and his war policies. Especially after the Democrats assumed a congressional majority in the 2006 election but still rubber-stamped Bush's war budget, Sheehan denounced their abject surrender. In her May 2007 "Letter to the Democratic Congress," Sheehan excoriated the Democrats' capitulation to the continuance of the war.[19] Her anger led her briefly to "retire" from the antiwar movement, only to reemerge later in 2008 as a primary opponent of the Democratic Speaker of the House and Congresswoman from California, Nancy Pelosi. Even in her "resignation" letter, Sheehan asserted that "I will never give up trying to help people in the world who are harmed by the empire of the good old U. S. of A. . . . but I am finished working in, or outside this system. The system forcefully resists being helped and eats up the people who try to help it."[20]

A similar perspective emerged from another grieving parent, albeit a father rather than mother. While Andrew Bacevich had been an academic critic of the wars in Afghanistan and Iraq, the loss of his soldier son in the conflict led to an attack on the "Republican/Democratic duopoly of trivialized politics." Bacevich continued his denunciation of such trivialized politics that prevent "any serious accounting of how much our misadventure in Iraq is costing . . . (and) who actually pays."[21]

Sheehan also moved from the very specific criticism of the Bush administration to taking on both the Democratic Party establishment and the imperial presidency itself. Thus, although President Obama promised to end the wars after taking office, Sheehan demonstrated outside the White House on October 5, 2009, and was arrested with sixty others protesting Obama's continuation of the wars in Iraq and Afghanistan. As she noted in a 2010 article published in Al-Jazeera-English, "I have observed that it was one thing to be anti-Bush, but to be anti-war in the age of Obama is not to be tolerated by many people." Continuing to call out Obama for the targeting of some antiwar activists in the United States, Sheehan also wrote that "Obama has ominously declared himself judge, jury and executioner of anyone that he deems a national security 'threat.' These are the actions of a tyrant and another assault against our rights and against the rule of law from a person who promised 'complete transparency' from his administration."[22]

In moving beyond her early role as a grieving mother against a heartless Bush administration to a full-blown political dissident in the Age of Obama, Cindy Sheehan has managed to challenge the dominant order in each of her transformations. While sharing with Lila Lipscomb the iconic figure of the grieving mother becoming, in the process, a lightning rod for antiwar opposition, Cindy Sheehan has transcended the national and patriotic boundaries limiting the political challenges mounted by Lila Lipscomb and Military Families Speak Out. Sheehan's international and oppositional perspectives have greatly expanded the public meanings of the grieving mother and thus offered a much more radical critique of war and US imperial policies. Unfortunately, the mass movement that mobilized around such figures as Lipscomb and Sheehan during the Iraq War has not been sustained in the era of Obama's drone warfare. Not only have drones made the prosecution of the war even more remote, but the use of such weapons has further disconnected the executioners from their victims, making even more difficult a shared sense of empathy with the suffering of others.

Perhaps the key to transcending the imperial enclosures that prevent moving beyond identifying solely with the suffering of American mothers like Lipscomb and Sheehan is a much more inclusive and anti-imperial empathy. As media and imperialism critic Robert Jensen opines, "Empathy seems less forthcoming for . . . victims, especially when it is one's own government or society or culture that is systematizing the brutality. When the pain is caused by our government, we are channeled away from that empathy. The way we are educated and entertained keeps us from knowing about or understanding the pain of others in other parts of the world, and from understanding how our pleasure is connected to the pain of others. It is a combined intellectual, emotional, and moral failure—a failure to know, to feel, and to act."[23]

Certainly, grieving mothers like Sheehan and Lipscomb call on our individual and collective empathy, but only up to a point where their "otherness" is still recognizable in nationalistic terms. Going beyond the national and imperial boundaries requires a more radical engagement with what the political philosopher Wendy Farley calls the "eros" of empathy. For Farley, the "obliviousness of another's personhood" is part of the "illusions" or ideologies that inform individuals, communities, and nations.[24] Noting that the "reality of other persons is effectively concealed by a dense cloud of lies, misleading images, and intonations of moral grandeur," Farley designates "eros," or the empathy of the heart, as a "nondominating proximity [that] permits an understanding of others to emerge that would otherwise be impossible."[25]

On the other hand, empire and war have bred into the citizens of the United States an incapacity to rise above the "paranoid togetherness" that historian William Appleman Williams identifies as a constituent element of "empire as a way of life."[26] Williams underscores what he means by "empire as a way of life" in his definition of "way of life" as "the combination of patterns of thought and action, that, as it becomes habitual and institutionalized, defines the thrust and character of a culture and society."[27] Although Williams emphasizes the role of economics in shaping this way of life, he is also attuned to "politics, ideas, and psychology."[28]

To pierce the psychological underpinnings of imperial America as a way to liberate oneself further from the enervations of empire as a way of life and engage with an inclusive empathy, one can consider Robert Jay Lifton's analysis of the "superpower syndrome" of the United States. As a practicing psychiatrist and psychohistorian, Lifton is particularly well suited for probing the fantasies of "infinite power and control" that accompany "superpower syndrome."[29] Contending that the "American superpower is an artificial construct, widely perceived as illegitimate," Lifton also asserts that its "reign is . . . inherently unstable . . . and its reach for full-scale domination marks the beginning of its decline."[30]

As both an implicit and explicit critique of this "superpower syndrome," grieving mothers like Sheehan remind us of the very real death and destruction that accompany war and empire. Moreover, grieving mothers offer an opening into the eros of empathy. On the other hand, empathy can often be undermined by nationalist and masculinist fantasies of war and what psychologists Helene Moglen and Sheila Namir call the "dis-eases of othering." Hence their call for a more encompassing empathy is one that "necessitates recognition of being in the place of the other, imagining one's way into the space and place of the other."[31] To understand and expand that space and place of the other in psychological and political terms may start at the grieving mother in one's own backyard but must go beyond to be where all suffering others reside.

## Notes

1. Sara Ruddick, "The Rationality of Care," in *Women, Militarism, and War*, ed. J. B. Elshtain and S. Tobias (Savage, MD: Rowman and Littlefield, 1990), 240. For an overview of the long history of war that emphasizes gender, see Barbara Ehrenreich, *Blood Rites: Origins and History of the Passions of War* (New York: Owl, 1998).

2. Cynthia Weber, "*Fahrenheit 9/11*: The Temperature Where Morality Burns," *Journal of American Studies* 40, no. 1 (April 2006), 124.
3. Quoted in Lila Lipscomb interview, Democracy Now, August 2, 2004, http://www.democracynow.org/2004/8/2/lila_lipscomb.
4. Emma Brockes, "The Lie that Killed My Son," *Guardian*, July 7, 2004.
5. Weber, "*Fahrenheit 9/11*," 126.
6. Laura Knudson, "Cindy Sheehan and the Rhetoric of Motherhood: A Textual Analysis," *Peace and Change* 34, no. 2 (April 2009), 165–66.
7. Quoted in ibid., 166.
8. Ibid., 167.
9. Quoted in Tina Managhan, "Grieving Dead Soldiers, Disavowing Loss: Cindy Sheehan and the Im/possibility of the American Antiwar Movement," *Geopolitics* 16, no. 2 (May 2011), 448.
10. Ibid., 446–47.
11. On the "new American way of war" and citizen removal, see Adrian Lewis, *The American Culture of War: The History of US Military Force from WWII to Operation Iraqi Freedom* (New York: Routledge, 2007), 377–99. On emotional connections to the aggrieved in war, see Scott Sigmund Gartner, "Ties to the Dead: Connections to Iraq War and 9/11 Casualties and Disapproval of the President," *American Sociological Review* 73, no. 4 (August 2008): 690–95.
12. Nancy Fraser, *Justice Interruptus: Critical Reflections on the "Postsocialist" Condition* (New York: Routledge, 1997), 75.
13. Managhan, "Grieving Dead Soldiers," 445.
14. Quoted in ibid., 450.
15. Cindy Sheehan, *Peace Mom: A Mother's Journey through Heartache to Activism* (New York: Atria, 2006), 213.
16. Cindy Sheehan, "Matriotism," *Huffington Post*, January 22, 2006, http://www.huffingtonpost.com/cindy-sheehan/matriotism/b/14283.html.
17. Ziauddin Sardar and Merryl Wyn Davies, *Why Do People Hate America?* (New York: The Disinformation Co., 2002), 140. Sardar and Davies underscore this point by their critical readings of network television programs, such as NBC's *West Wing* and ABC's *Alias*, that represent the rest of the world through jingoistic images and simplistic discourse. See ibid., 15–38 and 63–65.
18. For two incisive studies of the media distortions propagated by the Bush administration and replicated in the corporate media, see Sheldon Rampton and John Stauber, *Weapons of Mass Deception: The Uses of Propaganda in Bush's War on Iraq* (New York: Penguin, 2003); and Danny Schechter, *When News Lies: Media Complicity and the Iraq War* (New York: Select, 2006).
19. Cindy Sheehan, "Letter to Democratic Congress," May 26, 2007, http://www.axisoflogic.com/artman/publish/Article_24669.shtml.

On the larger context for Sheehan's anger at the Democratic Party's exploitation of the antiwar movement, see "The Partisan Dynamics of Contention: Demobilization of the Antiwar Movement in the United States, 2007–2009," *Mobilization: An International Journal* 16, no. 1 (2011): esp. 46–47.
20. Cindy Sheehan, "Good Riddance Attention Whore," *Daily Kos*, May 28, 2007, http://www.dailykos.com/story/2007/5/28/12530/1525.
21. Andrew Bacevich, "I Lost My Son to a War I Oppose," *Washington Post*, May 27, 2007, B01.
22. Cindy Sheehan, "Dissent in the Age of Obama," *Al-Jazeera-English*, October 5, 2010.
23. Robert Jensen, *Citizens of the Empire* (San Francisco: City Lights, 2004), 98.
24. Wendy Farley, *Eros for the Other: Retaining Truth in a Pluralistic World* (University Park: Pennsylvania State University Press, 1996), 17–25.
25. Ibid., 30 and 69.
26. William Appleman Williams, *Empire as a Way of Life* (New York: Oxford University Press, 1982), 221.
27. Ibid., 4.
28. Ibid., 84.
29. Robert Jay Lifton, *Superpower Syndrome: America's Apocalyptic Confrontation with the World* (New York: Nation, 2003), 178.
30. Ibid., 191–92.
31. Helene Moglen and Sheila Namir, "War and the Dis-eases of Othering," *International Journal of Applied Psychoanalytic Studies* 3, no. 2 (June 2006): 212. On the masculinist fantasies of war, see Ehrenreich, *Blood Rites*, 117–31.

## Selected Bibliography

Ehrenreich, Barbara. *Blood Rites: Origins and History of the Passions of War*. New York: Owl, 1998.
Farley, Wendy. *Eros for the Other: Retaining Truth in a Pluralistic World*. University Park: Pennsylvania State University Press, 1996.
Fraser, Nancy. *Justice Interruptus: Critical Reflections on the "Postsocialist" Condition*. New York: Routledge, 1997.
Gartner, Scott Sigmund. "Ties to the Dead: Connections to Iraq War and 9/11 Casualties and Disapproval of the President." *American Sociological Review* 73, no. 4 (August 2008): 690–95.
Jensen, Robert. *Citizens of the Empire*. San Francisco: City Lights, 2004.
Knudson, Laura. "Cindy Sheehan and the Rhetoric of Motherhood: A Textual Analysis." *Peace and Change* 34, no. 2 (April 2009): 164–83.
Lewis, Adrian. *The American Culture of War: The History of US Military Force from WWII to Operation Iraqi Freedom*. New York: Routledge, 2007.

Lifton, Robert Jay. *Superpower Syndrome: America's Apocalyptic Confrontation with the World.* New York: Nation, 2003.

Managhan, Tina. "Grieving Dead Soldiers, Disavowing Loss: Cindy Sheehan and the Im/possibility of the American Antiwar Movement." *Geopolitics* 16, no. 2 (May 2011): 438–66.

Moglen, Helene, and Sheila Namir. "War and the Dis-eases of Othering." *International Journal of Applied Psychoanalytic Studies* 3, no. 2 (June 2006): 206–18.

Rampton, Sheldon, and John Stauber. *Weapons of Mass Deception: The Uses of Propaganda in Bush's War on Iraq.* New York: Penguin, 2003.

Ruddick, Sara. "The Rationality of Care." In *Women, Militarism, and War*, edited by Jean Bethke Elshtain and Sheila Tobias, 229–54. Savage, MD: Rowman and Littlefield, 1990.

Sardar, Ziauddin, and Merryl Wyn Davies. *Why Do People Hate America?* New York: The Disinformation Co., 2002.

Schechter, Danny. *When News Lies: Media Complicity and the Iraq War.* New York: Select, 2006.

Sheehan, Cindy. *Peace Mom: A Mother's Journey through Heartache to Activism.* New York: Atria, 2006.

Weber, Cynthia. "*Fahrenheit 9/11:* The Temperature Where Morality Burns." *Journal of American Studies* 40, no. 1 (April 2006), 113–31.

Williams, William Appleman. *Empire as a Way of Life.* New York: Oxford University Press, 1982.

# Notes on Contributors

**Dana Cooper** is an associate professor of history at Stephen F. Austin State University. Her most recent works include an edited volume, *Transatlantic Relations and Modern Diplomacy: An Interdisciplinary Examination* (Routledge, 2013), and *Informal Ambassadors: American Women, Transatlantic Marriages, and Anglo-American Relations, 1865–1945* (Kent State University Press, forthcoming, 2014).

**Tracy Crowe Morey** received her PhD from the University of Toronto and currently teaches in the Hispanic and Latin American Studies Program in the Department of Modern Languages, Literatures, and Cultures at Brock University. Her most recent research and scholarship reflect an interest in the historical memory boom of the Spanish Civil War as represented in literature and the arts as well as women's testimonial literature in the various contexts of the Americas.

**Annika A. Culver** serves as an assistant professor of East Asian history at Florida State University (FSU), where she is also affiliated with the Institute for World War II and the Human Experience. In addition, she is a scholar in Cohort II of the US-Japan Network for the Future. Her latest book, *Glorify the Empire: Japanese Avant-Garde Propaganda in Manchukuo*, investigates how formerly left-wing Japanese intellectuals portrayed Japanese-occupied Northeast China in their often equivocal writings, photography, and art promoting a fascist regime from 1932 to 1945. Culver specializes in researching Japanese imperialism, Sino-Japanese cultural connections, and US-Japan relations. Her latest projects center on how Japanese companies advertised Japanese imperial modernity in Western-oriented products sold throughout the Empire, and a study on a Harvard-trained American ornithologist's view of US-occupied postwar Japan.

**Mohamed Haji Ingiriis** is a Somali scholar specializing in Somali Studies. He is now a researcher at the Help Somalia Foundation in London. He is also a book reviews editor for the *Journal of the Anglo-Somali Society*. Previously studying at the Katholieke Universiteit Leuven, he obtained an MA in History from the Departments of Anthropology and History at Goldsmiths, University of London, and an MSc in Organisation and Community Development from the Department of Social Sciences and Humanities at London Metropolitan University. Both his Master's theses were achieved with a distinction. His academic articles have been published in such peer-refereed journals as the *Journal of Eastern African Studies*, *African Renaissance*, *Northeast African Studies*, and *The Northern Mariner*. His book reviews have appeared in the *Journal of Modern African Studies*, *African Affairs*, *Review of African Political Economy*, *Africa Today*, *Canadian Journal of African Studies*, and *Journal of the Anglo-Somali Society*. Further book reviews and review essays will feature in the forthcoming issues of *Cahiers d'Études Africaines*, *Journal of Conflict and Peacebuilding Review*, and *Journal of African and Asian Studies*.

**Udi Lebel** is an associate professor and head of the Department of Sociology and Anthropology at Ariel University and research fellow at the Samaria and Jordan Rift R&D Center, Israel. His main research interests are political psychology, civil-military relations, politics of collective memory, and commemoration; bereavement, death, and dying; and security communities. His latest book is *Politics of Memory—The Israeli Underground's Struggle for Inclusion in the National Pantheon and Military Commemoralization* (Routledge).

**Michael Loadenthal** is a Doctoral Candidate and Dean's Fellow at the School for Conflict Analysis and Resolution (George Mason University) and for the past four years an Adjunct Professor in the Program on Justice and Peace (Georgetown University). In 2010, he completed a Master's degree at the Centre for the Study of Terrorism and Political Violence (University of St. Andrews), focusing his study on social movements, political violence, and contemporary statecraft. He has conducted ethnographic fieldwork in a variety of national locales, including the Occupied Palestinian Territories. Currently, he splits his time between raising his daughters, teaching theory, photographing graffiti, writing constantly, and agitating for a better world. He regularly publishes propaganda and political theory under a variety of pseudonyms.

**Salvador Jimenez Murguia** is an associate professor of sociology at Akita International University and Paul Orfalea Fellow of Global and

International Studies at UC Santa Barbara. His research focuses on Japanese Cultural Studies.

Associate Professor **John Navin** is a member of the history faculty at Coastal Carolina University. A specialist in Early American history, he writes about colonial families, religious communities, and exploited or oppressed groups. He earned a Bachelor's degree in English at UMass/Boston, a Master's degree in American Studies at Boston College, and a Doctorate in History at Brandeis University. A former marketing communications executive, Dr. Navin served as Associate Dean of Humanities and Fine Arts at Coastal Carolina University from 2001 to 2008. He is the author of numerous articles and is currently writing a book about the racial dynamics of Charleston, South Carolina.

**Benjamin A. Peters** is an assistant professor of politics and fellow of comparative culture at Miyazaki International College in Kyushu, Japan. His research and writing center on the right to peace and institutional constraint on militarism.

Born in Australia, **Claire Phelan** received a Master's degree in Defense Studies before moving to the United States to complete a PhD in History at Texas Christian University. She serves as an Assistant Professor of History at the University of Mary Hardin-Baylor in Texas. She is the recipient of a number of awards, including a Cuffee Memorial Fellowship, a Greenwich Maritime Museum Research Fellowship, a Walsh Foundation Fellowship, and a Nokia Research Award in Women's History. She regularly presents at maritime history conferences both in the United States and overseas.

**Lorraine Ryan** is a lecturer in Hispanic Studies in the University of Birmingham, England. Her publications, which have appeared in *Romance Studies, Bulletin of Spanish Studies, Modern Language Review, Memory Studies, Hispania, Journal of Sociology*, and the *Hispanic Research Journal*, center on collective and cultural memory in contemporary Spain. In 2013, she was awarded the Outstanding Scholarly Publication Prize by the AATSP (American Association of Teachers of Spanish and Portuguese). Her monograph on the representation of spatiality in Contemporary Spanish memory narratives will be published in the Ashgate New Hispanisms Series in 2014.

**Cristina Santos** received her PhD from the University of Toronto and currently teaches in the Hispanic and Latin American Studies Program in the Department of Modern Languages, Literatures, and Cultures at Brock University. Her research reflects an interest in investigating the monstrous depictions of women as aberrations of feminine nature vis-à-vis the socioculturally proscribed norm. She also investigates the construct of the "monstrous" in testimony as the construction of a personal and communal sense of identity that challenges official history.

**Fatin Shabbar** is currently a final year PhD candidate and a tutor at the University of South Australia in the School of Psychology, Social work and Social Policy. She completed a Social Work degree (with first-class honors) in 2009 at the same university. Fatin Shabbar's research background includes Iraq and Middle East politics, Iraqi women, war and motherhood, Islam, westernization and postcolonial feminism. In addition to her academic work, Fatin Shabbar is also a senior counsellor at TAFE SA (Technical and Further Education South Australia) and a secretary-general of Iraqi Women's Voice of South Australia.

**Elena Shabliy** is a PhD candidate at Tulane University. In 2005, she graduated *magna cum laude* from Lomonosov Moscow State University with a BA and an MA in German language and Western literature. In 2009, she earned an Interdisciplinary Master of Liberal Arts degree at Tulane University.

**Francis Shor** is a professor in the History Department at Wayne State University. His wide-ranging interests and publications include the fields of utopian studies, comparative labor and gender studies, civil rights and antiwar social movements, twentieth-century US social-cultural studies, and US imperialism and its antagonists in the world. The latter interest is reflected in the publication of his latest book, *Dying Empire: US Imperialism and Global Resistance* (Routledge, 2010).

**Lyrica Taylor** is an assistant professor of art history at Azusa Pacific University, California, and focuses on the history of Modern British Art. She received her PhD in Art History from the University of Maryland, College Park. Taylor has presented her research at multiple conferences, including at the Universities of Oxford, London, Edinburgh, and Leeds; the College Art Association (US); the Art Association of Australia and New Zealand; and the Association of

Art Historians (UK). She has held internships at Tate Britain; the Huntington Library, Art Collections, and Botanical Gardens; the Smithsonian National Portrait Gallery; and the National Endowment for the Arts.

**Amitabh Vikram Dwivedi**, a linguist by profession, has been working as an assistant professor in the School of Languages and Literature at Shri Mata Vaishno Devi University, Katra, India. He documents endangered languages, and he is associated with the language revitalization program. His recent publications, *A Linguistic Grammar of Hadoti* (2012) and *A Grammar of Bhadarwahi* (2013) by LINCOM EUROPA Academic Publications (Germany), register the lesser known Indo-Aryan languages in India. His descriptive grammar on Dogri language is forthcoming.

# INDEX

Abbas, Al, 211, 212
Abdullah (Karbala martyr), 211, 212
Abzug, Bella, 5
Africa: motherhood and war in, 10–11, 225–35
African Americans, 28, 51
Agents for the Relief of Seamen, 47
Aguirre, Carmen, 62, 65–66, 68
Ahmad, Amal Zaki, 189–90
Akber, Ali Al, 211, 212
al-Aqsa Intifada, 182–83, 193–95
al-Aqsa Martyrs Brigade, 182, 193
Alday, Conchita. *See* Tijerino, Doris
Alfonsín, Raul, 90
Algonquian tribe, 30
Allende, Salvador, 67
al-Manar, 190
al-Qaeda, 188, 213, 245
Anglo-Americans: as mothers in war, 19–27, 31
Another Mother for Peace, 6
Arafat, Suha al-Taweel, 198
Arafat, Yasser, 182
Aramburu, Cardinal Juan Carlos, 89
Araucanians, 65
Argall, Samuel, 17
Argentina: motherhood and war in, 8, 62–63, 66, 68, 70–71, 74, 85–91
Argentine National Commission for the Disappeared (CONADEP), 90
Arita Hachirô, 99
Asai Kan'emon, 108

ascriptive motherhood, 129–35, 138–39
Asghar, Ali Al. *See* Abdullah
Asia: motherhood and war in, 10, 95–110, 115–25
*Atarashiki tsuchi*. *See New Earth*
atomic bomb, 147, 152, 244
Australia, 228
Austria: compulsory military service in, 4
Auxiliary Territorial Services (ATS), 171
Avedon, Barbara, 6
Azurduy de Padilla, Juana, 66

Ba'ath Party, 207–8, 212–13; and Shi'a Muslims, 216–17
Baneen, Om Al, 211, 212, 213
Begin, Manachem, 160, 172
Belli, Gioconda, 65, 70, 71
Ben-Gurion, David: and motherhood, 165–66, 170, 171–72, 173
Ben-Yisahi, Ron, 162
Bignone, Reynaldo Benito, 90
Bin-Akheel, Muslim, 211
Blue Star Mothers Club, 8–9
Bonafini, Hebe, 90
Brazil: compulsory military service in, 4
Briantspuddle War Memorial, 149
Buck, Pearl, 104
Bush, George W.: as oppositional figure for Iraq War mothers, 242–47

## 260    INDEX

Cabinet Information Bureau (CIB), 116
Camp Casey, 244
Canada, 105; motherhood and war in, 4, 8; and Native American captivity, 21, 24, 25, 27, 28
Carlotto, Estela Barnes de, 90
Carter, Jimmy: compulsory military service and, 3
Castillo, Carmen, 62, 71–73
Catawba tribe, 29
Catholic Church, 24; in Argentina, 89; in Spain, 128, 136
Chechnya, 6–7
Cherokee tribe, 19, 29, 30
Chickasaw tribe, 29
Chile: motherhood and war in, 62, 67–68, 71, 87
China: compulsory military service in, 4. *See also* Manchuria, China; Qin Empire
Choctaw tribe, 29
Cihuacoatl, 63–64
Civil War, Somali. *See* Somali Civil War
Civil War, Spanish. *See* Spanish Civil War
Civil War, US. *See* US Civil War
Claydon, England, 149
Coatlicue, 63–64
Cold War, 2–3
CoMadres, 87
Committee of Soldiers' Mothers, 6–7
compulsory military service, 1, 3–4, 117, 208
Crawford, Texas, 243, 244
Creek tribe, 29, 30, 31
Cuba: motherhood and war in, 68, 71–73

Dirty War, 10, 86–91
Djibouti, 228
Dorset, England, 149

*East of Eden*, 105
Edo era, 117

Educational Kamishibai Federation, 116
Egypt, 172, 182; compulsory military service in, 4
El Salvador: motherhood and war in, 8, 87
Elmi, Asha Haji, 228, 232–33
Embargo Act (1807), 46, 48
England, 17, 29, 54, 56; compulsory military service in, 2
Epstein, Jacob, 153–54
Esopus tribe, 18, 23, 24
Esopus War, 24
Ethiopia, 225, 228; compulsory military service in, 2
Europe, 171, 228; compulsory military service in, 4; cultural influence in Americas of, 32, 63, 85; motherhood and war in, 10, 127–39, 145–55
European Parliament, 90

*Fahrenheit 9/11*, 242
Falmouth, Maine, 20
Farhat, Maryam Mohammad Yousif. *See* Um Nidal
fascism, 105–6
Fatah, 181, 182, 183, 193
Federala, La (*guerrera*), 66
Figueroa, María Isabel, 70–71
*Figure (Requiem)* (Barbara Hepworth sculpture), 152
First Lebanese War, 160, 162
Fort Loudoun, South Carolina, 28
Fort Mims, Alabama, 32
Fort Vause, Virginia, 19
Foucault, Michel, 130, 137
Four Mothers, The, 159–60, 161–62
France: compulsory military service in, 2; and impressment, 50, 53, 57; in North America, 16, 19, 20, 22, 24, 25, 27, 32
Franco, Francisco, 127–29
Francoist Spain: official view on motherhood of, 128–35; opposition to official view of motherhood in, 135–38

# INDEX

Franklin, Benjamin, 25
Frente Sandinista de Liberación Nacional (FSLN): mothers in, 62, 67, 68–70

Gabo, Naum, 146
Gates, Sir Thomas, 15
Gaza Strip, 181, 182, 187, 188, 194
George III (king), 32
Germany, 105; film of, 101, 104
Gill, Eric, 149
Gnadenhutten, Ohio, 32
Gold Star Mothers Club, 8–9
*Good Earth, The*, 104
Grandmothers of Plaza de Mayo, 90, 91
Great Britain, 4, 46; motherhood and war in, 145–55
Greater East Asia Co-Prosperity Sphere, 98–99
Great Swamp Fight, 18–19, 31
Greece, 149; compulsory military service in, 4
Guber, Ephraim, 171
Guber, Rivka, 170–73
Guber, Zvi, 171
Gulf War, 208

Hamas, 161, 162; as opposition to Israel, 182, 183, 185, 187, 193–94, 196, 198–99, 200; as political party, 187–88
Hamas Charter, 200
Hammarskjöld, Dag, 152
*Hanatsubaki*, 96, 106
Harbin, China, 101–2
Haverhill, Massachusetts, 27
Hepworth, Barbara, 145–55
Hezbollah, 161, 190, 196
*Histadrut* Labor Federation, 171
*Hôshû (Homare no kazoku)* (*Abundant Harvest [Family of Distinction]*) (Asai Kan'emon painting), 108–9
Hussein, Imam: family of, 211–12, 214; martyrdom of, 209–10, 211, 213–14, 219

Hussein, Saddam, 245; cult of, 207–8, 216; and Shi'a Muslims, 212–13, 217

Imperial Rescript on Education (1890), 117, 118
Imperial Rescript to Soldiers (1882), 117–18
impressment, 9, 45–57
*Infant* (Barbara Hepworth sculpture), 153
*Inheriting Our Mothers' Gardens*, 215
Iran, 190, 210; compulsory military service in, 4
Iraq: motherhood and war in, 207–19
Iraq-Iran War, 208
Iraq-Kuwait War, 208
Iraq War: motherhood and war in, 241–48
Ishiwara Kanji, 99
Islam: and martyrdom, 184–87, 190–99; and motherhood, 182–83, 187–90, 215–18. *See also* Shi'a Islam
Islamic Jihad, 181, 182, 183
Islamic Resistance Movement. *See* Hamas
Israel: compulsory military service in, 4; fatherhood and war in, 8; motherhood and war in, 8, 10, 159–75; as target of Palestinian militancy, 181, 184–90, 192, 194–99
Israel Defense Forces (IDF): mothers of soldiers in, 159–61, 163, 169, 171, 173, 174, 175; and Palestine, 182, 193
Israeli Independence War, 164, 168, 171
Italy, 146; fascism in, 105–6

Jamestown, Virginia, 15, 17
Japan: conscription in, 117; motherhood and war in, 10, 95–110, 115–25

Japan Memorial Society for Students Killed in the War, 120
Johnson, Lyndon, 3, 5–6
Josefa (*guerrera*), 66

*kaitaku-sha* (rural pioneer woman), 96, 99–100, 107
*kamikaze*, 10, 115–25
Kantô Army, 95, 98, 102
Karbala, Battle of: description of, 209–10; in memory, 209–15, 218–19; rituals of, 213
King Philip, 30
King Philip's War, 18, 28, 30, 31
King William's War, 25
*kokutai* (essence of the nation), 118, 119, 124
Kuwait, 208
*kyôwa* (harmony or concord), 99

Laila (Karbala martyr mother), 211, 212, 213
Lancaster, Massachusetts, 19
Las Ventas, 137–38
Latin America: motherhood and war in, 9–10, 61–74, 85–91
Lebanese War, First. *See* First Lebanese War
Lebanon, 190; Israeli presence in, 159–61, 163, 173, 174
Lebanon War, Second. *See* Second Lebanon War
*Lebensraum* (living space), 105
Leeds School of Art, 146
Lewis, David, 150
Lipscomb, Lila, 11, 241–43, 245, 247

*machismo* (masculine virtues), 85
Madonna, 108, 145–55
*Madonna and Child* (Barbara Hepworth painting), 148, 149–51
*Madonna and Child* (Barbara Hepworth sculpture), 148–55
Madres de Plaza de Mayo. *See* Mothers of Plaza de Mayo
Madrid, Spain, 137, 138

Maine, 20–21, 27
Malayan Emergency, 146; described, 148–49
Malinche, La, 64
Manchukuo. *See* Manchuria, China
Manchuria, China: Japanese colonization of, 95–110
Manchuria Colonial Development Company, 101, 102
Manchurian Incident, 99, 100
*Manshû Gurafu*: Manchuria portrayed in, 95–110
*Maquette for "The Unknown Political Prisoner"* (Barbara Hepworth sculpture), 152
Marchi, Margarita, 71
*marianismo* (feminine virtues), 85–86
Marine Family Network Parents, 9
Marinis, Hugo de, 62
Massachusetts, 24, 27, 28
Mather, Cotton: description of Native American raids by, 26, 27
Mather, Increase: description of Native American raids by, 18–19, 20, 23, 28
Matsuoka Yôsuke, 99
McCormick-Deering tractors, 104
Meiji era: administrative reforms in, 116–17
Meneses, Pascuala, 66
Metacomet. *See* King Philip
Mexican Revolution, 64–65
Mexico: compulsory military service in, 4; motherhood and war in, 63–65
Miantonomi, 17
Middle East: motherhood and war in, 10, 159–75, 181–202, 207–19
Military Families Speak Out, 242, 247
MIR. *See* Revolutionary Left Movement
Moholy-Nagy, László, 146
Mondrian, Piet, 146
Monroe, James, 55

## Index

Montoneros, 62
Moore, Henry, 149, 153–54
Moore, Michael, 242
Moro de López, Juana, 66
Mothers against Silence, 160
mothers: general societal pressures on, 4–5; in Islamic culture, 182–83, 187–90, 215–18
Mothers of Plaza de Mayo, 10, 61, 74, 85–91
Muhammad (prophet), 188, 209
Muklasa tribe, 29
Munich Conference, 147
Mystic Fort, 31
Mystic River, 17

*nabad-dhalin* (peace building), 232
Napoleon, 2, 57
Napoleonic Wars, 46, 56
Narragansett tribe, 17
National Reorganization (Argentina), 88
Native Americans: as mothers in war, 16–19, 24, 25–26, 27–33. See also *individual tribes*
Navon, Yitzchak, 172
Nechamkin, Aryeh, 162
*New Earth*, 101, 104
Newman, Paul, 6
New Netherland, 18, 23, 24
Nicaragua, 17; motherhood and war in, 62–63, 65, 67, 68–70
Nicholson, Ben, 146–47
*nidal* (political struggle), 209
Nogawa Takashi, 106
North America, 228; motherhood and war in, 9, 11, 15–33, 45–57, 241–48
Northern Ireland: motherhood and war in, 8
North Korea: compulsory military service in, 4
Norway: compulsory military service in, 4

Obama, Barack, 246–47
Olmstead, Mildred Scott, 7–8

Paiz, Nora, 65
Palestine: motherhood and war in, 8, 181–202
Palestinian Authority, 182, 183, 190
Palestinian Authority TV, 196
Partido Peronista Feminino. See Peronista Women's Party
Paspahegh tribe, 15
Paul VI (pope), 89
Pax Materna, 6
Pederson, Michael, 242
Pelosi, Nancy, 246
Pennsylvania, 2, 19, 22
Pequot War, 17–18, 27, 28, 31
Perón, Isabel, 88
Perón, María Eva Duarte de, 85
Peronista Women's Party, 85
Plaza de Mayo, 86. See also Grandmothers of Plaza de Mayo; Mothers of Plaza de Mayo
Pocahontas, 17
Pontiac's Rebellion, 32
Popular Front for the Liberation of Palestine (PFLP), 185
Proceso, El. See National Reorganization
*Project (Monument to the Spanish Civil War)* (Barbara Hepworth sculpture), 152

Qasim, Al, 211, 212, 214
Qin Empire: conscription in, 2
Queen Anne's War, 28

Rabab, Al (Karbala martyr mother), 211
Rabin, Yitzchak: and motherhood, 166
Ramleh (Karbala martyr mother), 211
Reagan, Ronald: compulsory military service and, 3
Return Plan, The, 67–68
Revolutionary Left Movement (MIR), 62, 67, 71
Reynolds, Debbie, 6

Rodríguez, Carmen, 62, 65–66, 67–68, 71
Rolfe, John, 17
Roosevelt, Franklin Delano: compulsory military service and, 3
Rowlandson, Mary: captivity of, 19, 20, 21, 23–24
Royal Air Force, 148
Royal College of Art, 146
Russia, 102, 103; compulsory military service in, 4; motherhood and war in, 6–7
*ryôsai kenbô* (Good Wife, Wise Mother), 109

San Antonio, Texas, 32
Sand Creek, Colorado, 32
Sandinistas. *See* Frente Sandinista de Liberación Nacional (FSLN)
Sanjiang Province, China, 104
Save Somali Women and Children (SSWC), 232
Schalit, Gilead, 162
Second Lebanon War, 159, 161
Second Sino-Japanese War, 98. *See also* World War II
Selassie, Haile, 2
Selective Service System, 5
*Sengentai*, 106
Seven Years War, 32
Shapira, Miriam, 170
Shari'ati, Ali, 210
Sharon, Ariel, 182
Sheehan, Casey, 243
Sheehan, Cindy: opposition to Iraq War of, 11, 241–42, 243–47, 248
*Shenandoah*, 1, 11
Shenandoah doctrine, 1–2, 5
Shi'a Islam: under Saddam Hussein, 207–19
Shigemitsu Mamoru, 99
Shimaki Kensaku, 106
*Single Form* (Barbara Hepworth sculpture), 152

Skeaping, John, 146, 148, 149
Skeaping, Paul, 146; biography of, 148–49; effect on Barbara Hepworth's art of, 149–55
Sneh, Ephraim, 162
Somalia: motherhood and war in, 225–35
Somali Civil War, 225–26, 227–28
Somoza, Anastasio, 65, 68–69
South Korea: compulsory military service in, 4
South Manchuria Railway Company (SMRC): portrayal of Manchuria by, 96, 99, 100–102, 104, 107, 109–10
Soviet Union, 98, 102, 103; and military service, 8
Spahr, Adriana, 62
Spain, 50; motherhood and war in, 10, 127–39
Spanish Civil War, 127; effect on Barbara Hepworth on, 147, 152. *See also* Francoist Spain
Spanish Second Republic: womens' roles in, 127–29, 134
Steinbeck, John, 105
Stern, Elazar, 162
Stewart, Jimmy, 1, 11
St. Ives, England: Barbara Hepworth's *Madonna and Child* in, 145, 147, 148, 149, 155
storytelling, 215–18
Sughra, Fatima Al, 211

Tanaka Chigaku, 118–19
Tangu Truce, 98
Tatsuo Kawai, 99
Ta'ziyeh, 214
Tieli City, China, 104
Tijerino, Doris, 62, 65, 68–70, 71
Tokunaga Sunao, 106
total war, 30–31, 95, 98
Treaty of Paris (1763), 19, 32
Truman, Harry S.: compulsory military service and, 3

## Index

Tuscarora tribe, 29
*Two Figures (Heroes)* (Barbara Hepworth painting), 148, 151–52

*Umeyo fuyaseyo* (Give birth and multiply), 107–8
Um Nidal, 187–89, 191
Underhill, John, 17
United Kingdom: compulsory military service in, 4; motherhood and war in, 8. See also *constituent nations*
United Nations, 152, 208, 233
United States: compulsory military service in, 3; conscription in, 2–3; emigration to, 229; land use in, 205; motherhood and war in, 5–7, 8–9, 45–57, 241–48; products of, 104
US Civil War, 1, 11; conscription in, 2

victimological militarism, 174–75
Videla, Jorge Rafael, 90, 91
Vietnam War, 1; conscription in, 3; motherhood and war in, 5–6, 9, 241
Villaflor, Azucena, 86

War of 1812, 47, 50; motherhood and war in, 7
wars on terror: compulsory military service in, 4; motherhood and war in, 9
Washington, George, 52; compulsory military service and, 3
Webster, Daniel, 7

Wells, Maine, 26
West Bank, 175, 181, 182
Westos tribe, 28–29, 31
Wethersfield, Connecticut, 17
Williams, Roger, 17–18
Williamson, John, 148
Wilson, Dagmar, 5
Wilson, Woodrow: compulsory military service and, 3
Women's International League for Peace and Freedom, 8
Women Strike for Peace, 5–6
Woodward, Joanna, 6
World War I: and Barbara Hepworth, 149, 155; conscription in, 2; motherhood and war in, 8, 9
World War II: and Barbara Hepworth, 145, 146, 155; conscription in, 2; motherhood and war in, 9, 10, 95–110, 115–25
Wounded Knee, South Dakota, 32

*Yad leBanim* (Memorial for the Sons), 170, 172
Yamada Seizaburô, 106
Yamagata Aritomo, 117
Yamassee War, 29
*Yamato minzoku* (Japanese race), 103–4
*Yamato-nadeshiko* (true Japanese maiden), 96–97
*Yiddeshe Mama* (Jewish Mother), 159–70, 171, 173–75
Yoshida Shōin, 123

Zahra, Al Saydah Fatima't Al, 211, 212

Printed in the United States of America